HOW DID CHRISTIANITY BEGIN?

Michael F. Bird is lecturer in New Testament at the Highland Theological College in Dingwall, Scotland. He is the author of *Jesus and the Origins of the Gentile Mission* (T&T Clark, 2006), *The Saving Righteousness of God* (Paternoster, 2007) and *A Bird's-Eye View of Paul* (InterVarsity Press, 2008).

James G. Crossley is lecturer in New Testament at the University of Sheffield (UK). He is the author of *The Date of Mark's Gospel: Insight from the Law in Earliest Christianity* (T&T Clark, 2004), *Why Christianity Happened: A Sociohistorical Analysis of Christian Origins 26–50 CE* (Westminster John Knox, 2006) and *Jesus in An Age of Terror: Scholarly Projects for a New American Century* (Equinox, forthcoming).

Maurice Casey is Emeritus Professor of New Testament Studies at the University of Nottingham (UK). He is the author of several books including *From Jewish Prophet to Gentile God* (Westminster John Knox, 1991), *Aramaic Sources of Mark's Gospel* (Cambridge University Press, 1998), *An Aramaic Approach to Q* (Cambridge University Press, 2002) and *The Solution to the 'Son of Man' Problem* (T&T Clark, 2007).

Scot McKnight is Karl A. Olsson Professor in Religious Studies at North Park University, Chicago, USA. He is the author of more than twenty books, including *Galatians* (Zondervan, 1993), *A New Vision for Israel: The Teachings of Jesus in National Context* (Eerdmans, 1999), *Jesus and His Death* (Baylor University Press, 2005) and *Embracing Grace: A Gospel for All of Us* and *The Real Mary* (both published by SPCK, 2007), as well as the co-editor, with J. D. G. Dunn, of *The Historical Jesus in Current Study* (Eisenbrauns, 2005).

HOW DID CHRISTIANITY BEGIN?

A believer and non-believer examine the evidence

MICHAEL F. BIRD
AND
JAMES G. CROSSLEY

First published jointly in 2008 in Great Britain by SPCK
and in the United States by
Hendrickson Publishers, Inc.

Society for Promoting Christian Knowledge
36 Causton Street
London SW1P 4ST

Hendrickson Publishers, Inc.
P.O. Box 3473
Peabody
Massachusetts 01961-3473

British Library Cataloguing-in-Publication Data
A catalogue record for this book is available from the British Library

SPCK ISBN 978–0–281–05850–1
Hendrickson Publishers ISBN 978–1–59856–341–2

1 3 5 7 9 10 8 6 4 2

Typeset by Graphicraft Ltd, Hong Kong
Printed in Great Britain by Ashford Colour Press

Produced on paper from sustainable forests

Contents

Contents

Preface

This volume constitutes a dialogue and a debate about the birth of Christianity between two scholars from two distinct viewpoints: a Christian from the evangelical tradition (Michael F. Bird) and a secularist (James G. Crossley). It tackles a wide array of subjects, such as the historical Jesus, the resurrection, Paul, the Gospels, and the early Church and gives evangelical and secular perspectives on each topic.

The book arose through the interaction of the authors on the internet through their respective internet blogs, called 'Euangelion' by Michael Bird and 'Earliest Christian History' by James Crossley.[1] Then at the Society of Biblical Literature conference in Philadelphia 2005, Michael and James got together and came up with the idea of writing a book about the origins of Christianity together where they would have a chance to present the arguments and viewpoints of their own respective positions and enable readers to evaluate and size-up the relative value of each side of the argument. In many ways this book is similar to the volume by N. T. Wright and Marcus Borg called *The Meaning of Jesus: Two Visions* (San Francisco: Harper, 1999). The differences are (1) whereas Borg and Wright represent a contrast of evangelical and liberal versions of modern Christianity, the differences between Crossley and Bird are more acute since the contrast is between an evangelical and a secularist; and (2) the subject matter is more comprehensive and covers the beginnings of early Christianity from Jesus to the end of the first century.

James Crossley, according to Michael Bird, is a likeable agnostic with a quick wit and a mind like a steel trap. James is a former electrician now biblical scholar who teaches at Sheffield University. He has written on the historical Jesus and Christian origins and his current research interests include the political contexts of New Testament scholarship. He did his PhD at the University of Nottingham on the dating of Mark's Gospel and the role of the Law in Christian origins and early Judaism. James professes no religious commitments and is committed to studying the Bible and early Christianity from a secular point of view, that is, without any religious commitments and without recourse to miraculous explanations. James often gets mistaken for being an evangelical because he is willing to argue for

---

[1] See <http://euangelizomai.blogspot.com/> and <http://earliestchristianhistory.blogspot.com/> (checked 10 April 2008).

positions which are usually regarded as being conservative, such as dating the Gospel of Mark to the early 40s of the first century. The most redeeming characteristic of James Crossley, in Michael Bird's opinion, is that he is not an angry or militant secularist and he is willing to listen to and respect others with whom he disagrees.

Michael Bird, according to James Crossley, is one of the most tolerant evangelicals around, who, aside from openly engaging with a secularist, has even attempted to heal a deep wound in contemporary Reformed thought over the issue of salvation and works, and with some success by all accounts. Anyone with a brief knowledge of post-Reformation schisms will know that it takes a brave person to do such a thing. Michael Bird is tutor in New Testament at the Highland Theological College and completed his PhD at the University of Queensland on the historical Jesus and the Gentiles, in which he argued that the seeds of the later gentile mission can be found in the teaching of Jesus. Michael Bird comes from a non-religious background and found faith in what might seem to many an unusual context: working as a paratrooper and in military intelligence. Michael Bird is a prolific writer covering major areas, such as the historical Jesus, Pauline theology and Christian origins.

A few points of clarification are in order. First, when Bird identifies himself as an evangelical Christian he means that he believes in the saving and transforming power of the gospel and is committed to the historical doctrines of orthodox Christianity. What is more, not all Christians would necessarily agree with all of his views of Jesus, Paul and the early Church. Similarly, when Crossley identifies himself as a secularist he means that he studies Christian origins without any personal religious commitment (implicit or explicit), a major emphasis on social-historical explanations and, most significantly, a different perspective from the overwhelming majority of the discipline. Crossley does not intend this to be anything like a fixed definition of a 'secularist', just one that usefully describes the kinds of work he does on Christian origins.

Second, Bird and Crossley do not necessarily disagree on everything about Christian origins. In many cases though, when we do agree on something it is often for very different reasons. As such we have limited the topics to areas that will primarily manifest our differences and present opportunities for us to explain and defend our distinctive viewpoints.

Third, it is also our conviction that, despite our different presuppositions and style of argumentation, we both have something to contribute to the ongoing discussion of the New Testament and the birth of Christianity. There is a sense in which 'iron sharpens iron' and through engagements such as this one we are able to clarify, expound and defend our own views as well as learn from what others with different perspectives and varied viewpoints have to say.

This book covers the areas of the historical Jesus, the resurrection of Jesus, the apostle Paul, the Gospels and the shape of early Christianity. Each chapter looks at one of these topics in turn and includes an initial essay, a response and a counter-response. As such, a conversation gradually develops between the authors. We have also invited two other scholars, who are also from different ends of the spectrum, to contribute responses to this book: Dr Scot McKnight (North Park University, Chicago, USA) and Professor Emeritus Maurice Casey (Nottingham University, UK). Both are experienced teachers and scholars and bring to this book their vast experience in writing about Jesus, Paul and the early Church. McKnight will respond to Crossley's views and Casey will respond to Bird's views. We thought it fitting to give the final word to two scholars who are more seasoned and experienced than ourselves and see how our arguments and analysis fare in their judgment.

Our deepest thanks go to Rebecca Mulhearn of SPCK, who has supported our project from the beginning and provided us with many helpful ideas and suggestions along the way. We remain grateful to our many friends in the world of biblioblogs who have encouraged us in our studies and spurred us on to present the best case we can for our respective positions.

Michael Bird offers this book in dedication to his family (Mum, Dad and Dean) for their willingness to endure a family member who has 'gone religious'. And thanks to several friends such as David Campbell and Matt Montonini who read parts and made comments. James Crossley would like to dedicate this book to the usual suspects: Pamela Crossley, Richard Crossley and Caroline Watt. He would also like to thank his Sheffield colleague, the Pauline expert Barry Matlock, for a variety of conversations on Pauline theology which helped clarify parts of the chapter on Paul (everything in that chapter is of course the responsibility of James Crossley). We also would like to express our willingness to sell the movie rights of this book which we think would make a fine sequel to the *The Da Vinci Code*, particularly given that we actually do know something about early Christian history.

Abbreviations

Bibliographical abbreviations

AB	Anchor Bible
ABRL	Anchor Bible Reference Library
ANET	*Ancient Near Eastern Texts relating to the Old Testament*, ed. J. B. Pritchard
BBR	*Bulletin for Biblical Research*
Bib	*Biblica*
BTB	*Biblical Theology Bulletin*
COQG	Christian Origins and the Question of God
JGRChJ	*Journal of Greco-Roman Christianity and Judaism*
JSNT	*Journal for the Study of the New Testament*
JTS	*Journal of Theological Studies*
LHJS	Library of Historical Jesus Studies
LNTS	Library of New Testament Studies
NSBT	New Studies in Biblical Theology
NTS	*New Testament Studies*
PGM	*Papyri graecae magicae: Die griechischen Zauberpapyri*, ed. K. Preisendanz
SNTS	Society for New Testament Studies
TSAJ	Texte und Studien zum antiken Judentum
WTJ	*Westminster Theological Journal*

Ancient literature

Acts Pil.	*Acts of Pilate*
Aeschylus	
Ag.	*Agamemnon*
Eum.	*Eumenides*
Supplices	*Suppliant Women*
Aristides, *Apol.*	*Apology*
Aristotle	
Metaph.	*Metaphysics*
Arnobius, *Adv. Gent.*	*Adversus nationes*
As. Mos.	*Assumption of Moses*
B. Meṣ.	*Baba Meṣiʿa*

Did.	*Didache*
Ep. Arist.	*Aristeas*
Epictetus, *Diatr.*	*Diatribai (Dissertations)*
Epiphanius, *Pan.*	*Panarion (Adversus haereses)*
'Erub.	*'Erubin*
Eusebius, *Hist. eccl.*	*Historia ecclesiastica (Ecclesiastical History)*
Gen. Rab.	*Genesis Rabbah*
Gos. Eb.	*Gospel of the Ebionites*
Gos. Pet.	*Gospel of Peter*
Gos. Thom.	*Gospel of Thomas*
Ḥul.	*Ḥullin*
Ignatius, *Magn.*	*To the Magnesians*
Irenaeus, *Haer.*	*Adversus haereses*
John Chrysostom	
Adv. Jud.	*Adversus Judaeos*
Josephus	
Ag. Ap.	*Against Apion*
Ant.	*Jewish Antiquities*
J.W.	*Jewish War*
Jub.	*Jubilees*
Justin Martyr	
1 Apol.	*First Apology*
Dial.	*Dialogue with Trypho*
Juvenal, *Sat.*	*Satires*
L.A.B.	*Liber antiquitatum biblicarum (Pseudo-Philo)*
Liv. Pro.	*Lives of the Prophets*
Origen	
Cels.	*Contra Celsum*
Comm. Jo.	*Commentarii in evangelium Joannis*
Pesaḥ	*Pesaḥim*
Philo of Alexandria	
Flacc.	*In Flaccum*
Good Person	*That Every Good Person Is Free*
Her.	*Quis rerum divinarum heres sit*
Legat.	*Legatio ad Gaium*
Migration	*On the Migration of Abraham*
Mos.	*De vita Mosis*
Opif.	*De opificio mundi*
QE	*Questions and Answers on Exodus*
Spec. Laws	*On the Special Laws*

Pliny the Younger
   Ep.   *Epistulae*
Plutarch
   Comm. not.   *De communibus notitiis contra stoicos*
   Is. Os.   *De Iside et Osiride*
Prot. Jas   *Protoevangelium of James*
Pseudo-Philo, *see L.A.B.*
Pss. Sol.   *Psalms of Solomon*
Šabb.   *Šabbat*
Sanh.   *Sanhedrin*
Sib. Or.   *Sibylline Oracles*
Suetonius
   Aug.   *Divus Augustus*
   Claud.   *Divus Claudius*
Ta'an   *Ta'anit*
Tacitus, *Ann.*   *Annales*
Tertullian, *Spect.*   *De spectaculis (The Shows)*
Tg. Onq.   *Targum Onqelos*
T. Job   *Testament of Job*
T. Levi   *Testament of Levi*
T. Mos.   *Testament of Moses*

Introduction

Michael F. Bird: the Christian view on the birth of Christianity

According to Martin Dibelius: 'In the beginning was the sermon.'[1] What that means is that at the root of Christianity was the proclamation of certain events pertaining to Jesus and the explanation of these events by the followers of Jesus. And so began what we now call Christianity and it began with a bang! Jesus was crucified in Judea some time around 30 CE, and by 49 CE (a mere 19 years later) the Roman emperor Claudius was making imperial policy about Christians in relation to disputes in Rome among the Jewish population concerning a certain 'Chrestus' who we may identify with 'Christ' (Acts 18.2; Suetonius, *Claud.* 25.4). How do we get from Judea to Rome in so short a time? What happened, when, where, who, how and what does it mean? To look briefly at those questions is the task before us now.

In our study of Christian origins we are dealing with reports and interpretations, facts and faith, history and theology. What sets me apart from James Crossley is that I accept the interpretation of the events by the earliest witnesses, I share their faith, and I expound the theology that they have bequeathed to us. That is why I am an 'evangelical' Christian, which I take to mean *someone who identifies with the faith of historic Christianity and believes in the saving and transforming power of the evangel, that is, the good news about Jesus the Christ.* That will obviously influence the way that I approach the historical task. As Frank Thielman writes:

> Whereas both the New Testament theologian and the secular historian are interested in the history to which the canonical texts give access, they differ on the importance that they grant to the perspectives of the texts themselves. Historians who stand outside the church employ every means at their disposal to render the perspectives of the canonical texts inoperative in their thinking. The texts then provide the raw data with which the secular historian attempts to reconstruct the story of early Christianity according to another perspective. The New Testament theologians, however, through the basic insight of faith, want to embrace the perspectives of the texts on

---

[1] Martin Dibelius, *From Tradition to Gospel* (Cambridge: James Clarke, 1971), 12–15; in German: *Im Anfang war die Predigt.*

the events that provoked their composition. The perspectives of the texts on the history of early Christianity are not husks to be peeled away so that the historian might see more clearly. They are not merely historical data that provide information about early Christian religion. For New Testament theologians who regard the texts as authoritative, the perspectives of the texts speak of their true significance. They are, in other words, objects of faith.[2]

I am a reader of the history of early Christianity, the texts and artefacts, the sociology and its relevant contexts, but I read it sympathetically. For me, the Bible is not an assortment of documents about religious ideas from antiquity but it is Scripture and has sacred value in the faith community to which I belong. Does that make me biased then? To be perfectly truthful, it certainly does, and I cannot avoid that. But let me say two things to those who might dismiss my historical labours prematurely as too partisan and lacking in objectivity. First, as a Christian my task is not to peddle my presuppositions and call them evidence. Rather, I hope to carry out the kind of open and critical enquiry that might vindicate those presuppositions.[3] Second, I would vouch for myself by saying that, even as a believer, I am genuinely interested in history and truth in its own right. If I were to be persuaded that certain events did not take place (e.g. the resurrection) then I would have to seriously reconsider my current expression of faith and perhaps even abandon it altogether.[4] Suffice to say, that has not happened to date. On the contrary, my faith has grown and been enriched by my historical study. Over time I have changed my mind on many theological issues as a result of my historical ventures, but I have not yet felt the temptation to chuck it all in as it were.

As I study early Christianity, I see a number of sequential stories: the story of Israel, the story of the Jews under foreign hegemony, the story of Jesus, the story of the early Church, and also the story of God. Thus, what I want to do in this book is provide a commentary on these narratives by looking at the main threads in the various plots and subplots: Jesus, the resurrection, the Gospels, Paul and the early Church, and pay attention to the flash-points along the way. I hope in the end to provide a compelling and entertaining narration of early Christianity that tells us something of Jesus, the first Christians and even of God.

---

[2] Frank Thielman, *Theology of the New Testament: A Canonical and Synthetic Approach* (Grand Rapids, MI: Zondervan, 2005), 31–2.

[3] Bruce D. Chilton, 'An Evangelical and Critical Approach to the Sayings of Jesus', *Themelios* 3 (1978), 74–85 (85).

[4] I think here of Gerd Lüdemann and Bart Ehrman in particular, as examples of scholars who have abandoned faith owing to their scholarly endeavours.

James G. Crossley: the secular view on the birth of Christianity

Whatever route either of us would take in this competing book on Christian origins, the passages/evidence and narrative outline could only be selective. That much is obvious but it begs the questions: Why choose certain passages/pieces of evidence? And why choose a certain narrative? What I will do is use the preselected areas (Jesus, resurrection, Paul, Gospels and Christianity in the Roman Empire) to explain some of the key reasons why Christianity became a major religion in its own right, often constructing its identity over against the Roman and Jewish worlds while at the same time being embedded in both. Three key areas, among numerous others, set Christianity apart from its Jewish heritage: Law observance (or lack of), Gentiles and the full deification of a human being, Jesus. Judaism, in contrast, was known, partly, for its observance of the Law, its stress on Jewish ethnicity, and its god who certainly did not become a human being. At the same time, Christianity's Jewish and scriptural heritage of hostility to other cults or views of the divine, among other things, provided one mechanism for a distinctive identity to be constructed over against the Roman world. Of course, identity is much messier and much more complex than this simple outline, but in general terms, and in terms of orthodox Christianity, the above factors became known as some of the distinctive features. The question now is how Christianity got to these distinctive features.

The approach I will take will be what may generally be called 'secular', if by secular we mean the kind of approach that might typically be used in humanities departments outside theology and biblical studies. Here, I will provide some fairly conventional approaches developed by historians outside theology and biblical studies and sometimes fruitfully applied to the historical study of Christian origins. This will involve looking at broader social and economic trends, combined with individual decisions, that led to the emergence of Christianity as a distinctive religion. In this respect, the famous pre-inclusive language statement of Karl Marx is worth recalling:

> Men make their own history, but they do not make it just as they please; they do not make it under circumstances chosen by themselves, but under circumstances directly encountered, given and transmitted from the past.[5]

---

[5] K. Marx, 'Eighteenth Brumaire of Louis Bonaparte', in K. Marx and F. Engels, *Collected Works: Volume 11 1851–1853* (London: Lawrence & Wishart, 1979), 99–197.

But not unlike Christianity as described above, I too have a heritage that I cannot (and will not) totally shake off, namely, the various approaches advanced in biblical studies and even – heaven forbid – theological approaches. Indeed, the very thematic structure of this book is one of classical studies of Christian origins grounded in theological approaches to the ancient texts. This is hardly a surprise, as theology is deeply embedded in its historical context, and theology too, as we will see, plays its part in the emergence of Christianity, even if this has been massively overstated in scholarship. But, on this level too, my choice of areas to study sharply focus the secular–evangelical/Christian debate on the full divinity of Jesus and the non-observance of at least key parts of the Law (not to mention the resurrection!), which have been massive identity markers for Christian tradition.

Contrary to what has been written about me in various reviews and elsewhere, I do not deplore theological approaches, theology, history of ideas, Christianity or religion, etc. I have stressed this elsewhere and stress it again (and again) and consequently I can now only hope people do not add words and sentiments that are not present (cf. Rev. 22.18–20). What I want to do is provide an explanation for the emergence of Christianity that is not heavily grounded in theology, the supernatural, and/or ideas but one that is heavily grounded in socio-historical explanation. I do not wish to demolish anyone's worldview or religious beliefs but, at the same time, I have no desire to endorse them for the sake of historical research that comes up smelling of Christian roses. But then why have a book between a believer and non-believer if there are no points of argument?

To anticipate a certain type of reaction, I am not arguing that my secular perspective is 'more objective' or somehow inherently superior to an evangelical or indeed any other approach, though, obviously, I do think my explanation is, to the best of my knowledge, a better account of the evidence, just as, presumably, Michael Bird thinks his account is better than mine. If neither of us were arrogant enough to think like this then there would be little point in being involved in doing a book like this. And this really hits at the heart of this book: Who has got the better account of Christian origins?

1

The historical Jesus

James G. Crossley

Perhaps not unfairly, I have sometimes been accused by Christian scholars of both liberal and conservative dispositions of having too many conservative evangelical traits when it comes to the historical Jesus. For example, I think that there is a lot of useful historical information about Jesus' life and teaching that can be gleaned from the Gospels of Matthew, Mark and Luke (though not John – see my chapter on the Gospels). To add to the confusion, I believe the following: famous terms for Jesus such as 'son of man' and 'son of God' really were being used by or of Jesus when he was alive; Jesus really did practise healing and exorcism; and Jesus really did predict his imminent death and probably thought it had some important atoning function. So why bother writing a chapter that sounds, so far at least, *virtually evangelical*?

One key point of difference here is not simply facts but *interpretation* of the facts. In each case mentioned above, and for all the dramatic claims that Jesus may have made, I do not think there were any claims made that were too out of the ordinary in Jesus' first-century context. I do not think there was anything supernatural at work, or, better, at least nothing that cannot be paralleled cross-culturally. I should also add further remarks concerning what will become the wider narrative thread in my contributions to this book, namely, that Jesus and Christianity were the product of broader social, economic and historical trends. It was, I would stress, Jesus' reactions in this context – intentionally or, as I think is more likely, unintentionally – that tapped into these trends and got the ball rolling in the origins of Christianity. In other words, Christian origins are perfectly explicable in terms of normal this-worldly historical explanation and Jesus plays a small part in such developments.

I have mentioned that crucial developments in distinguishing Christianity as a religion in its own right involved Law, Gentiles and Christology and that these will be the focus of my contributions to this book. The historical figure of Jesus and the ways in which he did – and did not – contribute to these crucial developments is our first task and it should become clear that Jesus' socio-economic context can shed some light on this.

Jesus growing up

Jesus was born sometime close to the end of the first century BCE in Galilee. If we judge Jesus' birth as presented by Matthew and Luke in terms of conventional historical standards, my guess is that we would have to say that we know next to nothing about the specifics of Jesus' birth other than that the circumstances were probably like that of any conventional peasant birth and that he had two normal human parents, probably Joseph and Mary. There were plenty of dramatic stories in the ancient world about the births (and deaths) of figures deemed significant, including rulers such as Alexander the Great. In Jewish tradition, there are stories of the matriarchs giving birth where God directly intervenes. The retellings of these stories are also significant and, as Roger Aus has shown in detail, there are plenty of close parallels between Matthew's story of Mary and the stories of certain matriarchs in rabbinic literature.[1] In all these cases, it would be extremely difficult to find historians who would take them as anything other than imaginative storytelling and, by the standards of conventional historical research, there is no good reason why the Gospel accounts of the miraculous conception of Jesus should be taken any differently. But even if the source for Matthew and Luke got (say) material from Mary herself, we are then left with the problem of Mary telling a bemused Joseph and the world that the reason she mysteriously became pregnant was because the Holy Spirit made her so. (How many fiancés can you see buying that?)

Incidentally, the principle of parallel stories in the ancient world applies to miracles in general. Miracles were attributed to different figures across the ancient world and so it is unsurprising that miracles attributed to Jesus occur in the Gospels and, by the standards of conventional historical research, they are of little historical value in the reconstruction of the events of Jesus' life. I will return to the dubious use of the miraculous in historical research in my chapter on resurrection. In contrast, there are far more significant issues in terms of explaining Christian origins. There are a whole range of interesting details of social history that can illuminate what it might have been like for Jesus growing up in Nazareth, but two key events probably would have shaped his life and the emergence of

---

[1] R. D. Aus, *Matthew 1—2 and the Virginal Conception in Light of Palestinian and Hellenistic Judaic Traditions on the Birth of Israel's First Redeemer Moses* (Studies in Judaism; Landham: University Press of America, 2004).

Christianity more than any other: the building and rebuilding of two major urban centres in Galilee, Tiberias and Sepphoris respectively.[2]

These building projects are important for the historical study of Jesus and Christian origins because social historians have pointed out that social change involving urbanization can lead to peasant unrest, with reactions ranging from utopias to millenarian movements.[3] There are endless and important debates over whether urbanization was a benefit for the Galilean populace but in terms of social change this does not necessarily matter too much. What is important, as social historians have pointed out, is the *perception* that new change is for the worse.[4] We know that there were dramatic changes in Galilee and not everyone thought such changes were for the better. For example, by the time of the Jewish war of 66–70 CE, the Jewish historian Josephus records that there was great hatred toward Sepphoris and Tiberias. We also have a stress on harsh socio-economic conditions across the Gospel tradition (Mark 12.1–12; Matt. 5.25/Luke 12.57–59; Matt. 5.40; Matt. 5.42/Luke 6.35; Matt. 6.12; 18.23–35; Matt. 9.37–38; 20.1–8; 25.31–46; Luke 4.18; 6.20–21; 13.27; 15.17; 16.1–8; 19—21), suggesting that there were voices recorded in this tradition who did not think social change was for the better.

This social background can explain a great deal about the emergence of Jesus' ministry. There are various reasons to suggest that it was not just coincidence that the Jesus movement emerged in Galilee at the time of undeniable social change and it is to these reasons we now turn.

In general terms, it has long been noted that Jesus appears similar to the prophetic-type figures (e.g. John the Baptist in Matt. 3 and Theudas in Acts 5.36) who emerged during the period of Roman influence and rule in Palestine. Furthermore, while Jesus was no bandit, he did have some very harsh things to say about the rich. In the ferocious Parable of the Rich Man and Lazarus (Luke 16.19–31), the poor man Lazarus gets reward in the afterlife whereas the rich man goes straight to a fiery afterlife. There is no mention in this parable that the rich man suffers because he abused his wealth or the like. He suffers for the simple reason that he is rich. This

---

[2] See, e.g., J. D. Crossan, *The Birth of Christianity: Discovering What Happened in the Years Immediately after the Execution of Jesus* (New York: HarperCollins; Edinburgh: T&T Clark, 1998), 151–235.

[3] See, e.g., J. C. Scott, 'Protest and Profanation: Agrarian Revolt and the Little Tradition, *Part I*', *Theory and Society* 4 (1977), 1–38 (e.g. 17); J. C. Scott, 'Protest and Profanation: Agrarian Revolt and the Little Tradition, *Part II*', *Theory and Society* 4 (1977), 211–46; J. H. Kautsky, *The Politics of Aristocratic Empires* (Chapel Hill: University of North Carolina, 1982), 318.

[4] See, e.g., E. J. Hobsbawm, *Uncommon People: Resistance, Rebellion and Jazz* (London: Abacus, 1998), 224.

is the only reason the parable gives: 'Child, remember that during your lifetime you received your good things, and Lazarus in like manner evil things; but now he is comforted here, and you are in agony' (Luke 16.25).

Comments such as these are significant because there was a long tradition grounded in the Hebrew Bible/Old Testament of wealth being a sign of blessing here on earth. This continued into the Judaism at the time of Jesus. However, in times of serious social change, the obvious injustices of such 'reward theology' can get highlighted. In broadly contemporaneous Judaism, the document *1 Enoch* reversed reward theology so that rewards and riches in this life were no longer a sign of favour but were actually a sign that an individual was damned! True rewards will come in the life to come.

Jesus was following in the footsteps of *1 Enoch* in his attacks on the rich. We have already seen the Parable of the Rich Man and Lazarus but the logic and problems of critiquing traditional 'reward theology' are perhaps most worked out in Mark 10.17–31. Mark 10.17–31 as a whole may or may not go back to an incident in Jesus' life but it certainly reflects ideas surrounding the problems of rich people not *really* being blessed on earth. The unusualness of the shift in reward from this life to the life to come is the best historical explanation for the perplexed reactions of the disciples (Mark 10.24, 26). That this passage as a whole held such sharp views on wealth gains further confirmation from the fact that textual traditions felt the need to alter the passage to make it more palatable for the more wealthy Christians (10.24, 25). Obviously, this would not have been done if in the passage Jesus' teaching on wealth was not so disturbingly stark.

There is some evidence that Jesus' teaching had some concern for the repentance of the rich. People of some means were far more likely to serve mammon, store up treasures on earth (Matt. 6.19–21; Luke 12.33–34), worry about what clothes to wear, what food to eat, and about prosperity (Matt. 6.25–34; Luke 12.22–32), a view made clear in *1 Enoch* (*1 Enoch* 97–98, 102). This concern for the repentance of the rich was also reflected in Jesus' controversial association with people labelled 'the sinners' (cf. Mark 2.15–17; Matt. 11.19/Luke 7.34; Luke 15.1–2) who, contrary to popular belief, were not the common everyday folk looked down on by people like the Pharisees. Rather, whenever the phrase 'the sinners' occurs in early Judaism and whenever social class is mentioned these people are always identified as rich or, to be more precise, oppressive rich,[5] and it is notable

---

[5] J. G. Crossley, *Why Christianity Happened: A Sociohistorical Account of Christian Origins 26–50 CE* (Louisville: Westminster John Knox Press, 2006), chapter 3.

that the sinners are associated with tax collectors and good living in the Gospel tradition (Mark 2.15–17; Matt. 11.19/Luke 7.34; Luke 15.1–2; 19.1–9). As with Jesus' teaching on the rich, it appears that Jesus called for such people to *repent* (cf. Mark 2.15–17; 14.3; Luke 15; 19.1–9; cf. Luke 7.36–50), which in early Judaism meant fellow Jews perceived to be wrongdoers (re-)turning to proper observance of the commandments and renouncing their previous ways. But whether or not Jesus was successful in getting such unpleasant people like 'sinners' and tax collectors to repent is another question.

Kingdom of God

I noted above that in the context of social change associated with urbanization projects such as Tiberias and Sepphoris, millenarian and utopian ideals were often found in reactions stemming from the peasantry. An excellent example of this is Jesus' teaching on the 'kingdom of God'.

It is widely agreed that Jesus, like Jews before and after him, used the term 'kingdom of God'. Precisely what Jesus *meant* by kingdom of God is not so clear. In general terms I would go along with those who suggest that for Jesus the phrase referred to the kingdom of both the present and the future. What *present* might generally mean for many Jews from around Jesus' time is that God rules the entire universe, as we see in the book of Daniel (Dan. 4.31–32). But it was clear that Jews were not ruling the world and that the world was far from being a perfect place for Jews – even though their God ruled all – or indeed virtually anyone else in the ancient world. Consequently, God's kingdom would come in the *future*, about which the book of Daniel was also clear (Dan. 2.44; cf. Dan. 7).

The book of Daniel is a good example because it holds both present and future kingdoms together without seeing this as a contradiction, just like the Gospel tradition does. Think of a passage like Mark 4.30–32 where Jesus compares the kingdom to a mustard seed which is small but it grows and eventually becomes the greatest of the shrubs. The book of Daniel is also a good example because we know from reading between the lines of the work of the first-century CE Jewish historian Josephus that Daniel was being read in dramatic terms where the present rulers of the world, Rome, would be overthrown by a final kingdom.

Quite what this dramatic new kingdom would look like is uncertain and many answers are educated guesses. There has been some heated debate as to whether this was a literal 'end-of-the-world' scenario or more down-to-earth socio-political change. It is actually very difficult to be precise because we do not have surveys of what people thought and there are no convenient explanations in the Gospel tradition. It is sometimes argued that first-century people would not have read a lot of the dramatic language associated with predictions of times to come (e.g. Mark 1.15; 9.1) literally because they were 'sophisticated' readers or the like. Yet, for all we know, among Jesus' audience there may well have been a range of interpreters, some interpreting more 'symbolically' or 'metaphorically' than others, just as there have been in different societies throughout human history. But we can say that in the tradition in which Jesus found himself there was an expectation for God to intervene dramatically in human history. Indeed some, such as people responsible for a commentary on the book of Habakkuk, found among the Dead Sea Scrolls, predicted the date of the 'end times' and got it wrong, as they virtually admitted when talking of the final age being prolonged (1QpHab 7).

A big question is this: when did *Jesus* think that the kingdom of God would arrive? This has been a real problem for Christian scholars because there has been a powerful scholarly tradition arguing that Jesus predicted the imminent kingdom within the lifetime of some of his audience. Jesus was not as specific as the Habakkuk Commentary from the Dead Sea Scrolls but he was precise enough. As Jesus says in Mark 9.1, 'there are some standing here who will not taste death until they see that the kingdom of God has come with power'. This reflects other teachings of Jesus which are not quite as specific but do point to something happening soon (e.g. Mark 1.15). This means that, like the Habakkuk Commentary from the Dead Sea Scrolls, Jesus got his prediction wrong. The earliest Christians, including Paul, continued to believe something dramatic was going to happen soon. Yet when those who had stood by Jesus were no longer alive the timeframe was stretched too far, causing problems for the first Christians. John's Gospel, for example, written towards the end of the first century or the beginning of the second, drops all references to 'the kingdom of God' save two where the kingdom of God now refers to entry into John's version of Christianity (John 3), not to mention John's problems with the second coming not happening (John 21). Like the authors of the Habakkuk Commentary, Christians had to deal with the problem of a mistaken prediction by employing creative reinterpretation (cf. 2 Peter 3).

Law and conflict

When discussing the role of the Law in the teaching of Jesus it is important to think of the Law or, what Jews would call the Torah (effectively the first five books of the Bible and the laws and commandments they contain), on two levels: (1) biblical law, that is, the laws as explicitly stated in the Bible; and (2) the interpretation or expansion of biblical law to new situations. It is often thought, especially by many Christian interpreters, that when Jesus comes into conflict over the Law in the Gospel tradition, he is rejecting the former, that is the validity of biblical laws, when in fact it is clear, at least from the Synoptic Gospels, that Jesus' disputes with his contemporaries concern the latter, that is, some of the *interpretations* or *expansions* of biblical law.

I do not think that Jesus ever doubted the validity of the biblical laws. In fact, in some instances Jesus endorsed certain *expansions* or *interpretations* of the Law. A classic case of many people believing that Jesus overrode or rejected biblical law when in fact he was actually engaging with interpretation or expansion of biblical law is that connected with the 'eye for an eye' ruling of Exodus 21.24. Matthew 5.38–42 records the strongest version of the contrast: 'But I say to you, Do not resist an evildoer. But if anyone strikes you on the right cheek, turn the other also.' Unlike other Gospel traditions concerning the Law, we are not told that Jesus' words here led to conflict, something we would surely have expected if Jesus had done something as dramatic as overturn a commandment. But this lack of conflict should not be surprising because Jesus does not do anything so dramatic. From the available evidence, it seems that the dominant interpretation of Exodus 21.24, at least among the Pharisees and later rabbis, was that it should definitely *not* be interpreted literally in terms of violent retribution. We see in Jewish legal sources, particularly in those written down by the rabbis, that if someone was injured then financial compensation was the way to resolve the situation (e.g. *m. B. Qam* 8.1; *b. B. Qam* 83b–84a; *Tg. Ps.-J.* Exod. 21.24; *Mek.* Exod. 21.24 [III:67–69]). However, there were literal, violent interpretations of Exodus 21.24 against which groups such as the Pharisees reacted (cf. *Jub.* 4.31; *m. Mak.* 1.6). It appears that the words attributed to Jesus stand in this tradition of rejecting the violent interpretation.

Jesus' rejection of the violent interpretation of Exodus 21.24 would have some relevance if at least some of Jesus' teachings were aimed at people deemed 'sinners', people who we saw could have had some skills in the area of violent retaliation. Of course, it will take more historical investigation to show whether or not Jesus interpreted Exodus 21.24 but, as Jesus was never said to react against the non-violent interpretation, it would be extremely difficult to make the traditional case that Jesus rejected outright the biblical law of Exodus 21.24.

But how do we explain Jesus' view of the Law causing conflict with those dedicated to the expansion of the Law? For a start it seems fairly clear that groups in early Judaism did engage in some heated debates, as Josephus, a Jewish historian writing in the first century CE, tells us (*Ant.* 13.297–98). Such disputes among groups could range from the basic argument to the particularly brutal, such as the disputes between the people responsible for the Dead Sea Scrolls and their opponents (e.g. 4Q171 4).

Let us take the example of Sabbath observance because this is one of the areas where Jesus clashes with opponents over the interpretation of the Law. The following example is a Jewish dispute over whether fallen fruit should be picked up on the Sabbath, an *expansion* of biblical law that is paralleled at the time of Jesus (*Jub.* 2.29; CD 10.17–23; *Philo, Mos.* 2.22): 'Six rules did the men of Jericho make . . . For three the Sages criticised them . . . [2] they eat on the Sabbath fruit which had fallen under a tree . . . (*m. Pesaḥ* 4.8)'.

We might compare this with the dispute over the plucking of grain on the Sabbath in Mark 2.23–28: 'One Sabbath he was going through the cornfields; and as they made their way his disciples began to pluck heads of grain. The Pharisees said to him, "Look, why are they doing what is not lawful on the Sabbath?" (Mark 2.23–24)'. Nowhere in biblical law is plucking grain on the Sabbath forbidden so we must be dealing with a dispute over the interpretation and expansion of biblical law.

As with other disputes over the interpretation of biblical law, the Gospels suggest that Jesus' disputes over the Sabbath were bitter. Think of Mark 3.6 which is the response to Jesus healing a man on the Sabbath. This incident comes just after Jesus has been accused by the Pharisees of unlawfully plucking grain on the Sabbath in Mark 2.23–28. In Mark 3.1–6 it appears that Jesus is developing a key aspect of Sabbath law in early Judaism by controversially extending the long-established principle that the duty to save life, which includes his healing ministry, overrules the duty to observe the Sabbath (cf. 1 Macc. 2.40–41). Compare the following:

> Any matter of doubt as to danger to life overrides the prohibitions of the Sabbath. (*m. Yoma* 8.6)

> Is it lawful to do good or to do harm on the Sabbath, to save life or to kill? (Mark 3.4)

All the above Sabbath discussion shows that the Sabbath disputes mentioned in the Gospels were very much at home in an early Jewish context and had little concern for Christianity. Whether or not they precisely go back to the life and teaching of Jesus, they show that the key synoptic evidence does not have Jesus contradicting any biblical Sabbath law.

Other disputes were not portrayed as escalating out of control. Mark 7.1–23 is a very good example of Jesus being remembered as a figure who clashed over interpretation of the Law. It has scribes and Pharisees asking why Jesus' disciples do not wash their hands before eating ordinary food. The role of hand-washing in Pharisaic and rabbinic thought requires much more detailed analysis than is usually given when discussed in historical Jesus and Gospel studies, but in basic terms hand-washing is an expansion of biblical purity laws designed to keep the insides pure by preventing the transmission of impurity from hands-to-food-to-eater via the ultra-defiling nature of a liquid. Jesus' response in Mark 7.15 appears to be a rejection of this expansion of biblical purity laws.

This would already imply that Jesus kept the biblical purity laws. It may seem strange to many Christians that Jesus observed biblical purity laws but there is nothing in the synoptic tradition that has Jesus attacking any biblical purity law. Sometimes people refer to Jesus coming into contact with impure people (e.g. Mark 5) but this happened to many Jews all the time. If they could, all they had to do was to make themselves pure again through the regulations set out in scriptural texts.

There are other disputes over the interpretation recorded in the Synoptic Gospels (e.g. Matt. 23) and in all cases there is no serious evidence that Jesus' view went beyond the boundaries of disputes known in early Judaism. Whether all of the Gospel passages discussed above go back to the historical Jesus requires a great deal more analysis than can be offered here but the key point to note is that there is a strong tradition of Jesus being engaged in internal Jewish legal disputes that have little to do with what is known about the early Church after Jesus' death. As the early Church was including more and more non-observant people from an early date (approximately 10 to 15 years after Jesus' death – see my chapter on Paul) then there is a strong chance that this tradition of Jesus as legal debater stems from the historical Jesus himself.

Jesus' last week

Whatever we make of Mark 3.6, Jesus' actions on the Sabbath did not manage to get him killed. Instead, Jesus appears to have been killed for doing something in the Jerusalem Temple (Mark 11.15–17). So what did Jesus do that was so upsetting? The traditional view that Jesus pushed for the end of the sacrificial system never had any serious evidence to support it. Rather it appears that Jesus was angry over perceived economic exploitation of poorer people.[6] Note the stress on the economic aspects of the Temple in Mark 11.15–18.

---

[6] C. A. Evans, *Jesus and His Contemporaries: Comparative Studies* (Leiden: Brill, 1995), chapter 9.

We know that Jesus was not the only first-century Jew concerned with the role of the dove-sellers. The first-century figure Simon ben Gamaliel was strongly critical of the inflated price of doves for sacrifice (*m. Ker.* 1.7). Similarly, the Dead Sea Scrolls (e.g. 1QpHab) were extremely critical of what they perceived as a corrupt Temple that exploited people. In this context, the words of Jesus make sense when he contrasts what he sees as the ideal function of the Temple ('a house of prayer') with what he hyperbolically sees as its present state ('a den of robbers').

It is sometimes argued that Jesus' action in the Temple was an instance of symbolic destruction. While a case can be made for Jesus predicting the destruction of the Temple owing to its present corruption, possibly hoping for its rebuilding (cf. Mark 14.58–59; 15.29), I am not convinced that his actions in the Temple were an act of prophetic symbolism. When prophetic actions are described in the scriptures they are usually explained and explicitly *interpreted* (e.g. Isa. 20.3; Jer. 19.1–13; 27–28; Ezek. 4—5; 12.1–16; 24.15–24). As there is no such explanation in Mark 11 it is difficult to accept such a view.

Another common argument related to Jesus' actions in the Temple is that Jesus established an alternative Temple system and took on an alternative role as priest or high priest, all in opposition to the Jerusalem Temple system. This seems to me to be letting Christian theology sneak into the debate under the pretence of Jesus' 'Jewish-ness', the common idea that Jesus *is* Jewish . . . but not *that* Jewish. And I am not just being overly suspicious here either.

For a start, no one in the synoptic tradition criticizes Jesus for starting an alternative Temple movement or setting himself up as an alternative priest or high priest, something we might expect had Jesus done something so dramatic. There is also nothing in the synoptic tradition which has Jesus replacing the Temple system.[7] Some people think that the reference to sins being 'forgiven' in Mark 2.1–12 has Jesus taking on a priestly function. However, it is not entirely clear how the Greek ought to be translated: it could equally be talking about sins being 'released', a vivid image of the paralysed man able to move his limbs again. But even if we translate it as 'forgiven', the phrase uses a 'divine passive' to suggest that the forgiveness comes from God ('your sins have been forgiven [by God]') and God was more than capable of forgiving sins outside the Temple in early Judaism (e.g. Ecclus. 3.30). Additionally, Jesus is assumed to have had an entirely positive attitude toward the ideal function of the Temple,

---

[7] See now the critique in D. Catchpole, *Jesus People: The Historical Jesus and the Beginnings of Community* (London: Darton, Longman & Todd; Grand Rapids: Baker, 2006).

even if he thought the present system corrupt. Look at Mark 1.44; Matt. 5.23–24; and 23.16–22, for instance.

So if we have passages favouring the ideal function of the Temple, no clear passages where Jesus says he replaces the Temple, and no explicit criticism of Jesus starting up an alternative system, then it is historically more plausible that Jesus accepted the ideal function of the Temple and did not set himself up in contrast to the Temple.

After his actions in the Temple, Jesus would have been well aware that he could be killed. In fact there is a good chance that Jesus knew he would have been killed prior to his actions in the Temple. His mentor, John the Baptist, had already been killed for prophetic activities, so Jesus would have to expect the worst. It also seems that Jesus developed a martyr theology whereby his death would have some benefit for others. In a tradition of martyrdom recalled annually at the Jewish festival of Hanukkah, there was a significant development whereby the sacrifice of the martyrs had some kind of atoning function for Jews with reference to the Law (e.g. 2 Macc. 7).

There are some Gospel traditions which point to a clear atoning function, such as Mark 10.45; 14.24. We might expect that if Jesus said such things he is best understood following martyr theology in early Judaism. But do not these traditions say that Jesus' death is for 'the many'? Well, yes, obviously; but we should not get carried away with the idea that this phrase refers to all humanity, Jew and gentile alike. We know that this phrase is used in early Judaism to refer to a particular group. In the Dead Sea Scrolls, the phrase 'the many' referred to the group (probably the Essenes) responsible for writing and collecting the scrolls (e.g. 1QS 6; CD 13.7; 14.7). It does not necessarily follow, therefore, that if Jesus used the phrase 'the many' in a context where his death was seen to have an atoning function he was making reference beyond the boundaries of Judaism in any significant way.

Moreover, if Jesus did develop a martyr theology, there is further evidence that he would have been concerned with Jews *primarily*. The reason for this is that typical of Jesus' ministry was a *primary* concern for Jews with little concern for Gentiles (see especially Matt. 10.5–6). Jesus' meeting with a gentile woman in Mark 7.24–30 (if accurate) is portrayed as exceptional but does imply that Gentiles will get something; Gentiles are, though, definitely second-class citizens in the times to come: 'Let the children [Jews] be fed first, for it is not fair to take the children's food and throw it to the dogs [Gentiles]' (Mark 7.27; at cf. Matt. 5.47; Luke 12.30/ Matt. 6.32). There are some passages which are sometimes read as a future and better hope for the Gentiles (e.g. Luke 10.13–14/Matt. 11.20–22; Luke

11.31–32/Matt. 12.41–42; Matt. 8.11–12/Luke 13.28–29), which would be in line with some mainstream Jewish views, but even here there has been some questioning of whether gentile salvation is even in mind in such passages.

Who was Jesus? – Healer and exorcist? Son of Man? Son of God? Messiah?

Jesus was famously remembered as someone who healed the sick and exorcized demons. It is often pointed out that this material does not show too many signs of interference by the early Church and could well reflect events from the life of Jesus. In fact, Jesus was hardly the only healer and exorcist around, as he notes himself (Mark 9.38–40), and as we know from non-Christian sources (e.g. Josephus, *Ant.* 8.45–49). But it should be stressed that this does not mean that there is something supernatural or miraculous happening. In Jesus' culture, illness and disease were interpreted in terms of the demonic. Yes, Jesus may well have healed people and have been perceived to have exorcized demons but this is nothing new in a cross-cultural context. Psychosomatic illnesses, including things similar to what the Gospel writers called a 'paralytic' (someone unable to move their limbs properly; cf. Mark 2.1–12), with accompanying healing by a traditional authoritative healer, are attested in many cultures, as are acts perceived to be exorcisms. Clearly these issues can be explained as social and psychological in origin and there is, in terms of historical analysis, no good reason why we should make an exception for Jesus' healings and exorcisms.

According to the Gospel tradition, 'the Son of Man' was a title for Jesus. That this was actually a significant *title* for Jesus during his lifetime is highly unlikely. The 'son of man problem' is notoriously difficult but some basic comments can be made. First, in Aramaic, the language in which Jesus spoke, the phrase in its most basic form simply means 'man' or 'human being'. Second, there was no dramatic title 'the Son of Man' in early Judaism. Many scholars refer to Daniel 7.13, 'I saw one like a human being [literally, 'son of man'] coming with the clouds of heaven' (NRSV). But 'son of man' simply means 'a human being', as the NRSV translation makes clear. Third, at the time of Jesus, the phrase 'son of man' was not a Greek phrase (though it occurs in translations of Semitic texts), and when translated into Greek it not only sounds unusual for a Greek speaker but also has a stronger force with the potential for sounding like a title. We will return to this in due course. Fourth, those suggestions by certain evangelical scholars (e.g. N. T. Wright) that the use of the term based on Daniel 7.13 can in some way be used to refer to the fall of Jerusalem are problematic for a number of reasons, the primary one being that there is no use whereby anyone might possibly understand the phrase meaning 'human being' to be referring to Jerusalem issues or anything related.[8]

I just said that the basic form of the phrase 'son of man' in Aramaic refers to 'man' or 'human being'. We now need to make some qualifications. The phrase can use the Aramaic equivalent of the English and Greek definite article, 'the', though it does not have to do so. In other words, the Aramaic phrase can be literally translated 'the son of man' or '(a) son of man', both meaning more or less the same thing in Aramaic. In Aramaic, the phrase takes on another usage. As experts in the area of son of man studies have shown, the phrase can be used to refer to a more general category of human beings but also with reference to the individual, not unlike the use of 'one' in English. It has long been noted that the Aramaic idiom is often used in situations where speakers find themselves in contexts of danger or death, or in situations requiring humility or modesty: all such themes are echoed in son of man sayings in the Gospels and may reflect an underlying Aramaic idiom used by the historical Jesus.[9]

There are several examples in the teaching of Jesus where the phrase is used in a fairly conventional Aramaic sense. Perhaps the clearest example is in Mark 2.23–28. After a dispute over the Sabbath, Jesus says the following: 'The sabbath was made for humankind, and not humankind for the sabbath; so the Son of Man is lord even of the sabbath' (Mark 2.27–28). Based on this saying alone, it would seem that there is some parallelism in verses 27–28, allowing the saying to have a general frame of reference but with particular reference also to the speaker, Jesus. The general element picks up generalized sayings concerning the authority of humans over the Sabbath in early Judaism (cf. Exod. 16.29; *Jub.* 2.17; *Mek.* Exod. 31.12–17). But there is a clear implication in the Marcan passage that Jesus is defending and referring to his own argument on Sabbath observance. A further argument in favour of the general-yet-specific son of man usage in the teaching of Jesus is how Matthew and Luke deal with Mark 2.27–28: both drop the general Mark 2.27 ('The sabbath was made for humankind, and not humankind for the sabbath') and keep 2.28 ('so the Son of Man is lord even of the sabbath') thereby heightening the reference to Jesus alone and dropping the idiomatic use of son of man retained in Mark.

---

[8] N. T. Wright, *Jesus and the Victory of God* (London: SPCK, 1996).
[9] For a comprehensive study see now M. Casey, *The Solution to the 'Son of Man' Problem* (London and New York: Continuum/T&T Clark, 2007).

There are son of man sayings that are clearly inventions of the early Church. In Mark 13.26 there is a clear reference to Daniel 7.13, 'Then they will see "the Son of Man coming in clouds" with great power and glory.' Yet Mark 13 is almost entirely secondary and tells us more about the early Church than the historical Jesus.[10] The saying also refers to the second coming of Jesus, an idea developed by the early Church and not by the historical Jesus. The similar saying in Mark 14.62 does not have a strong case for being authentic either. For a start, it seems like a second coming saying. But it was supposedly said during Jesus' trial (itself historically problematic) so it immediately becomes questionable: how did the Gospel tradition come across what Jesus supposedly said? And should we not be a little suspicious that Mark came across a saying of Jesus that perfectly mirrored his own Christianized theology?

But, clearly, 'the Son of Man' did become a title for Jesus at some point. The probable reason for this process from an Aramaic idiom to a Greek title is that Jesus used the phrase of himself with reference to others but when translated into Greek it is not only unusual but can also take on a form of a title, as it would if translated into English: *the* Son of Man. The phrase simply does not have this titular force in Aramaic. All this means that the phrase 'son of man' is an Aramaic idiom that was used by Jesus and many other people in early Judaism but did not denote anything particularly special and places Jesus firmly within Judaism with no concern for starting anything radically new in the sense that he would be *the* Son of Man to inaugurate a new age for all, or anything like that.

In an even more negative sense, the phrase 'son of God' does not necessarily denote the second person of the Trinity, the most unbelievable human being with major divine characteristics, or anything of the kind. As has long been noted, the phrase 'son of God', in early Judaism at least, can have a range of meanings, from Israelites, good Jews and kings to angelic figures (e.g. Gen. 6.2, 4; Exod. 4.22; Deut. 32.5–6, 18–19; 32.8; 2 Sam. 7.14; Ps. 2.7; 29.1; 89.7; Jer. 31.20; Dan. 3.25; Hos. 11.1). Tellingly, later Jewish literature could say that God called the charismatic Hanina ben Dosa 'my son' (*b. Ta'an.* 24b; *b. Ber.* 17b; *b. Ḥul.* 86a). This example (among many others) shows how deeply embedded the language of God's son was in Judaism because it continued long after the highly elevated uses in Christianity were established.

---

[10] See J. G. Crossley, *The Date of Mark's Gospel: Insight from the Law in Earliest Christianity* (London and New York: T&T Clark/Continuum, 2004), 19–43.

Jesus as 'son of God' was a favourite title of the early Christian Church.[11] But it was also one that was developing and being reinterpreted from a very early time, already suggesting that Jesus may have used it – assuming for the moment that he used it at all – in a more mundane sense. Matthew edits Mark to stress the stronger sense of the term 'Son' (Mark 6.52/Matt. 14.33; Mark 8.29/Matt. 16.16; Mark 15.30/Matt. 27.40; Mark 15.32/Matt. 27.43). With John's Gospel the phrase 'the Son of God' is used in an extremely strong sense where equality with God is explicitly mentioned (e.g. John 5). There is nothing like this in the Synoptic Gospels so presumably the historical Jesus never said anything similar to that which appears in John's Gospel, otherwise it is almost incomprehensible that the other Gospels would have left it out. We also have another strong saying in material common to Matthew and Luke where coming to God is through the Son alone (Matt. 11.27/Luke 10.22), an issue to which I shall return in my chapter on the Gospels. This too is suggestive of later invention as it is a Christianized formulation not developed elsewhere in the Synoptic Gospels, something we might expect with such a dramatic saying. Calling Jesus 'the Son (of God)' is therefore an observable development (see my chapter on Paul).

The strongest case for Jesus being described as God's Son is in the context of Jesus' exorcisms (e.g. Mark 3.11; 5.7). In this sense, it is more like the Jewish charismatic figures such as Hanina ben Dosa than any claim to be the actual Son of God.[12] Again, once Christians started to develop the figure of Jesus after his death it is not difficult to see how the more spectacular use of 'Son of God' would have contributed to making Jesus the one and only Son of God. Another strong case for Jesus using related language is his use of 'father' in contexts which would imply that he was a good son, like other good Jews. The teaching of Jesus as son coheres remarkably well with figures such as Honi the Circle-Drawer, the first-century Jewish holy man believed to be a miracle worker:

> Simeon b. Shatah said to him, '. . . For you importune before the Omnipresent, so he does what you want, like a son who importunes his father, so he does what he wants.' (*m. Ta'an.* 3.8)

> Is there anyone among you who, if your child asks for bread, will give a stone? Or if the child asks for a fish, will give a snake? If you then, who are

---

[11] M. Casey, *From Jewish Prophet to Gentile God: The Origins and Development of New Testament Christology* (Louisville: Westminster John Knox Press; Cambridge: James Clarke, 1991), 44–46.

[12] On Jesus and charismatic holy men, see esp. G. Vermes, *Jesus the Jew: A Historian's Reading of the Gospels* (London: SCM Press, 1973).

evil, know how to give good gifts to your children, how much more will your Father in heaven give good things to those who ask him!

(Matt. 7.9–11; cf. Matt. 6.9–13; Luke 11.2–4, 11–13)

The term 'the Messiah' (literally, 'anointed'; 'Christ' in Greek) was another key term for the first Christians. It is, however, unlikely that Jesus used it of himself: he does not use it in the earliest Gospel, Mark, and it does not occur in our other earliest source behind Matthew and Luke, a hypothetical source conventionally labelled 'Q'. Conversely, the title is widely used in New Testament and other early Christian documents. Moreover, the phrase 'the Messiah' was probably not a technical title in early Judaism at the time of Jesus. It has long been noted not only that there are different types of 'messianic' figures (e.g. priestly, royal, prophetic) but also that the word 'Messiah' was qualified in early Judaism to describe what kind of 'messiah' or anointed figure was in mind.[13] For example, one document from the Dead Sea Scrolls (4Q252 5) refers to 'the Messiah of righteousness, the branch of David'. Consequently, there was no such absolute title 'the Messiah' by the time of Jesus. I would suggest that the reason why Christians crystallized these separate strands into an absolute title, '*the* Messiah', was to make Jesus the not-to-be-rivalled, not-to-be-contested, supreme figure in early Judaism, ruling out any potential rivals from priestly, royal and prophetic strands in this all-encompassing term.

Conclusions

We have seen throughout this chapter that Jesus – for all the dramatic claims he may have made – does not do anything unparalleled in early Judaism. He remains a figure within Judaism and had little, if any, concern for developing his message among the Gentiles/non-Jews, let alone starting a new religion. Critics of the reconstruction of Jesus as a 'fairly ordinary' human being, such as the figure I have presented, argue that such a figure could not have started a movement among the Gentiles, let alone sown the seeds of a new religion. Such views tend to ignore conventional historical developments and long-, medium- and short-term trends (social, economic, political, etc.) and focus far too heavily on Jesus' ideas being the most important spur. This owes too much to the figure of Jesus being the centre of Christian theology and little to a conventional historical mindset. We will return to the role of the individual Jesus and the broader historical trends in due course, but in the next chapter I will turn to the other

---

[13] M. de Jonge, 'The Use of the Word "Anointed" in the Time of Jesus', *Novum Testamentum* 8 (1966), 132–48.

classic argument, usually from evangelical circles, for the development of Christianity: the bodily resurrection of Jesus.

Michael F. Bird

Several years ago I was speaking at a church in Brisbane, Australia, to a group of Asian university students about Jesus. After this particular sermon a young Japanese student asked: 'What is Jesus?' She was apparently confused by what the subject matter of my sermon even was. By analogy I'm asking something similar here: what and who is the historical Jesus? I think the question is an important one. Who is the flesh-and-blood human being called Jesus of Nazareth who walked the plains of Palestine and the shores of the Sea of Galilee? Who is the man who earned the fury of the Judean leadership, who was crucified on a Roman cross, and was so *remembered* by Christians in the first century as the Son of God? That is what I am setting out to address in this chapter.

The historical Jesus

For a working definition we might say that the historical Jesus is the picture of Jesus that emerges through the application of historical tools and by the formation of historical hypotheses. The 'historical Jesus' is not a positivistic or objective history of Jesus, but it comprises a fallible portrait of Jesus that emerges from dialogue with the textual history of early Christianity and in partnership with other readers of that history.[14] We must also keep in mind that regardless of how the early Church interpreted the significance of Jesus it did not abandon his historical message and person. Ernst Käsemann argued that the primitive Church never lost interest in the life history of Jesus as being properly basic for faith.[15] Since 'Jesus' is not a metaphor for a cache of timeless theological truths we are committed, whether we like it or not, to the task of exploring and investigating the person of Jesus in his historical context. To know Christ is more than knowing that he is divine and human, more than knowing that he died for our sins; it is a matter of knowing about his teachings and understanding how Jesus relates to Israel, to his followers and to his own contemporaries. This would suggest that historical study of Jesus is in fact a

---

[14] Michael F. Bird, *Jesus and the Origins of the Gentile Mission* (LNTS 331; London: T&T Clark, 2006), 23; and see also the excellent discussion in Scot McKnight, *Jesus and His Death: Historiography, the Historical Jesus, and Atonement Theory* (Waco, TX: Baylor, 2005), 28–46.

[15] Ernst Käsemann, 'The Problem of the Historical Jesus', *Essays on New Testament Themes* (trans. W. J. Montague; London: SCM Press, 1964).

necessary task of discipleship.[16] The nature of faith (in a historical person) and the nature of God's revelation (in the sphere of space–time history) demand that we participate in what is known as the *Quest for the Historical Jesus.*[17] Even if you're an atheist you need to ponder: 'Who is this Jesus that I don't believe in?' The answer might surprise the most ardent sceptics when they find out that the Jesus in whom they disbelieve is radically different from the Jesus of Nazareth.

The virgin conception

According to the Apostles' Creed, a second-century statement of faith, Jesus 'was conceived of the Holy Spirit, born of the Virgin Mary'. The affirmation of the virgin birth by Christians in the second century was maintained amid those who postulated a purely human birth (e.g. Cerinthus, Carpocrates and groups who became known as the Ebionites) and those who denied Jesus any human birth (e.g. Marcion).[18] When Christians of the second century made belief in the virgin birth part of their creeds and confessions they were essentially following the testimony bequeathed to them in the Gospels. The Gospels of Luke and Matthew both narrate that Jesus was born through miraculous conception when the Holy Spirit came upon a young Galilean girl named Mary. This is ordinarily called the virgin birth or, more properly, the virgin conception. These stories are absent from Mark and John although we have reason to think that they might presuppose them (see, e.g., Mark 6.3; and John 8.39–41). The accounts in Luke and Matthew have their own peculiar emphases and there are variations in the details as one would expect from stories such as these that circulated orally in the early Church. Still, there appears to be a common narrative thread to the Matthean and Lucan birth narratives:

1 Jesus' birth in relation to the reign of Herod the Great.
2 Mary is a virgin, betrothed to Joseph, but their relationship is not yet consummated.
3 Joseph is of Davidic descent.
4 The birth is announced by angels.
5 Jesus is the Son of David.
6 Jesus is conceived by the Holy Spirit.

---

[16] N. T. Wright, *The Challenge of Jesus* (London: SPCK, 2000), 14–15.

[17] See Michael F. Bird, 'Should Evangelicals Participate in the "Third Quest for the Historical Jesus?"', *Themelios* 29 (2004), 5–14; Michael Pahl, 'Is Jesus Lost? Evangelicals and the Search for the Historical Jesus', *Themelios* 31 (2006), 6–19.

[18] Michael F. Bird, 'Birth of Jesus', in *Encyclopedia of the Historical Jesus*, ed. Craig A. Evans (New York: Routledge, 2008), 71–4.

7 Joseph plays no role in the conception.

8 The name 'Jesus' is divinely given.

9 An angel refers to Jesus as 'Saviour'.

10 Jesus is born after Mary and Joseph have come to live together.

11 Jesus is born in Bethlehem.

12 Jesus' family settles in Nazareth.[19]

Several reasons are often given for taking the virgin conception to be a myth dressed up in the garb of a historical narrative. First, several scholars argue that the birth stories have been written-up in order to portray Jesus as fulfilling biblical prophecy. The Lucan annunciation narratives are heavily influenced by Old Testament prototypes like the child born to Hannah (1 Sam. 1—3), and Matthew's depiction of Herod the Great parallels the account of Pharaoh's cruelty to the Hebrews and Moses' birth as national deliverer (Exod. 1—2). While it is clear that the Evangelists have modelled the birth narratives after Old Testament stories about barren women having children, it seems unlikely that they have conjured up the virgin conception out of thin air based purely on Old Testament precedents. Most barren women conceived through natural means whereas in the virgin conception we have something unparalleled in Jewish scriptural traditions. What is more, in primitive Christian exegesis the Old Testament provided the hermeneutical grid through which traditional material was interpreted and modelled rather than comprising the creative pool from which it was formulated.

Second, Matthew's quotation of the Old Testament may appear erratic at points. For instance, Matthew 1.23 cites Isaiah 7.14 which reads: 'the virgin shall conceive and bear a son'. Not only was this passage not treated as a messianic prophecy in Jewish interpretation, which associated the son with a child born during the time of Ahaz and Isaiah, but the Hebrew word *'almâh* means a woman of marriageable age and not necessarily a virgin. The notion of virginity is probably imported from the Septuagint (a Greek translation of the Hebrew text for Greek-speaking Jews) through the word *parthenos* that implies more explicitly a 'virgin'. So is Matthew a proponent of a bad translation? While *'almâh* is not a technical term for *virgo intacta* the idea of virginity could be connoted, depending on the context. In any case, a virgin conception is clearly not predicted in the Hebrew text of Isaiah 7.14, but Matthew's citation does not demand an exact correspondence of events as much as it postulates a correlation of patterns or types between Isaiah's narrative and his own birth story. The coming

---

[19] Joseph A. Fitzmyer, *Luke* (2 vols; AB; New York: Doubleday, 1983), 1.307.

of God's anointed, the manifestation of God's presence, and the rescue of Israel through a child born to a young girl brings to Matthew's mind Isaiah 7 as an obvious prophetic precedent again repeated at a new juncture of redemptive history.

Third, in the sphere of comparative religions certain sages or heroes were said to have been born of miraculous circumstances involving gods (e.g. Perseus, Plato, Alexander the Great). According to the Roman historian Suetonius (*Aug.* 94.4) the birth of the emperor Augustus came about by his mother being impregnated by the god Apollo. Based on these comparisons several scholars suppose that Christians borrowed from pagan birth stories and fabricated their own mythic narrative in order to make Jesus look equally heroic and divine. One should keep in mind that analogy does not mean genealogy; there is no indication that Luke and Matthew use Graeco-Roman birth stories as their sources. The birth narratives also possess a distinctive Palestinian character and reflect the piety of Jewish Christianity (especially the Lucan hymns attributed to Mary and Zechariah). Additionally, other mythic birth stories such as that of Augustus imply some human–divine sexual union which is absent from the Gospels. Thus the purported parallels are not quite as parallel as is often supposed.[20]

What one thinks of a virgin conception will depend entirely upon what presuppositions one has and whether one believes in a God who can and does intervene in human affairs in such a way. On the one hand, miraculous birth stories are not entirely unique in the sphere of religious history and the birth narratives are invested with theological meaning by the Evangelists. On the other hand, there is a sound platform of evidence that could be said to imply a miraculous birth:

1 Paul speaks of Jesus as 'born of woman' (Gal. 4.4; cf. Rom. 1.3; Phil. 2.7).
2 Jesus is called the 'son of Mary' and not the son of Joseph in Mark 6.3.
3 There was in circulation a Jewish polemic that presupposes that there was something suspicious about the circumstances surrounding Jesus' birth including the insinuation that he was a *mamzer* or illegitimate (John 8.41; *Gos. Thom.* 105; Tertullian, *Spect.* 30.6; *Prot. Jas* 13–16; *Acts Pil.* 2.3) and born to a Roman soldier called 'Panthera', a play on the Greek word *parthenos*, meaning 'virgin' (Origen, *Cels.* 1.28, 32).
4 There is no reason for taking the birth narratives as being altogether different from the rest of the Gospels which contain historical

---

[20] For early Christian responses to the allegation that the virgin birth was borrowed from pagan myths of divine–human intercourse, see Justin, *Dial.* 67–70; *1 Apol.* 33; and Origen, *Cels.* 1.37.

narratives set in the parameters of a Graeco-Roman biography or historiography.[21]

Thus, while the evidence does not prove a virgin birth, it is at least consistent with it. What we can say for certain is that Jesus' paternity was enigmatic from the start.[22] That is the fact that Crossley must explain and yet he does not attempt to do so other than say that historians would consider the birth accounts 'imaginative storytelling' (see page 2). Ultimately, whether one chooses to accept the virgin conception will depend upon one's theological and philosophical convictions as well as one's faith in the ancient Church's witness to Jesus. All I can say is that in early 2007 it was reported in the news that a female Komodo dragon named Flora conceived through parthenogenesis (i.e. reproduction without the aid of a male). I cannot help but think that if a Komodo dragon can do it, why not God?[23]

Miracles

There is perhaps no area of historical research and philosophical enquiry that will separate Evangelicals and Secularists more than the question of miracles. To begin with, what is a miracle? A *miracle* is an extraordinary event that is brought about by a god and possesses religious significance.[24] A *miracle story* is a short narrative that includes a miraculous event as the climax of the account. In the Gospels Jesus is reported to have performed 36 independent miracles consisting of exorcisms, healings, resuscitations and nature-miracles.[25] But how plausible is a miracle when it comes to history, especially the historical Jesus?

There are several philosophical and scientific objections to miracles. The philosopher David Hume argued that a miracle is a violation of the unalterable laws of nature and miracles are therefore impossible. The theologian Rudolf Bultmann maintained that miracles are part of the mythic husk that the message of the New Testament is contained in and can be disregarded as they are foreign to the world of modern man. Others point out that there were various miracles purported to have been performed

---

[21] See further, Richard A. Burridge, *What Are the Gospels? A Comparison with Graeco-Roman Biography* (2nd edn; Grand Rapids, MI: Eerdmans, 2004).

[22] Markus Bockmuehl, *This Jesus: Martyr, Lord, Messiah* (Edinburgh: T&T Clark, 1994), 33.

[23] I owe this analogy to Ben Witherington: <http://benwitherington.blogspot.com/2007/01/virginal-conception-and-political.html> (cited 25 January 2007).

[24] Richard Swinburne, *The Concept of Miracles* (London: Macmillan, 1970), 1.

[25] See the list in B. L. Blackburn, 'Miracles and Miracle Stories', in *Dictionary of Jesus and the Gospels*, eds Joel B. Green, Scot McKnight and I. Howard Marshall (Downers Grove, IL: IVP, 1992), 549–60 (551).

by persons in the ancient world such as Rabbi Honi the Circle-Drawer and Apollonius of Tyana and we do not believe in such legends about them, so why should we believe in miraculous legends about Jesus? There are several responses that I can make here. Against Hume not everyone is a default atheist and if it is possible that God exists then it is equally possible that this God may actually choose to intervene in the affairs of human beings. Miracles are not necessarily a violation of the laws of nature as much as they are acts where God temporarily overpowers nature. An aeroplane does not violate Newton's law of gravity as much as it is able to nullify its effect with its own power. Bultmann's objection is Eurocentric and peoples of other cultures in Africa, Asia and South America have no a priori problem with miracles. What is more, Bultmann essentially swaps a theistic worldview for a deistic one where God is the absentee landlord who no longer interacts in the world as he is purported to have done in the Gospels. The question of religious parallels is more interesting. Still, one unique facet of Jesus' miracles that sets him apart from other miracle-workers is that he claims to perform these miracles with a sense of unmediated authority and is not simply a medium for some higher power. These signs or mighty deeds performed by Jesus are regarded as the proof that Israel's story is reaching its gripping conclusion through him. These mighty acts of Jesus also have better historical attestation than that for any other miracle-worker in the ancient world, including the likes of Apollonius of Tyana whose miraculous works are extant only in the account of the third-century writer Flavius Philostratus.

There are also several reasons why the miracles of Jesus have historical plausibility. First, the Gospels portray Jesus as performing mighty deeds of healings, miracles and exorcisms which attracted crowds and made him popular. That is eminently plausible, as Morton Smith wrote that 'the gospels represent Jesus as attracting attention primarily as a miracle worker, and winning his followers by miracles. The gospels do so because he did so.'[26] That fits into a first-century context where various popular prophets such as the Samaritan (Josephus, *Ant.* 18.85–87), Theudas (Josephus, *Ant.* 20.97–98; Acts 5.36), the Egyptian (Josephus, *Ant.* 20.169–171; *J.W.* 2.261–263; Acts 21.38) and Jonathan the refugee (Josephus, *Life* 424–425; *J.W.* 7.437–442) all attracted significant crowds by fostering hope in presenting the signs of deliverance. Second, such miracles are attested in every stratum of the Gospel tradition (Mark, material common to Luke and Matthew, material unique to Luke, Matthew and John). Third, Jesus is even

---

[26] Morton Smith, *Jesus the Magician* (San Francisco: Harper & Row, 1978), 10.

reported as being a miracle-worker outside of the Gospels including the Jewish *Tosefta* (*t. Ḥul.* 2.22–23) and by Josephus (*Ant.* 18.64). The Jewish and pagan authors accuse him of sorcery and magic precisely because of his reputation as a miracle-worker (*b. Sanh.* 43a; Origen, *Cels.* 1.6, 38, 68, 160; Quadratus in Eusebius, *Hist. eccl.* 4.3.2; Justin, *Dial.* 68). In the magical papyri incantations were given in Jesus' name which assumes the efficacy of Jesus' name in healings and exorcisms (*PGM* 4.3019–30; cf. Acts 19.13–19; Arnobius, *Adv. Gent.* 1.43; and use of Jesus' name in healing was prohibited by the later rabbis). Fourth, many of these miracle stories include embarrassing elements that the early Church would be unlikely to invent, such as the claim that Jesus could not perform many miracles in Nazareth because of a lack of faith (Mark 6.4–6) and the admission that Jesus' signs did not convince the inhabitants of Capernaum, Bethsaida and Chorazin (Luke 10.13–15/Matt. 11.20–24). What is more, much of the anti-Jesus rhetoric that one finds in the Gospels presupposes that Jesus was doing miraculous deeds. This includes the accusation that Jesus performs miracles by the power of Beelzebub (Mark 3.22–23; Luke 11.19/Matt. 12.27), the sarcastic calls for Jesus to do in his hometown what he did in Capernaum (Luke 4.23), and Herod's mocking of Jesus' miraculous abilities (Luke 23.8–11). Fifth, that Jesus was identified as 'a prophet' by the crowds (Mark 6.15; Matt. 21.11, 46; Luke 7.16, 39; 24.19; John 4.19; 9.17) and 'the prophet' by his followers (Deut. 18.15, 19; and Acts 3.22–23; 7.37; cf. John 6.14; 7.40) was probably spurred on by belief in his miracle-working abilities. This evidence does not prove every single miracle that Jesus performed and it does not indicate that every reported miracle had a supernatural source, but it does show that the miracle stories are part of the most authentic core of the tradition and Jesus was remembered by his followers and known by his contemporaries as being a miracle-worker. John Meier writes:

> Viewed globally, the tradition of Jesus' miracles is more firmly supported by the criteria of historicity than are a number of other well-known and often readily accepted traditions about his life and ministry . . . Put dramatically but with not too much exaggeration: if the miracle tradition from Jesus' public ministry were to be rejected *in toto* as unhistorical, so should every other Gospel tradition about him.[27]

In terms of Jesus' ministry these 'signs' (*sēmeia*) or 'mighty deeds' (*dunamis*) had a threefold function: (1) they indicate the presence and

---

[27] John P. Meier, *A Marginal Jew: Rethinking the Historical Jesus* (ABRL; 3 vols; New York: Doubleday, 1994), 2.630.

power of the future age operating in Jesus (e.g. Matt. 12.28; Luke 11.20); (2) they testify to Jesus as God's eschatological agent; and (3) they evoke faith by performing the signs that indicate that Israel's restoration is at hand. At the same time, Jesus rejected demands for him to do miraculous signs on cue in order to authenticate his identity (Mark 8.11–13; John 6.30) and he reportedly rebuked the crowds for treating him like a move-able feast because of his feeding miracle (John 6.26). Jesus was opposed to those who became fixated on the signs of the kingdom while ignoring the message of the kingdom to repent and believe in the gospel.

The message of Jesus: the kingdom and the king

Closely related to the miracles of Jesus is the message of Jesus. The Synoptic Gospels imply that the central theme of Jesus' message was the kingdom of God (Mark 1.14–15; Matt. 4.23; 9.35; Luke 4.43; 8.1; 9.11). This phrase occurs frequently on the lips of Jesus and in some Jewish writings contemporary with Jesus (e.g. *As. Mos.* 10.1–3; *Wis.* 10.10; *Pss. Sol.* 17.3; 1QM 12.6–10), but there is a paucity of references to it in the Old Testament. More common in the Old Testament is the theme of God as 'king'. In one sense God already is king of Israel (e.g. 1 Sam. 8.7; Ps. 24.8–10; 29.10), but in another sense there was a hope that God would yet show himself as king. For example, in Psalm 145.8–13 the Psalmist praises Yahweh's compassion and love and announces that Yahweh's kingdom is an everlasting kingdom and expresses the hope that all nations would praise Israel's God. In Isaiah 52.7, there is the announce-ment of glad tidings of peace and salvation as the coming reign of Yahweh will spell an end to Israel's exile in Babylon and mark the beginning of the restoration of the Jewish nation from virtual death. In Daniel 7, we encounter this mysterious figure called 'one like a son of man' who is granted an everlasting kingdom. At the end of Obadiah there is the prom-ise that, when Israel's exile is over, the kingdom would become the Lord's. We see that Yahweh's kingdom, kingship and reign are bound up with a certain matrix of political and religious hopes, including a new exodus, the return of the twelve tribes to Palestine, the advent of a messianic figure (or figures) to defeat Israel's enemies and reign in righteousness, a new or purified temple, the establishment of pure worship and a righteous people, the return of Yahweh to Zion, abundant prosperity, a renewed covenant, and the subjugation or admission of the Gentiles. This is what we call eschatology; it is about the future of Israel and the nations. The Jewish view was that Yahweh would not allow Israel to languish in exile or under foreign oppression for ever, but would remember his covenant with Israel, and what God did for Israel would eventually spill over to affect the gentile nations. When all of this occurred, it would be the day that God finally became king.

Thus, when Jesus begins his ministry in Galilee proclaiming the gospel of the kingdom of God, he was not talking about a social programme for society nor was he telling people how to get to heaven. Rather, he was proclaiming that Israel's God was now acting in a dramatic way to make good his promises that had been announced in the prophets; in other words, God was at last becoming king and displaying his kingship through this particular Jewish prophet to achieve the renewal and restoration of Israel. Viewed this way the 'kingdom' is not a timeless metaphor nor a purely political entity, but it is a way of speaking of the dynamic rule or reign of God that is now invading the present. This kingdom cannot be forced (Matt. 11.12/Luke 16.16) but it must be entered (Mark 9.47; 10.15, 23–25; John 3.5). This kingdom is simultaneously present in Jesus' exorcisms, miracles, preaching, and in the experience of the Spirit, and yet it also awaits a future consummation. Jesus calls for faith in God given the appearance of the kingdom and also calls for repentance of sins based on the coming judgment associated with the kingdom's final manifestation.

The parables of Jesus are not (as it is often said) 'earthly stories with heavenly meanings'. Jesus' parables represent a form of subversive speech that strike at the jugular of the beliefs, aspirations and worldviews of his audience by retelling the story of Israel, God, the Messiah and the kingdom in a provocative and arresting way so as to undermine alternative perceptions of Israel's story and identity (as held by the Pharisees, proto-Zealots, Sadducees, Herodians, etc.). That is why many of the parables are spoken by Jesus in contexts of hostility and opposition. Even when the content of the parables appears largely didactic rather than polemical there still remains a tacit element of unexpected reversal in their narrative climax (see the parables of the Prodigal Son [Luke 15.11–32], Day Labourers [Matt. 20.1–16] and Vineyard Tenants [Mark 12.1–12]). The parables bring to light what Jesus means by 'kingdom' and it may not be the same as that of his contemporaries, such as the zealot-minded Judeans or the Herodian collaborators or the ruling priests of the temple. N. T. Wright notes that: 'Jesus was articulating *a new way of understanding the fulfilment of Israel's hope*.'[28] Thus Jesus' parables cannot be reduced to quaint vignettes about theology, ethics or social protest (though it may touch upon these), but are related to the larger context of this hope for the deliverance of the Jewish nation. The parables of Jesus are only

---

[28] N. T. Wright, *Jesus and the Victory of God* (COQG 2; London: SPCK, 1996), 176 (italics original).

adequately grasped against the larger backdrop of his public ministry as one who comes to effect the restoration of Israel.

In contrast, Crossley thinks that Jesus was wrong about his teachings on the arrival of the kingdom of God in the near future. But this is because of a fundamental misreading of these texts in their literary, political and ideological context. First, in the mind of several Jewish authors the arrival of the kingdom could extend over time, in and through a series of dramatic events that could invade the present (e.g. *Jub.* 23; *1 Enoch* 91.12–17) and so the Habakkuk Commentary at Qumran with its belief in the imminence of the end was not necessarily the default option. Second, sayings about the purported imminence of the coming kingdom can arguably be identified with events other than the end of the physical order. Mark 9.1 is sandwiched in a context where Jesus connects his messianic identity and the kingdom to his appointed destiny to die in Jerusalem amid the messianic woes. Mark 13.30 is part of the discourse of Mark 13 that focuses on the destruction of the temple not the end of the world. The destruction of the temple represents the coming of the Son of Man in judgment and his resultant vindication as the prophet who opposed the temple. Jesus' enigmatic reply to Caiaphas in Mark 14.62 is not about his return from heaven but is a vivid metaphor for his vindication and co-enthronement with God that he is to experience after his sufferings (see Luke and Matthew, who add '*from now on* you will see the Son of Man'). Third, the notion of some delay or uncertainty about the coming of the kingdom is ubiquitous throughout the Gospel tradition and, therefore, unlikely to be something that was made up later.[29] Moreover, Victoria Balabanski has pointed out that if the early Church was disappointed by the failure of Christ to return, such a disappointment is not uniformly reflected in the key texts. The intensity of hope for Christ's return fluctuated in some contexts and there was no definite tendency towards diminished eschatological enthusiasm since Matthew actually intensifies rather than plays down Mark's eschatological material.[30]

Jesus' preferred self-designation was 'Son of Man' and this title in the Gospels is central for spelling out Jesus' relation to the coming kingdom. The title 'Son of Man' is one of the most confusing topics in New Testament studies and I am loath to enter into this debate (particularly when I know that Maurice Casey is writing a response against me and he is

---

[29] On the so-called *parousia* sayings, see Timo Laato, *De ignorantia Christi: zur Parusieverzögerung in den synoptischen Evangelien* (Lund: Scriptura, 2002).

[30] Victoria Balabanski, *Eschatology in the Making: Mark, Matthew and the Didache* (SNTS 97; Cambridge: Cambridge University Press, 1997).

perhaps *the* expert on the subject [see page 33]). Suffice to say, I do believe that the designation was used by Jesus of himself and in a quasi-titular sense. There is a case to be made that in Aramaic the phrase 'son of man' can be a generic form of 'human' or else it can comprise a manner of self-reference like 'I' or 'someone in my position' and this fits certain contexts (e.g. Matt. 8.20/Luke 9.58; and Mark 3.27–28), although it has also been debated to what extent this idiomatic usage was current in the first century. What is more, we do know that some Jews were reading Daniel 7.13 about the 'Son of Man' messianically. Documents like *4 Ezra* and parts of *1 Enoch*, probably written in the same century in which Jesus lived, clearly make the Son of Man a messianic figure. On the lips of Jesus 'Son of Man' is a deliberately veiled and cryptic messianic claim; it speaks of a role more than a title.

That leads to the question, did Jesus think of himself as the Messiah or the king of the coming kingdom? That Jesus was crucified owing to a perceived messianic claim is evident from the question posed to him by the High Priest at his trial (Mark 14.61) and from the titulus 'King of the Jews' on the cross (Mark 15.26; John 19.19). Why was this allegation made against Jesus and why was Jesus mocked as a messianic pretender? Crossley never engages this question and he finds the impulse towards Jesus' messiahship in the post-Easter period. There remain, nevertheless, strong indications that Jesus did make an implicit claim to be the Messiah and that it was determinative for him being handed over to the Romans. In the first place, there is absolutely no reason why Jesus' resurrection should be said to necessitate his messianic identity since 'resurrected' does not equal 'Messiah'. Against Crossley more specifically, the early Christians did not need the title 'Messiah' to portray Jesus as the 'supreme figure' who brooks no rivals since the titles 'Lord', 'Prince' and 'Son of God' achieved that far better than did the title 'Messiah'. Second, elements of Jesus' pre-passion ministry have messianic overtones. Jesus' action in preaching a gospel and his work of healings and exorcisms correspond with the messianic vocation as spelled out in the *Messianic Apocalypse* from Qumran: 'He will heal the badly wounded and will make the dead alive, he will proclaim good news to the poor' (4Q521 2.12). In fact, in a pericope from Q (Luke 7.18–23/Matt. 11.2–6) Jesus answers an explicit messianic question from followers of John the Baptist with an answer along the lines of 4Q521, 'Go and tell John what you have seen and heard: the blind receive their sight, the lame walk, the lepers are cleansed, the deaf hear, the dead are raised, and the poor have good news brought to them' (Luke 7.22/Matt. 11.5). Third, Jesus' ministry in Jerusalem in his final days can be said to have a messianic motif in so far as the triumphal entry, the cleansing of the temple and parabolic utterances like the Parable of the Tenants all point in the direction of a carefully crafted messianic claim. Ben Meyer wrote, 'the entry into Jerusalem and the cleansing of the Temple constituted a messianic demonstration, a messianic critique, a messianic fulfilment event, and a sign of the messianic restoration of Israel'.[31] Jesus may never have explicitly claimed the title 'Messiah', given its militaristic associations, but he certainly did act out the role in ways that were provocative and telling.

Another aspect of Jesus' message for us to consider was his view of the Torah or Jewish Law, out of which Crossley makes a lot. I concur with Crossley that Jesus was essentially Law-observant, but we should also keep in mind that relaxation of certain commands and intensification of other commands was a common feature in Jewish prophetic renewal movements. That is why Jesus prohibits divorce when the Law allows it (Mark 10.1–12) and why he forbids a would-be disciple from burying his father which the Law explicitly commands (Matt. 8.22–23/Luke 9.59–60). I am also much more confident, in sharp contrast to Crossley, that Jesus did see a place for the Gentiles in the kingdom and I have argued elsewhere that Jesus believed that a transformed Israel would transform the world.[32] While I do not think that Jesus abrogated the Law, he did, like other Jews, relativize purity beneath morality and refused to make certain interpretations of the food laws the distinctive boundary marker of covenant identity (e.g. Mark 7.1–23).

Did Jesus think that he was God?

The American scholar John Knox wrote: 'I, for one, simply cannot imagine a sane human being, of any historical period or culture, entertaining the thoughts about himself which the Gospels, as they stand, often attribute to him [Jesus].'[33] On this view, to think that Jesus regarded himself to be in any sense 'God' is said to be improbable. After all, there is no reason to see Jesus as anything other than a good monotheist. Jesus proclaims the kingdom of God, the gospel of God (e.g. Mark 1.14–15); he prays to God as Father (Mark 14.36; Luke 11.1–4/Matt. 6.9–13; John 11.41–42); he affirms the Jewish confession of God, the *Shema* of Deuteronomy 6.4 (Mark 12.29–30), and he calls for steadfast devotion to God (Luke 16.13/Matt. 6.24). And yet the Nicene Creed, a fourth-century Christian statement of faith, declares that Christians believe in

---

[31] Ben F. Meyer, *The Aims of Jesus* (London: SCM Press, 1979), 199.

[32] Bird, *Jesus and the Origins of the Gentile Mission*.

[33] John Knox, *The Death of Christ: The Cross in New Testament History and Faith* (Nashville: Abingdon, 1959), 58.

'one Lord Jesus Christ, the only-begotten Son of God, begotten of the Father before all worlds, God of God, Light of Light, Very God of Very God'. Was the deity of Christ something concocted by creative minds such as Paul and John as Christianity spread out into the wider Graeco-Roman world where Christian beliefs became intermingled with pagan beliefs of divinized beings and then popularized by the post-Constantine Church? Or, did Jesus have a consciousness of himself as being divine and called to exercise divine prerogatives? I shall defend the latter.

To begin with, it is necessary to explode the popular caricature of Jesus which presents Jesus as announcing: 'Hi, I'm God. I'm going to die on the cross for your sins. But first of all I'm going to teach you how to be a good Christian and how to get to heaven. And after that I thought it would be fitting if you all worshipped me as the second member of the Trinity.' This might seem a rather naïve way to understand Jesus' identity, but it is a sketch of Jesus that many Bible-believing Christians have. When I argue that Jesus understood himself to be in a sense divine, this is not what I am talking about.

The place to start is with Jesus as the 'Son'. There are multiply attested units where Jesus refers to himself as the 'Son' and so refers to his unique filial relation to God and his special role in ushering in the kingdom (Luke 10.22/Matt. 11.27; Mark 12.1–12; John 3.35–36; 5.19–47; 6.45–46). This is confirmed by Jesus' own experience of God in baptism (Mark 1.11), during temptation (Matt. 4.1–11/Luke 4.1–13) and revelation (Luke 10.21–22/Matt. 11.25–27). Jesus expressed a sense of unmediated divine authority that led the authorities to query him about its origin (Mark 11.27–33) and public opinion was that he spoke with a *unique* authority that set him apart from the scribes (Mark 1.22, 27; cf. Matt. 8.9/Luke 7.8). Jesus also reconfigures divine commandments based on his own authority (e.g. Matt. 5.21, 27, 33, 38, 43).

Claims to speak for God do not imply divinity as several prophetic figures often claimed to speak for God, but no one regarded them as divine. But in the case of Jesus this authority became unusually acute. Jesus pronounces the forgiveness of sins which leads to a charge of blasphemy (Mark 2.5, 10; cf. Luke 7.36–50). The charge, 'Who can forgive sins but God alone?' (Mark 2.7) demonstrates that Jesus appropriated the role of the priest in relation to atonement, but outside of the cultus, and thus with an independent authority and with independent access to God. Here Jesus does not claim to be a rogue priest, but he offers the forgiveness that was only available through the divinely instituted system of sacrifices (cult of Yahweh) at the place of God's dwelling (temple of Yahweh). While it is true that one can find examples of forgiveness of sins outside of the cultus (e.g. Ecclus. 3.30, which Crossley mentions, and I would add 4QprNab 242.4 from Qumran), Crossley has not explained the reason for the allegation of blasphemy. If Jesus meant, 'Your sins have been forgiven *by God*' then how would that evoke the response 'Who can forgive sins but God alone?'? The 'God alone' part is crucial as Jesus was perceived as providing that which only God can provide.

We can add that Jesus' eschatology implies a Christology. Not only is the kingdom coming but also Jesus is the one who inaugurates it through his mighty deeds, exorcisms, healings, and preaching. In Luke 11.20, Jesus is remembered as saying: 'But if it is by the finger of God that I cast out the demons, then the kingdom of God has come to you.' It is simplistic therefore to say that Jesus proclaimed the kingdom and that the Church proclaimed Jesus. Jesus' proclamation of the kingdom always carried with it an implied self-reference as he is the agent bringing it into effect. It is response to Jesus' message that determines one's standing in the covenant and entrance into the kingdom (Mark 1.15; 8.34—9.1; 12.1–12; Matt. 7.24–27; 21.31; Luke 10.16/Matt. 10.40; John 13.20). Moreover, there are instances where Jesus apparently refers to himself as one who is like Wisdom (Matt. 11.28–30; Luke 7.35/Matt. 11.19; Luke 11.49), is greater than the temple (Matt. 12.6) and greater than Satan (Mark 3.27; Luke 11.21–22/Matt. 12.29). Torah, Wisdom and temple were symbols of God's presence with his people and were in a sense incarnational, and it is these symbols that Jesus associates with his own vocation and identity.[34] Jesus' use of Psalm 110 in Mark 12.35–37 testifies to his belief that the Messiah is somehow more than a Son of David and destined for an enthronement on par with Daniel 7.13–14 (see also *1 Enoch* 55.4; 62.3–5). In Luke 19.44, Jesus is remembered as saying: 'and they will not leave within you one stone upon another; because you did not recognize the time of your visitation'. The background to this saying is probably Ezekiel 34, which depicts the coming of God in the coming of the Davidic Shepherd-King. Wright is correct when he posits Jesus as entering Jerusalem believing that he is embodying the return of God to Zion and offering divine salvation to the populace of Jerusalem.[35]

Crossley brazenly dismisses the authenticity of the 'Johannine Thunderbolt' in Matthew 11.27/Luke 10.22 (see page 15) on the grounds that this is a 'Christianized formulation'. Yet we have here a saying attributed to Jesus

---

[34] On the pre-existence of Jesus in the Synoptic Gospels, see Simon Gathercole, *The Pre-Existent Son: Recovering the Christologies of Matthew, Mark and Luke* (Grand Rapids, MI: Eerdmans, 2006).

[35] Wright, *Jesus and the Victory of God*, 631–53.

that clearly elevates his status and role in the divine design and it comes from a source (probably 'Q') that is quite early. I suspect that the real reason why Crossley brushes it aside so quickly is because it might show that John's Christology is not quite as foreign to the historical Jesus as he thinks.

In early Christianity there arose rather quickly the integration of Jesus into patterns of worship. Religious devotion became largely binitarian,[36] centred on Jesus and God, and Jesus was accordingly regarded as participating in the divine identity, which goes back as early as the Aramaic-speaking Church; for example, in 1 Corinthians 16.22 the Aramaic word *mara* or 'Lord' (e.g. *maranatha*) is used of Jesus. When the early Christians mentioned God they had to mention Jesus as well, and whenever they mentioned Jesus they felt constrained to mention God in the same breath.[37] It is important to realize that although Christianity was still within the domain of monotheism it has developed into *messianic monotheism*, where the very meaning of 'God' is redefined in view of the resurrection and exaltation of Jesus (John 1.1–14; Rom. 9.5; 1 Cor. 8.6; 16.22; Phil. 2.5–11; Col. 1.15–20). Yet this has pre-Easter antecedents since Jesus' claim to authority, his claim to act and speak on behalf of God, his mission to embody the presence of God in Jerusalem is the presupposition for the binitarian Christ-devotion of the primitive Church. Jesus afforded himself a role in the divine design that was unprecedented and blurred the line between author and agent. Jesus is a prophet, and *more* than a prophet, and it is this 'more' that prompted deeper reflection in light of his resurrection and exaltation as to how Jesus related to the identity and personification of God. The worship patterns of the primitive Church did not occur *ex nihilo*, belief in the resurrection and exaltation of Jesus would not be sufficient of itself to effect the belief that Jesus had been co-enthroned with God and incorporated into the divine identity. Rather, the seed bed upon which this faith in Jesus grew was out of Jesus' belief that he was the divine agent *par excellence*. As Craig Evans states: 'The New Testament deification of Jesus Christ, as seen especially in the theologies of Paul and the fourth evangelist, has its roots in the words and activities of the historical Jesus.'[38]

---

[36] Cf. Larry W. Hurtado, *Lord Jesus Christ: Devotion to Jesus in Earliest Christianity* (Grand Rapids, MI: Eerdmans, 2004).

[37] Marinius de Jonge, *God's Final Envoy: Early Christology and Jesus' Own View of His Mission* (Grand Rapids, MI: Eerdmans, 1998), 130.

[38] Craig A. Evans, 'The Historical Jesus and the Deified Christ: How Did the One Lead to the Other?' in *The Nature of Religious Language: A Colloquium*, ed. Stanley E. Porter (Sheffield: Sheffield Academic Press, 1996), 47–67 (67). I recommend also Raymond E. Brown, 'Did Jesus Know He was God?' *BTB* 15 (1985), 74–9.

Conclusions

So what is historical about the historical Jesus? In brief, I have argued that several things were, including doubts over Jesus' paternity, which are consistent with Christian claims of a virgin conception; he was widely known to have performed mighty deeds, healings, exorcisms; he spoke of the kingdom of God as the dynamic reign of God that was breaking in; he referred to himself as the 'Son of Man', which cryptically designated his unique authority and messianic role; Jesus had a high view of his own person and destiny as being bound up with the identity and mission of God; and his chief aim was to effect the restoration and regathering of Israel in a new exodus. Thus, the answer that I find myself drawn to by the phenomenon that is early Christianity is that Jesus was a miracle-worker, a prophet, a rabbi, a martyr, the Messiah and Lord.

This approach can be contrasted with Crossley in at least three ways.

1 Crossley is a materialist in that this world is all that there is and there is no possibility of a god intervening to establish his purposes for the human race. I do not share that assumption (which is what it is). Unless I become convinced that the universe just popped into existence by itself with no thought of a personal creative agent, and that human beings just happened to have evolved from amino acids into astronauts at random, I see no reason to adopt his materialist worldview.
2 Crossley plays the sociology hand very well but also very hard. Undoubtedly urbanization and the economic climate of Palestine shaped the contours of Jesus' message and how it was received. When Jesus said, 'blessed are the poor', he meant those of low status, economically and socially, not the affluently rich but spiritually poor. Yet we must not mistake *context* for *content*. The social environment of Jesus' ministry does not 'explain' the emergence of Jesus' ministry as much as it situates Jesus' teachings in a broader socio-economic context. Crossley is right to resist constructions of the historical Jesus that are little more than a cluster of theological ideas, but sometimes theological ideas matter hugely to the most economically deprived of people. It is a matter of getting the balance between sociology, economics and theology right, and I am not convinced that Crossley is there just yet.
3 Crossley is very dependent on cross-cultural comparisons for his conclusions. That is legitimate enough (I myself cite many non-Christian sources to make my point); methodologically, however, it can easily degenerate into parallel-o-mania where exhibit 'A' is little more than another version of exhibit 'B'. What is more, as I shall often say, analogy does not prove genealogy, and the formative causes for things Jesus

said and did cannot be explained away by comparative studies. People do and say things for religious reasons and those reasons cannot be reduced to sociological factors in a theological garb.

Response from James G. Crossley

Unfortunately space demands that I cannot respond to all of Bird's points. In passing, I am not convinced Bird has fully appreciated socio-historical methodology. Bird's discussion of the use of parallels (see pages 32–3) does not deal with the approach I advocate, though this may not be significant if Bird does not have my arguments in mind. As I have openly and polemically opposed the approaches Bird also critiques, and as every parallel I used is purposely backed up with evidence from Jesus' immediate context, there is no need to debate this further. In the abstract, we would actually seem to agree more than Bird seems to suggest.

Law and kingdom

On the Law, Bird refers to 'Jewish prophetic renewal movements' (see page 28) intensifying and relaxing commandments (from whose perspective – ours?) but I am not sure what he is talking about here. On relaxation and intensification (whatever he may mean by this) and the divorce passage mentioned (Mark 10.2–12) it is worth pointing out that similar Jewish views have been shown to exist by both myself and, more importantly, David Instone-Brewer.[39] On the saying, 'let the dead bury their dead' (Matt. 8.22–23/Luke 9.59–60), Bird references an old view on this being a 'relaxation' (see page 28). But there is nothing of the sort mentioned in the text and there is no acknowledgement of contemporary Jewish discussions which contradict Bird's statement.[40] Contrary to Bird's confidence, there is not a commandment referenced in this verse. There is not even the remotest sign of this saying being controversial in the Gospel contexts (compare Sabbath and purity disputes). Besides, the man's father is not going to be left unburied (the usual source of the scholarly view of controversy) because, as the passage says quite unambiguously, the dead man will be buried.

---

[39] D. Instone-Brewer, *Divorce and Remarriage in the Bible: The Social and Literary Context* (Grand Rapids/Cambridge: Eerdmans, 2002); Crossley, *Date of Mark's Gospel*, chapter 6.

[40] See M. Bockmuehl, 'Let the Dead Bury Their Dead (Matt. 8:22/Luke 9:60): Jesus and the Halakah', *JTS* 49 (1998), 553–81; C. H. T. Fletcher-Louis, ' "Leave the Dead to Bury Their Own Dead": Q 9.60 and the Redefinition of the People of God', *JSNT* 26 (2003), 39–68.

In Bird's discussion of the kingdom of God (see pages 24–6), the parallel texts which claim to spread the kingdom over time do precisely what texts such as Mark 9.1 do *not* do. Bird tries to wriggle out of the problematic situation by vaguely claiming that Mark 9.1 'is sandwiched in a context where Jesus connects his messianic identity and the kingdom to his appointed destiny to die in Jerusalem amid the messianic woes.' So what? Jesus still predicts the imminent coming of *the kingdom* in the middle of this.

Historicity and miracles

With other ancient texts in mind, statistically speaking we might reasonably expect *at least* a few Gospel verses to be inventions. This is a real problem for some evangelical approaches that claim every word of the Gospels is fact because it seems to compromise conventional historical practice, assuming that is what evangelicals want to be part of. In practice there are many examples from Bird's chapter that ought to be regarded as secondary, most obviously in his discussions of the miraculous, an issue to which I will return shortly. His discussion of the virgin birth (see pages 18–21) makes some dubious assumptions in terms of historical reconstruction. Bird does not back up his suggestion that Jesus' birth was enigmatic from the start. Jesus being 'born of a woman' (Gal. 4.4) is meaningless in terms of the virgin birth because I, like many others, was born that way too. Being called 'son of Mary' (Mark 6.3) can be explained in other ways (e.g. Joseph was long dead, a deliberately provocative allegation). Insinuations about Jesus' origins (e.g. John 8.41) are later than the birth narratives (Bird cites no early evidence) and so the assumption that Jesus had an unusual birth would have been present by this time and potentially up for debate. All of this merely shows, at best, that Jesus' birth was enigmatic from the earliest tradition available to Matthew and Luke. We have no idea how enigmatic his birth was during his life and in the first couple of decades following his death. Yet still the big problem will not go away: why is the virgin birth not in the earliest Gospel, Mark's Gospel?

On the historicity of miracles (see pages 21–4), Bird can cite as many multiple miracle traditions as he wants but they do not show Jesus really did perform supernatural miracles. All this shows is that some people *believed* Jesus performed supernatural miracles from an early date. On the issue of embarrassment (see page 23), Bird claims that the early Church would not have invented Jesus' inability to perform 'many miracles' in Nazareth because of a lack of faith (Mark 6.4–6). But we must be clear here: Mark 6.5–6 does not mention *miracles* that must be *supernatural*. The passage says, 'And he could do no deed of power there, except that he laid his hands on a few sick people and cured them. And he was amazed at their unbelief.' This can easily be explained in terms of non-supernatural cross-cultural healing of the sort we might associate with faith healers or shamans found throughout history right up to the present (see Casey's response, pages 183–94). There is clearly a problem in lumping miracles and healings/exorcisms together. Again, Jesus is *not*, as Bird claims, accused of performing *miracles* by the power of Beelzebub (Mark 3.22–23; Luke 11.19/Matt. 12.27). The problem is unambiguously with Jesus' *exorcisms* as the Gospels make perfectly clear (Mark 3.22–23; Matt. 12.27/Luke 11.19) and echoed in similar cross-cultural phenomena.

Christology and self-understanding

Bird's handling of the 'son of man' debate is problematic for the following reasons: he has not noticed an example of the generic 'son of man' several centuries prior to the second century CE (Sefire III, lines 14–17, not to mention Mark 2.27–28 being a particularly clear Gospel example); he does not properly engage with the basic idea that 'son of man' is a common and ordinary Semitic term for 'human being'; the Jewish texts he cites explicitly mention Daniel 7.13 so it is obvious that Daniel 7.13 is in mind in these Jewish texts; several Gospel texts do not reference Daniel 7.13 or anything vaguely 'messianic', etc. so it is difficult to see how anything other than a basic Semitic idiom is being used here; texts such as *1 Enoch*, with the best versions of the key sections remaining in Ethiopic, do not necessarily speak of the 'son of man' in relation to '*the* Messiah' in the strong sense and still retain the ordinary use of the term as 'human being'. Where Bird gets the language of 'cryptic' and 'veiled' from, I have no idea, but it cannot be the Gospel texts or the basic Semitic idiom.

Bird wants to defend the view that Jesus had 'a consciousness of himself as being divine and called to exercise divine prerogatives' (see page 29). But the only evidence for 'Son' to be taken in its strongest sense is either late or obviously secondary. Bird refers to 'multiply attested units' in support (see page 29). Three of these five are from John's Gospel (John 3.35–36; 5.19–47; 6.45–46) and include staggeringly high claims (e.g. making Jesus equal with God) that are simply *not* found in the Synoptic Gospels. If such spectacular things had been said in Jesus' lifetime, why were they left out of earlier tradition?

There is one, *and only one*, example given from material particular to Luke and Matthew (Luke 10.22/Matt. 11.27) that comes anywhere close. Bird makes some strange deductions in trying to work out my reasons for rejecting its historical accuracy when they were merely based on conventional historical method. For a start, Luke 10.22/Matt. 11.27 would restrict Jesus' message to Palestinian Jews and exclude Diaspora Jews, something that is not echoed anywhere else in the Jesus traditions. As an important aside, this saying only has the Son revealing the Father and there is nothing like the conflict over Jesus making himself God, such as we find in John's Gospel. That is a significant difference, even if both are not historically accurate, because Bird's language of 'Johannine thunderbolt' is overdone.

What this latter point also supports is the well-established scholarly observation that the title 'Son' visibly develops in the Gospel tradition. This is in fact further supported by the reference Bird makes to the earliest source, Mark (12.1–12). In Mark 12.1–12, the language is vague and parabolic, making no claims whatsoever to Jesus' divinity in any strong, or indeed weak, sense. The fact that Bird cannot provide significant early evidence of Jesus as Jesus-as-Son in a strong sense is telling because if Jesus really did say something as dramatic as Bird thinks he did why does it not occur anywhere else in Matthew, Mark or Luke?

Further evidence used to defend this 'divine' Jesus is the scholarly construct of Jesus and an alternative priestly system. The blasphemy charge over 'forgiveness' of sins (Mark 2.7) apparently 'demonstrates that Jesus appropriated the role of the priest in relation to atonement, but outside of the cultus . . . he offers the forgiveness that was only available through the divinely instituted system of sacrifices (cult of Yahweh) at the place of God's dwelling (temple of Yahweh)' (see page 29). Is there not a problem here with the fact that Jesus is never explicitly said to be acting as an alternative priest in the synoptic tradition and only ever endorses the ideal function of the temple system (Mark 1.44; Matt. 5.23–24; 23.16–22)? Bird also needs to answer this: if the healed man had to go to the Temple, which sins would be forgiven according to Jewish law and how would the priest go about forgiving the sins?

If we assume for a moment that historically there was a conflict over blasphemy underlying Mark 2.1–12, and if we note the idea that sins could be forgiven outside the Temple,[41] the conflict could alternatively be explained as concerning the authority to perform healings and exorcisms. This is precisely the conflict over blasphemy in Mark 3. But we should not assume that there really was a conflict because the scribes *think* Jesus did

---

[41] Bird suggests adding 4QprNab 242.4 from Qumran as an example (see page 30). I am not so sure. This Aramaic passage can be translated in a number of ways for a start. It was also collected among the Dead Sea Scrolls, by a group of people who did have some kind of alternative temple, so it is possible that it is not representative of people assuming the validity of the Jerusalem Temple.

something deemed blasphemous. Note: *think*. Jesus' opponents do not actually say anything. Mark tells us that they were angry inside, something which should strongly imply that this part of the story was an invention by Mark (how could the writer possibly have known what they were thinking?).

Bird claims that the 'worship patterns of the primitive Church did not occur *ex nihilo*, belief in the resurrection and exaltation of Jesus would not be sufficient of itself to effect the belief that Jesus had been co-enthroned with God and incorporated into the divine identity' (see page 31). An obvious response would be, *why not*? Why *should* the seeds of Jesus' deification have to be in his teaching? Not all believers thought of Jesus in such elevated terms. *Why not*? Given that Bird makes the assumption that claims of worship emerged from one person, Jesus, is it not theoretically possible for an alternative solution, namely, that *another* person (or persons) and their ideas were responsible for the worship of Jesus? We might add that there could be any number of social, theological, historical, economic, etc. reasons why the deification of Jesus could take place after his death and potentially run clean contrary to what Jesus believed about himself. And, if there is one thing we know about human beings, it is that they are more than capable of making things up.

Further reading

Arnal, W., *The Symbolic Jesus: Historical Scholarship, Judaism and the Construction of Contemporary Identity* (London and Oakville: Equinox, 2005).

Catchpole, D., *Jesus People: The Historical Jesus and the Beginnings of Community* (London: Darton, Longman & Todd; Grand Rapids: Baker, 2006).

Crossley, J. G., *Why Christianity Happened: A Sociohistorical Account of Christian Origins 26–50 CE* (Louisville: Westminster John Knox Press, 2006).

Herzog, W. R., *Prophet and Teacher: An Introduction to the Historical Jesus* (Louisville: Westminster John Knox Press, 2005).

Levine, A.-J., *The Misunderstood Jew: The Church and the Scandal of the Jewish Jesus* (San Francisco: HarperCollins, 2006).

Machen, J. G., *The Virgin Birth of Christ* (New York: Harper, 1930).

McKnight, Scot, *A New Vision for Israel: The Teachings of Jesus in National Context* (Grand Rapids, MI: Eerdmans, 1999).

Marshall, I. Howard, *The Origins of New Testament Christology* (Leicester: IVP, 1977).

Sanders, E. P., *The Historical Figure of Jesus* (London: Penguin, 1993).

Twelftree, Graham H., *Jesus the Miracle Worker* (Downers Grove, IL: IVP, 1999).

Witherington, Ben, *The Jesus Quest: The Third Search for the Jew of Nazareth* (Downers Grove, IL: IVP, 1997).

2

The resurrection

Michael F. Bird

I rather like the musical *Jesus Christ Superstar* with the one exception that Jesus' life ends in disarray, defeat and death – there is no resurrection, no prospect of vindication and no hope of a return. If Andrew Lloyd Webber and Tim Rice were to put *Little Red Riding Hood* on the stage I can only imagine that the finale would include the wolf reclining with a very full tummy – but that's not how the story goes! The tragic ending of *Superstar* would better describe another Jesus, Jesus ben Phameis, who died in Rome in the same century as Jesus of Nazareth. His funeral inscription reads:

> Traveller, my name is Jesus, and my father's name is Phameis;
> when descending into Hades I was 60 years of age.
> All of you should weep together for this man, who went at once to the
> hiding place of ages, to abide there in the dark.
> Will you also bewail me, dear Dositheos, because you are in need of
> shedding bitter tears upon my tomb?
> When I died I had no offspring, you will be my child instead.
> All of you, therefore, bewail me, Jesus the unhappy man.[1]

Evidently belief in a future resurrection was not unanimous among Jews. Neither was it the only post-mortem option doing the rounds in Jewish circles. Other options included reincarnation, the immortality of the soul, translation into heaven, some kind of shadowy existence in *sheol* (the Hebrew waiting place of the dead), leaving behind a good memory, or *apotheosis* (becoming a god): all were on the table. Even so, my objective in this chapter is to demonstrate that Andrew Lloyd Webber and Tim Rice were wrong and that *Superstar* is missing a crucial epilogue: the resurrection. Also, that Jesus ben Phameis need not have died in such despair. If he had encountered some of the Christians in Rome he might have heard that 'Jesus died

---

[1] S. Safrai and M. Stern (eds), *The Jewish People in the First Century: Historical Geography, Political History, Social, Cultural and Religious Life and Institutions* (2 vols; Amsterdam: Van Gorcum, 1974–6), 2.1043–4.

and rose'. The meaning of that phrase is that the God of Israel had done for Jesus in the middle of history what some Jews thought he would do for Israel at the end of history. Consequently, death and sin were not the last words, since redemption, reconciliation and renewal were realities that could be anticipated ahead of the final consummation. Thus, as a historian I believe that the 'logic of history' is that the reports of the empty tomb, the appearance stories and the genesis of the early Church are best explained by the hypothesis that Jesus' closest followers saw him alive shortly after his crucifixion.[2] As a Christian, I confess that 'He is risen – He is risen indeed!'

The burial and empty tomb

No one doubts that Jesus was crucified, since it is attested by the Gospels (e.g. Mark 15.24), the earliest Christian proclamation (e.g. Acts 2.23, 36; 4.10), Paul (1 Cor. 1.23; Gal. 3.1) and non-Christian authors too (Josephus, *Ant.* 18.64; Tacitus, *Ann.* 15.44.3). But as we move on to the subject of Jesus' burial and the discovery of an empty tomb then the debate starts.

According to the Gospels and Paul, Jesus was buried after his death (Matt. 27.56–61; Mark 15.42–47; Luke 23.50–55; John 19.38–42; 1 Cor. 15.4a). Moreover, we are told that he was buried by a sympathetic member of the Sanhedrin, Joseph of Arimathea, who placed Jesus' body in his own personal tomb (Matt. 27.57–61; Mark 15.43–47; Luke 23.50–56; John 19.38–42). An alternative to the burial account is that Jesus' body was left up on the cross as carrion for scavengers and the remains of his corpse were thrown in an unmarked grave. On this last option John Dominic Crossan writes: 'In normal circumstances the soldiers guarded the body until death and thereafter it was left for carrion crow, scavenger dog, or wild beasts to finish the brutal job. That nonburial consummated authority's dreadful warning to any observer and every passerby.'[3] On this reading, the story of the burial was invented by the early Church (i.e. Mark) in order to move Jesus' body from a criminal's grave to a more respectable tomb.

Although Crossan is fully aware that there are cases where victims of crucifixion did receive burial, he is at pains to emphasize that, given what we know of mass crucifixions in Palestine in the first-century, burial for those crucified was exceptional or extraordinary rather than the norm. Of course, Jesus was perceived precisely as being extraordinary by some of

---

[2] Paul Barnett, *Jesus and the Logic of History* (NSBT 3; Leicester: Apollos, 1997), 35.
[3] John Dominic Crossan, *Jesus: A Revolutionary Biography* (San Francisco: HarperSanFrancisco, 1994), 153.

his followers and sympathizers and they might well have attempted to give him a burial far more deserving of someone of his character and status given his ignominious death. Furthermore, there is textual and archaeo-logical evidence for burial after crucifixion. First, the Jewish philosopher of Alexandria, Philo, mentions the possibility of a crucified corpse being given back to his or her family for burial on the eve of a festival (Philo, *Flacc.* 83–85). Second, the discovery in 1968 of the bones of a crucified man named Jehoḥanan with a nail still lodged in his ankle found at Giv'at ha-Mivtar in north-eastern Jerusalem lends further credence to the view that burial after crucifixion was not unknown. Were these excep-tions? Probably not, since the Jews zealously obeyed the commandment of Deuteronomy 21.22–23 that executed criminals or hanging corpses should be buried before sunset (see John 19.31; Acts 13.27–29; 11QTemple 64.10–13; and Josephus, *J.W.* 4.317). A robust challenge to Crossan's argument also comes from Bruce Chilton:

> A straightforward reading of the Gospels' portrait of the burial has been challenged by revisionist scholars, who theorize that Jesus died in a mass crucifixion: the body was thrown into a common, shallow trench, to become carrion for vultures and scavenging dogs. This makes for vivid drama but implausible history. Pilate, after all, had been forced in the face of Jewish opposition to withdraw his military shields from public view in the city when he first acceded to power. What likelihood was there, especially after Sejanus' death [note: Sejanus was prefect of the Praetorian guard in Rome, who wielded considerable power and influence and was known to be vehemently anti-Jewish, see Philo, *Flacc.* 1.1; and *Legat.* 1.159–60, and Sejanus was executed by the Roman emperor Tiberius for treason in 31 CE], that he would get away with flagrantly exposing the corpse of an executed Jew beyond the interval permitted by the Torah, and encouraging its muti-lation by scavengers just outside Jerusalem? Revisionism can be productive. But it can also become more intent on explaining away traditional beliefs than on coming to grips with the evidence at hand, and I think this is a case in point . . .[4]

This goes to show that the hypothesis that Jesus' body *must* have been dumped into a mass grave with criminals and insurrectionists can be dis-proved.[5] Moreover, although some of Jesus' sympathizers may have felt com-pelled to bury him immediately after his death because of the shame of the cross, that is not the picture that we get from early Christian writers. Our earliest Gospel (Mark) and our earliest letter writer (Paul) both glory

---

[4] Bruce D. Chilton, *Rabbi Jesus: An Intimate Biography* (New York: Doubleday, 2000), 270.
[5] James H. Charlesworth, *Jesus within Judaism* (London: SPCK, 1989), 123.

and revel in the shame of the cross as a means of salvation (see Mark 8.34; 10.45; and 1 Cor. 1.18—2.2; Gal. 5.11; 6.12–14). The need or desire to cover up the dishonour and indignity of Jesus' death through an imaginative fiction is entirely absent from early interpreters.

That Jesus was buried seems *certain* given that the burial story is multiply attested by Mark's account, by the tradition that Paul cites in 1 Corinthians 15.3–8, which probably derives from Palestinian Christian circles in the 30s, and also by John's independent tradition. Jewish scruples about funeral rites also required that victims of crucifixion, however malevolent or despised they were, be buried before sundown. That Jesus was interred by Joseph of Arimathea is very *probable* since a Christian fictive account would be unlikely to depict a member of the Jewish Sanhedrin as undertaking this generous act for Jesus when Christian authors had a tendency to criticize and condemn the Judean leadership vehemently for their part in Jesus' death (e.g. John's version states that Joseph was a 'secret' disciple 'for fear of the Jews').

According to the Gospel accounts and as implied in Paul's tradition in 1 Corinthians 15.3–8, on the Sunday morning after his death several of Jesus' female disciples went to his burial site only to find the tomb empty and his body no longer there (Matt. 28.1–8; Mark 16.1–8; Luke 24.1–10; John 20.1–2). In our earliest Gospel, Mark, the ending is abrupt and perplexing. There are no resurrection appearances, the women are ordered to tell Peter and the disciples about the resurrection but they run away in fear and confusion, and it has a syntactically strange staccato ending with the Greek particle *gar* ('for'). Some early scribes sought to get around this by filling in the blanks with their own suggestions of what might have happened (see Mark 16.9–20) and some students of ancient manuscripts suppose that Mark's original ending has been lost to us. Several scholars regard the story as Mark's own creation and suppose that he fabricated the episode of the women's fear and failure so as to account for why no one until recently had heard of the empty tomb or resurrection. Not so. The reports of the empty tomb and resurrection appearances were anything but recent when Mark writes (probably in the 60s) as reports that Jesus 'died and rose' would have been in circulation for over a generation through traditional material of an early vintage, for example, 1 Corinthians 15.3–4; 2 Corinthians 5.15; 1 Thessalonians 4.14. Regardless, Mark has already set up his readers/hearers for an expectation for Jesus' resurrection (Mark 8.31; 9.31–32; 10.34; 14.28) and it is unlikely that he fails to meet those expectations even with his enigmatic finale. Mark's story actually presupposes the angelic announcement: 'He has been raised; he is not here' (Mark 16.6). That the women 'said nothing to anyone' (16.8) does not mean that they failed to inform the disciples of these astonishing events as the angel commanded them, but only that they kept it a secret from outsiders for reasons of fear. For example, in Mark 1.44 Jesus says to the healed leper: 'See that you say nothing to anyone; but go, show yourself to the priest.' By analogy the statement in Mark 16.8 might mean, 'they said nothing to anyone *except for the disciples*'. Moreover, groups with an apocalyptic orientation thought themselves to be privy to heavenly secrets that had to be concealed until an appointed time (see Dan. 12.4; and Rev. 22.10) and the women may have thought it better to keep quiet about what had transpired and to leave the decision about how and when to announce publicly what had happened to the other disciples.[6]

A few more pieces of evidence count in favour of the empty tomb. First, the lack of scriptural echoes and citations shows that the story has not been made up on the back of a catena of Old Testament proof texts. Second, in the ancient world a woman's testimony did not carry much weight. Now if someone were going to manufacture a miraculous story such as this, then I sincerely doubt that such a storyteller would make the truth of the incredible tale rest on the testimony of a few grief-stricken and frightened Jewish women whose report would most likely be cast aside as a womanish fantasy (as happened according to Luke 24.11, 'these words seemed to them an idle tale, and they did not believe them'). Third, the primitive Jewish polemic against the resurrection proclamation presupposes that the tomb was empty. The Jewish counter-claim that the disciples stole the body (Matt. 28.13; Justin, *Dial.* 108.2; *Gos. Pet.* 8.30) assumes that the tomb was somehow vacated by Jesus' corpse. Fourth, the early Christian preaching in Jerusalem sometime after Jesus' crucifixion would have been highly problematic if the whereabouts of the body were known to the Jewish authorities.

There are of course several possible objections to this conclusion. The women went to the wrong tomb, no one knew where the body was, or there were no witnesses to the empty tomb itself. Let's take the last objection as an example. It is argued that Paul cites no witnesses to an empty tomb in 1 Corinthians 15.4 and Mark has invented a post-burial empty tomb story and imputed its testimony to unreliable witnesses to somehow account for the fact that news of the empty tomb was not widely known. In response, we can note the words of Reginald Fuller:

> The silence of the women can hardly be explained as the Evangelist's device to account for the recent origin of the story; that is altogether too modern

---

[6] Richard Bauckham, *Gospel Women: Studies in the Named Women in the Gospels* (Grand Rapids, MI: Eerdmans, 2002), 289.

and rationalistic an explanation, and assumes that the early church was concerned, like the modern historical critics, with conflicting historical evidence. The early church expounded its traditions anew in new situations: it did not investigate them historically in order to discover their origin and *Sitz im Leben* [life-setting].[7]

What is more, we have already seen that divine secrets can have a specific function among apocalyptic groups concerning the veiling of other-worldly news until the appointed time. Some information is for insiders only and such a perspective probably goes back to Jesus himself (Mark 4.11). Even at the horizon of Mark's Gospel the secrecy motif is not one-sided and has a dual conceal–reveal function (Mark 4.22; 9.9). Mark has not conjured up the secrecy of Jesus' messianic identity or his empty tomb in order to explain why none of his Palestinian followers believed in them until relatively recently. On the contrary, both secrets are meant to be revealed when the followers learn that the Son of Man has been raised from the dead (Mark 9.9). We are also unaware of any first-century Christian group that repudiated the empty tomb and if Mark was trying to 'cover-up' lack of knowledge of the empty tomb then he would probably have had the news of the empty tomb on the lips of the angel himself in order to make it a divine revelation of something otherwise unknown. Again, another problem is motivation. If Christians like Paul could (so it goes) believe in the resurrection without an empty tomb then why would Mark feel compelled to invent one? What was the ultimate purpose of such a fabrication? To prove the resurrection? Christians already believed it. Finally, the whole passage in Mark 16.1–8 appears rooted in early Palestinian tradition: the very Torah-obedient action of the women in waiting for the end of the Sabbath; Jesus is called 'the Nazarene'; the reflection of the Jewish custom of anointing dead bodies with spices and perfumes; and the fact that this section has several words not found elsewhere in Mark (e.g. *diaginomai* [elapse]; *arōma* [spices]; *apokuliō* [roll away]; *sphodra* [exceedingly]; and *tromos* [trembling]). And what of Paul's failure to mention the empty tomb and any witnesses to it in 1 Corinthians 15? As Paul doesn't mention Pontius Pilate or Jerusalem either, does that count against them?[8] We might also keep in mind the old maxim: the absence of evidence is not evidence of absence. In sum, the conclusion I come to is the same as that of the Jewish scholar Geza Vermes:

---

[7] Reginald H. Fuller, *The Formation of the Resurrection Narratives* (London: SPCK, 1972), 52–3.
[8] Dale C. Allison, *Resurrecting Jesus: The Earliest Christian Tradition and Its Interpreters* (London: T&T Clark, 2005), 305–7.

[I]n the end, when every argument has been considered and weighed, the only conclusion acceptable to the historian must be that the opinions of the orthodox, the liberal sympathizer and the critical agnostic alike – and even perhaps of the disciples themselves – are simply interpretations of the one disconcerting fact: namely that the women who set out to pay their last respects to Jesus found to their consternation, not a body, but an empty tomb.[9]

The appearances

According to Paul, again in 1 Corinthians 15.3–8, the risen Jesus was seen by individuals and groups that included Jesus' followers, sceptics, unbelievers and even enemies. This early tradition interlocks with the multiple accounts in the Gospels that narrate persons seeing, hearing and touching the resurrected Jesus. There are clear divergences in the details provided by the Evangelists that do not appear to add up; indeed, we can speak of an excited bewilderment as to exactly where, when and who saw the risen Jesus and in what order, but this only adds to the realism. In the words of E. P. Sanders: 'Calculated deception should have produced greater unanimity. Instead, there seems to have been *competitors*: "I saw him first!" "No! I did." '[10] As we investigate the various stories of the appearances at the tomb, in a locked room, on a road out of Jerusalem, in Galilee and by the Lake of Tiberias we are led to the conclusion that several individuals and groups believed that they had genuinely seen Jesus alive in a physical mode of existence after his death.

We must also mention several alternatives to the resurrection appearances. First, it is sometimes argued that these appearances are a result of cognitive dissonance and arose as a way of compensating for failed expectations. For instance, when certain groups make predictions about Jesus' return on a foreordained date (e.g. Jehovah's Witnesses) and those predictions do not happen, it is common for groups to reinterpret rather than deny those expectations by saying things such as that Jesus returned in an invisible and spiritual way. Was belief in Jesus' resurrection a way of compensating for his shameful and unexpected death? Probably not:

1 If Jesus predicted his death and relatively immediate resurrection then these resurrection hopes precede the disciple's disappointment at his death.
2 Reinterpretation fostered by dissonance depends on a degree of temporal distance between the prophecy and its failure in order to allow

---

[9] Geza Vermes, *Jesus the Jew: A Historian's Reading of the Gospels* (London: SCM Press, 1973), 41.

[10] E. P. Sanders, *The Historical Figure of Jesus* (London: Penguin, 1993), 280.

hopes to fade and to force the mental cogs to click over to provide a reinterpretation of that failure. But belief in Jesus' resurrection was immediately after his death – within days not months or years.

3 Although the death of Jesus occasioned a moral lapse on the part of his disciples in abandoning him, in another sense it also confirmed to them Jesus' eschatological teaching that the suffering of the tribulation was dawning and the end of ages was approaching. In the words of Dale Allison the disciples were 'emotionally down but not theologically out'.[11]

Second, it is often pointed out that there are a number of religious parallels to the resurrection. In the oriental religions there were myths of dying and rising gods and there were Greek and Roman legends about empty tombs and unexpected appearances of the recently deceased (pagan critics of Christianity often invoked such parallels to explain the Gospel stories, e.g. Celsus as quoted in Origen, *Cels.* 2.55–58). None of the possible parallels concerns a crucified figure and Jesus' resurrection is bound up with a certain eschatology whereby his resurrection inaugurates the new age, something not paralleled in the religious history of Palestine.

Third, the most frequent explanation for the appearances (by secular and many Christian scholars) is that they were subjective visions. A lot is made of the word *ōphthē* ('appeared') in 1 Corinthians 15.5–8 as the same word can be used of visions, although it can also refer to seeing things in the ordinary sense too. But the biggest problem is why would the early Christian interpreters refer to a vision as a 'resurrection'? They could have said that they witnessed Jesus either as a ghost or as an apparition or as an angel, or claimed that his spirit had been exalted to heaven, all of which were tenable options. If the appearances were visions why did the disciples think that Jesus had been resurrected when 'resurrection' would have generated a whole host of confusing corollaries in what was already a really bad week? The general resurrection was meant to be physical, it was supposed to include everyone (or at least the righteous/wise), and was programmed to occur at the end of the age. The Jewish and Christian language of resurrection does not fit well as a visionary experience. Consider the following:

Isaiah 26.19: 'Your dead shall live, their bodies shall rise. O dwellers in the dust, awake and sing for joy!'

Daniel 12.2: 'And many of those who sleep in the dust of the earth shall awake, some to everlasting life, and some to shame and everlasting contempt.'

---

[11] Allison, *Resurrecting Jesus*, 322–3.

Sibylline Oracles 4.181–82: 'God will again fashion the bones and ashes of men, and he will raise up mortals again as they were before.'

2 Baruch 50.2: 'The earth will surely give back the dead at that time; it receives them now in order to keep them, not changing anything in their form.'

Josephus, *Against Apion* 2.218: 'God hath made this grant to those that observe these laws, even though they be obliged readily to die for them, that they shall come into being again, and at a certain revolution of things receive a better life than they had enjoyed before.'

L.A.B. 3.10: 'I will bring the dead to life and raise up those who are sleeping from the earth.'

Mishnah *Sotah* 9.15: Rabbi Phineas ben Jair said, 'the Holy Spirit leads to the resurrection of the dead. And the resurrection of the dead shall come through Elijah of blessed memory. Amen.'

Testament of Judah 25.1: 'And after this Abraham, Isaac, and Jacob will be resurrected to life and I and my brothers will be chiefs (wielding) our sceptre in Israel.'

Ignatius, *To the Smyrnaeans* 3.1: 'For I know that after his resurrection also he was still possessed of flesh, and I believe that he is so now.'

Justin, *Dialogue with Trypho* 80.5: 'I and others, who are right-minded Christians on all points, are assured that there will be a resurrection of the dead.'

The repeated phrase 'resurrection/raised from the dead' (cf. Luke 24.46; Acts 3.15; Rom. 1.4; Gal. 1.1; 1 Thess. 1.10; 1 Pet. 1.3) means literally *the standing up of dead bodies* and not *the appearance of someone who died*. We are talking about a physicality of some form that presupposes continuity between the former living body and a vivified post-mortem state. This is emphasized further in later Church writings with reference to the resurrection of the 'flesh' (Ignatius; Tertullian). In which case, the vocabulary of 'resurrection' is clearly a mismatch for the phenomenon of visionary experiences or hallucinations. It is no more legitimate to call a vision a resurrection appearance than it is to call a whale a fish instead of a mammal.

Fourth, it has become increasingly common to regard these visions as the projections of grief- and guilt-stricken persons experiencing the presence of someone after death. I have three problems with the claim that the resurrection appearances were visions borne out of bereavement.

1 I never ceased to be amazed that scholars who take a minimalist approach to history in the Gospels, who believe that the sources are so overlaid with theology, who urge the utmost caution before pronouncing any

story or saying as authentic, appear to suspend their scepticism as they make claims to know the interior mental events and psychological states of the disciples. I submit that it is these mental processes, if anything, that are inaccessible to us. I don't have a problem with scepticism, as long as it is consistent scepticism.

2 I do not think that visions, appearances or a sense of personal presence during bereavement would have lead to an instantaneous belief that a crucified man had been physically raised by God. There was a range of simpler options that would commend themselves for describing such visions during a time of grief. For instance, the disciples may have thought that Jesus had been transformed into an angel and visited them. Oddly enough, in Acts 10.1 during the imprisonment of Peter a group of Christians who had anticipated the worst were already beginning to experience emotional bereavement before Peter had even died. When Peter did turn up (quite unexpectedly) their grief at his apparent death led them to think that he had appeared to them as an angel, *but no one thought that the resurrected Peter was at the door.*

3 On the safe assumption that many people died in antiquity and their loved ones experienced the associated grief and loss, and people during this time would have had post-mortem experiences of the deceased as they do now, why didn't other mourners regard their loved one as resurrected? Why were the disciples the first, as far as we know, to claim that their recently departed friend had been resurrected? Again, why didn't the family of every Tobias, Dinah and Hershel killed on a Roman cross proclaim the resurrection of the deceased? Most probably because resurrection was known to be a physical, eschatological, corporate and single event, and whatever feelings, emotions, thoughts, and hopes that grief-induced visions evoked they did not feel or look anything like a resurrection.

So we are still stuck with the problem of why the disciples believed that their crucified leader was resurrected – not merely assumed into heaven, not translated to the bosom of Abraham, not morphed into an astral being, not transported to God's throne on a fiery chariot – but resurrected. I suspect that those who think it is easy to pigeonhole the resurrection narratives into the category of bereavement visions are trying to force a square peg into a round hole. The terminology of resurrection is a clear mismatch for the phenomenon of bereavement visions.[12]

---

[12] See further John J. Johnson, 'Were the Resurrection Appearances Hallucinations? Some Psychiatric and Psychological Considerations', *Churchman* 115 (2001), 227–38.

I want to add that the empty tomb and resurrection appearances are not two independent pieces of data: they are interlocking pieces of evidence. One cannot say that the tomb was empty (for whatever reason) but there were no appearances, nor can one suppose that there were appearances (of some subjective variety) but no empty tomb. In order to account for the origin of belief in Christ's resurrection we need to accept both the empty tomb and the resurrection appearances together. As N. T. Wright argues:

> Neither the empty tomb by itself . . . nor the appearances by themselves, could have generated the early Christian belief. The empty tomb alone would be a puzzle and a tragedy. Sightings of an apparently alive Jesus, by themselves, would have been classified as visions or hallucinations, which were well enough known in the ancient world.[13]

Resurrection as the cause of Christianity

What drives my studies of Christian origins are two questions: why did Christianity begin and why did it take the shape that it did? For me, any answer must include the notion that God raised Jesus from the dead. The growth of Christianity is a very complex subject with multiple religious, social, ethnic, cultural and historical factors at work. Some might want to find sociological explanations for this and rightly so as sociological considerations must be weaved into a holistic explanation of what actually happened. But I do not think that sociology is some kind of card that once laid on the table somehow trumps historical and religious explanations. Sociology can create religious beliefs, but religious beliefs can also create social dynamics. Theologians and sociologists need to remember that the door of cause-and-effect swings both ways on the socio-religious horizon. That said, I can take the sociological evidence seriously but still believe that at the root of it all the explanation of why there are Christians and a thing called Christianity today comes down to a religious and even supernatural reason: God raised Jesus from the dead. As Paul Barnett writes:

> In short, the logic of history, when applied to the study of Jesus means that the existence, momentum and direction of the early church are most plausibly explained by a powerful teacher who had a close relationship beforehand with his immediate circle, an influence radically reinforced by the confirmatory event of his resurrection from the dead.[14]

---

[13] N. T. Wright, *The Resurrection of the Son of God* (COQG 3; London: SPCK, 2003), 686; and see similarly Mark W. Waterman, *The Empty Tomb Tradition of Mark: Text, History, and Theological Struggles* (Los Angeles: Agathos, 2006), 211–12.

[14] Barnett, *Jesus and the Logic of History*, 35.

Conclusions

Christians and Secularists both believe that 'something' happened after Jesus' death that caused his followers to believe that he had been resurrected. We shall have to explain this 'something' by one of two ways. We could refuse to take the resurrection stories at face value and throw our lot in with scholars who propose alternative schemes of a stolen body, group hallucinations, hastily devised myths, grief-induced visions wrongly labelled 'resurrection', and regard the first Christians as sincerely religious but ultimately deluded by their own enthusiasm. Or we can take the word of a faith community that claims to embody the *memory* of Jesus and claims to be the custodian of the *testimony* to Jesus that is set before us now.[15] I choose the latter and here is why.

I believe in the resurrection of Jesus because it is the hypothesis that makes the most sense of the historical data before me: the texts, the history and the sociology. Someone might object and say: 'Look, dead men stay dead and they do not come back to life. You can rattle off reasons and evidences about your empty tomb and post-mortem appearances all you like, but that will not change the fact that *death is the journey from which no traveller returns!*' If someone is going to quote Shakespeare at me like that then I'll retort by quoting Brecht. In Bertolt Brecht's play *Life of Galileo*, Galileo is trying to prove to some friends that the earth revolves around the sun and not vice versa, and he tells his friends that all they have to do is look through the telescope and they'll be able to see all the evidence that they need. Yet before looking through the telescope his friends decide to have a scientific disputation first to determine whether or not the hypothesis of a non-Ptolemaic universe is in fact possible; they decide that it isn't possible and therefore refuse to look through the telescope at all. My point is that those who think that religion has a monopoly on dogmatism better think again, and unless the whole debate is going to be reduced to a slanging match between competing presuppositions we had all better be prepared to take the evidence seriously. As a good honest historian I do not think that there is irrefutable proof for the resurrection, there is no *coup de grâce* against the sceptic, some arguments work better than others, and I feel the gravity of certain secular objections. But on the whole I think the evidence still favours the resurrection.

I confess the resurrection of Jesus because it has inherent meaning, personally and theologically. Close to 15 years ago I began an experiment in

[15] Markus Bockmuehl, 'Resurrection', in *The Cambridge Companion to Jesus*, ed. Markus Bockmuehl (Cambridge: Cambridge University Press, 2001), 102–18 (110).

the laboratory of life that Jesus is the risen Lord. The experiment is not yet complete, but I do have some preliminary results. In August of 1994, I died to the world; through the discovery of faith I thereafter considered myself to be crucified with Christ, and now I live on by some strange and wonderful quickening whereby I exist in union with that same Jesus who could not be shackled by death and is exalted to God's right hand. From this union flows an unspeakable joy, an urge to worship, a sense of mission, and an odd feeling that I live in a world partially reborn. Now I realize that to some readers this is merely rank religiosity, such remarks are grossly subjective and unverifiable, and many will think that my historical study is driven entirely to validate my religious experience. After all, what does religious experience have to do with history? Well, first, the New Testament is not an assortment of theological doctrines and historical artefacts waiting for someone to come along and separate the two for us. The New Testament is a testimony to the religious experience of the early Christians. Second, despite the radical diversity in the New Testament itself, Luke Timothy Johnson advocates that the unity of the New Testament is grounded in the commonality of a religious experience centred on the presence of the risen Jesus.[16] The report of such experience does not necessitate that Jesus rose from the dead, yet a physical resurrection correlates with such faith-experiences and also interprets them. The experience generates a way of thinking and a new constellation of meaning for the believer. The resurrection is a way of speaking about what God did to Jesus and it also provides a window into what God intends for humanity. Jesus' resurrection is far more than proof of life after death or a metaphor for the continuing cause of God; it tells us something about God. The resurrection attests the power of God's goodness and the goodness of God's power.[17] Resurrection means that the curse of creation and the nexus of sin and death have been broken and will be swept aside. The vindication of the Messiah is also the vindication of those whom he represents. The resurrection opens up an alternative way of being human wholly different from the crass materialism of secularism. Finally, resurrection means that God's new creation is launched upon a surprised and unsuspecting world where new hopes are buoyed among oceans of terror and the stories of the Jesus-people are billboards in the global metropolis of things soon to come.

---

[16] Luke Timothy Johnson, *Religious Experience in Earliest Christianity: A Missing Dimension in New Testament Studies* (Minneapolis: Fortress, 1998), 184.

[17] Leander E. Keck, *Who Is Jesus? History in Perfect Tense* (Columbia: University of South Carolina, 2000), 129.

James G. Crossley

I don't think it possible to give a historically plausible account of how the early Christian movement developed, and how the New Testament was written, on the assumption that we are dealing with fraud, or myth or misunderstanding. Reputable historians are divided on this matter, but that is my critical judgement in the light of the evidence. And not mine alone. I recall Professor C. F. D. Moule, of Cambridge University, drawing attention to the indisputable fact of the existence of the Christian church from the earliest relevant time. He then asked pertinently, that if this fact, 'rips a great hole in history, a hole the size and shape of Resurrection, what does the secular historian propose to stop it up with?' More recently, Bishop Tom Wright, of Durham, has written massively, persuasively and positively about the bodily resurrection of Jesus. Once you can see that there is no a priori argument which renders miracles impossible or even implausible, his is a case to answer.[18]

Arguing for or against the bodily resurrection from the dead of a historical figure would almost certainly be regarded as something very strange for historians working in periods of history other than Christian origins. To argue that a person rising from the dead cannot only be shown to be historically accurate but that it was also the primary factor in the emergence of a new movement would take what is already bizarre beyond the realm of conventional historical research. But this is what happens in the study of Christian origins, where claims of doing 'good history' go hand-in-hand with invoking arguments about the dead *really* rising. So the quite sensible objection to those arguments – that is, how on earth it can be historically proved that a thing like that actually happened – has to take a back seat and arguments for and against have to be analysed because the strange debate is probably here to stay.

In fact, I am going to go one step further than saying that the resurrection cannot be proved and suggest that, by the usual judgments of historical research, the resurrection stories would be classed as inventions and certainly should *not* be used to explain *why* Christianity emerged. I am not the kind of secular-minded person who wants to persuade people that it did not happen but rather – and the difference is subtle – that in terms of conventional historical reconstruction the bodily resurrection should be dismissed as a historical event.

---

[18] P. Jensen, 'Boyer Lecture, 3: Jesus, Was He Miraculous?', 27 November 2005. Available at <http://abc.net.au/rn/boyerlectures/stories/2005/1510080.htm> (last accessed, 3 March 2007).

The resurrection did not take place

> Baudrillard's argument is not that nothing took place, but rather what took place was not a war.[19]

Our earliest and possibly independent sources for the bodily resurrection are very, very weak witnesses. They are Mark 16.1–8 and 1 Corinthians 15.3–8. I will start with 1 Corinthians, written 20-odd years after the death of Jesus but clearly using an old tradition:

> For I handed on to you as of first importance what I in turn had received: that Christ died for our sins in accordance with the scriptures, and that he was buried, and that he was raised on the third day in accordance with the scriptures, and that he appeared to Cephas [Peter], then to the twelve. Then he appeared to more than five hundred brothers and sisters at one time, most of whom are still alive, though some have died. Then he appeared to James, then to all the apostles. Last of all, as to someone untimely born, he appeared also to me.

It is sometimes argued by evangelical scholars that 1 Corinthians 15.4 ('that he was buried, and that he was raised') refers to bodily resurrection in the strongest sense: Jesus was literally and bodily *raised up* from the dead. Some readers will be surprised to know that not for the first time I agree with these evangelicals. The language of being 'raised' often does imply a bodily resurrection of the sort that would have left behind an empty tomb. But if this is so, what does this tell us? Well, this tells us that Paul *believed* that there was a bodily resurrection.

Let us look in more detail for we will see that the distance between me and such evangelicals gets wider. In 1 Corinthians 15.3–8 it is worth noting that Paul has what seems to be eyewitness accounts of *an appearance* of Jesus, including his own sighting of Jesus. All this proves is that certain people believed they saw Jesus, not that Jesus was really raised from the dead in a way that defies the laws of nature. In contrast to evidence of seeing Jesus, there is *no mention* of eyewitnesses to the empty tomb. On the empty tomb, all Paul has is a general tradition, a confession of *belief*, an assumption that Jesus was bodily raised and that therefore he must have left an empty tomb. That's all. It takes a staggering jump of logic to get to the supernatural from this evidence.

So, while Paul may well assume that the bodily raised Jesus left an empty tomb, it remains that there are *no* eyewitnesses to the empty tomb in Paul's tradition. Now let's look at what we *do* have with Paul's eyewitness

---

[19] Paul Patton, 'Introduction', in Jean Baudrillard, *The Gulf War Did Not Take Place*, (Bloomington: Indiana University Press, 1995), 1–21 (16).

accounts, and what we *do* have is a *vision*. Paul's vision is well known. Here is one version of it:

> Now as he was going along and approaching Damascus, suddenly a light from heaven flashed around him. He fell to the ground and heard a voice saying to him, 'Saul, Saul, why do you persecute me?' He asked, 'Who are you, Lord?' The reply came, 'I am Jesus, whom you are persecuting. But get up and enter the city, and you will be told what you are to do.' The men who were travelling with him stood speechless because they heard the voice but saw no one. (Acts 9.3–7)

If we assume that something like this occurred, then it would be nothing new in terms of the cross-cultural study of religion and society. People have visions in countless cultures and in countless contexts, in which accompanying great lights are common enough, and this goes well beyond 'grief visions' mentioned by Bird.[20] It does not mean that there is anything necessarily supernatural underlying such visions. Moreover, it is quite obvious that the cultural and religious context dictates the content of the vision. So, for instance, in Catholic cultures the Virgin Mary may be the centre of vision and not Zeus or some divinity from the Hindu supernatural world.

So what cultural and religious factors could have influenced the content of the visions of the first Christians? One important context would have been martyrdom in early Judaism where there was the idea, recalled annually at the festival of Hanukkah, of martyrs looking forward to being bodily resurrected. Here is one example:

> And when he was at his last breath, he said, 'You accursed wretch, you dismiss us from this present life, but the King of the universe will raise us up to an everlasting renewal of life, because we have died for his laws.' . . . 'I got these [hands] from Heaven, and because of his laws I disdain them, and from him I hope to get them back again.' (2 Macc. 7.9, 11)

This tradition of bodily resurrection is important because it seems clear enough (to me at least) that Jesus saw himself as a martyr who knew he was going to die (see my chapter on the historical Jesus [pages 11–12]). Consequently, this tradition of bodily resurrection tied in with martyrdom could potentially have been the driving force behind the cultural interpretation

---

[20] On the use of the cross-cultural study of visions and their applicability to the reconstruction of the resurrection appearances, see e.g. G. Lüdemann, *What Really Happened to Jesus: A Historical Approach to the Resurrection* (Louisville: Westminster John Knox, 1995); M. Goulder, 'The Baseless Fabric of a Vision', in *Resurrection Reconsidered*, ed. G. D'Costa (Oxford: Oneworld, 1996), 48–61; Allison, *Resurrecting Jesus*; J. G. Crossley, 'Against the Historical Plausibility of the Empty Tomb Story and the Bodily Resurrection: A Response to N. T. Wright', *Journal for the Study of the Historical Jesus* 3 (2005), 153–68.

of the visions of Jesus after his death. In other words, these visions could have been visions *interpreted* as a bodily raised Jesus. Bird claims that 'the vocabulary of "resurrection" is clearly a mismatch for the phenomenon of visionary experiences or hallucinations' (see page 46) but this is simply not the case if we understand the basic point that human visionary experiences can be interpreted in any number of ways in different cultures. Once again, we have the basic point that this does not imply that there was something supernatural underlying such visions or stories, which is presumably the implication of Bird's analysis.

It might be countered that visions are more 'ghostly' rather than bodily but (and against Bird's either/or option of *either* visions *or* bodily raised) in the context of earliest Christianity there was overlap in the descriptions between the ghostly and the bodily. As Mark's Gospel says in the story of the walking on water: 'But when they saw him walking on the lake, they thought it was a ghost and cried out' (6.49). Clearly, the ghostly was deemed to look sufficiently body-like to allow a writer to talk of such confusions. Then there is the strange case of Moses and Elijah in the story of the Transfiguration (Mark 9.2–8), both appearing with Jesus but suddenly disappearing. According to biblical tradition, Elijah did not die and went straight to heaven and in some Jewish traditions Moses was said to have not died. But whatever Mark assumes, the figures of Moses and Elijah in this Marcan context are not quite bodily in the sense of what bodies can do in everyday life.

So 1 Corinthians 15.3–8 is the first early piece of evidence that hardly supports the historical accuracy of the empty tomb and a bodily raised Jesus. The next is from Mark 16.1–8. Mark 16.1–8 is the other key piece of information because it is from the earliest Gospel. Matthew and Luke are based in large part on Mark's Gospel and it is *possible* that John's Gospel is based on Mark as well. Even if John's Gospel is not based on Mark, as is often argued by scholars, it is hopelessly inaccurate (see my chapter on the Gospels [pages 116–32]) and has virtually nothing to tell us about Jesus' life, never mind his alleged resurrection from the dead.

Mark 16 has a story of some women going to the tomb wondering who would roll away the massive tombstone so that they could get in. Then they saw that the stone had been rolled away and a young man dressed in white, presumably an angel, was there and calmly told the women that the man they were looking for, Jesus, had risen, and that the women should go and tell the disciples and Peter that Jesus is going ahead of them to *Galilee*. And in *Galilee* they will see Jesus. The frightened women fled and told no one because they were afraid. That is all Mark says. It is an abrupt end and there are endings added by later writers but these are almost certainly not original to Mark. Some scholars have argued for a lost ending to Mark. This may or may not be the case but positing a lost ending and then guessing what was in the lost ending does not strike me as a very solid basis for reconstructing the historical accuracy of the resurrection of Jesus.

What we are left with as the last verse of Mark is this: 'they said nothing to anyone, for they were afraid' (Mark 16.8). This strongly worded verse is all we have and it could easily be read as a story invented to explain why no one knew any details about the empty tomb. In other words, the women told no one out of fear and that is why, explains Mark, no one knows the whereabouts of the empty tomb.

Bird argues against such a view of Mark's empty tomb story by claiming that reports of 'the empty tomb and resurrection appearances were anything but recent when Mark writes (probably in the 60s)' (page 41). There are some of us who would not date Mark so late but let us assume the late date is true for the sake of argument. Few would dispute that the resurrection stories were known but that is not the point of the arguments of those, such as myself, who suggest that Mark's empty tomb story is designed to explain why no one knew of the whereabouts of the empty tomb. Bird adds that the claim that the women told no one out of fear probably implies that they told no one *except for the disciples*. Well, if this is the case, when and where? Bird claims Mark 1.44 as an analogy where Jesus tells the healed leper to tell no one but that he should show himself to the priest. This is not a good analogy because Mark actually says that the healed leper told people and that Jesus told him to show himself to the priest. This stands in stark contrast to no such indications in Mark 16.1–8.

It seems that there is a mild contradiction in Bird's argument on this issue when he tells us that there are signs of Mark 16.1–8 being an early Palestinian tradition, in the context of arguing against the secondary nature of the story. If we assume that it is, then why not make the argument that it was invented to explain why no one knew where the empty tomb was? Early does not necessarily equal historically accurate. Early equals early.

Whatever we make of Mark 16.8, now our second early source is very suspicious. This source has women telling *no one* of the resurrection while the other source, Paul, has *no* eyewitness in direct contrast to eyewitnesses to visions. This shows just how exceptionally fragile the arguments are in favour of the bodily resurrection. If this were any other academic discipline, this best available evidence would not be taken remotely seriously as sound evidence favouring the bodily resurrection. Moreover, people in the ancient world were more than happy to invent stories about their heroes and were not constrained by modern concepts of truth and historicity.

Indeed, the other Gospel accounts go along the lines of the fantastic and are typical enough of ancient storytelling. In the context of early Judaism, people invented stories about biblical characters, recent heroes, rabbis, holy men and so on. This practice of creative storytelling is not, as some conservative Christians have implied, to be equated with lying or a lack of morality. As early Jewish and Graeco-Roman literature amply shows, people were more than happy to make up stories about rulers, rabbis, holy men, great biblical figures, etc. and did so as they saw fit. More generally this kind of rewriting of history is *everywhere* in the ancient world, and the stuff of legend surrounded all sorts of people deemed great, from religious figures to emperors.

There is plenty of evidence that the first Christians were immersed in the world of creative storytelling that had minimal grounding in history. Such creative retelling was so common and so accepted a part of the cultural climate that it would be highly unlikely that the Gospels did *not* indulge in it. The Gospels do, after all, talk about their own Jewish hero, Jesus. Passages that might be judged to be creative rewriting might include stories of a dead man coming back to life and walking around and eating with people. In fact, we have one highly relevant passage which is quite obviously a human invention, Matthew 27.52–53: 'The tombs also were opened, and many bodies of the saints who had fallen asleep were raised. After his resurrection they came out of the tombs and entered the holy city and appeared to many.' My favourite attempt to avoid the blindingly obvious conclusion that this is a piece of fiction is by the conservative evangelical scholar N. T. Wright: 'Some stories are so odd that they may just have happened. This may be one of them, but in historical terms there is no way of finding out.'[21] Where this leaves historical research, I do not know, and we might want to ask ourselves the following: does this apply to sightings of Elvis, stories of fairies or tales of vampires?

But there are good reasons, other than it being a story about several people rising from the dead, to believe that the things mentioned in Matthew 27.52–53 did not happen. For a start, this story is not found in Mark's Gospel. It might be thought that Mark might just have recorded such a stunningly spectacular event if it had happened. He would hardly be ignorant of it if it had happened. The story is not mentioned elsewhere in the New Testament. Why? This story of the dead people rising from the

---

[21] Wright, *Resurrection of the Son of God*, 636.

tombs is not found in the work of the late-first-century CE Jewish historian Josephus. He knew of countless events in Jerusalem and it would be bizarre should he have omitted this. A bit of historical imagination shows how serious the problems are for a view that thinks the events of Matthew 27.52–53 happened. Think of a discussion between Josephus and his scribe. 'Well', the scribe says, 'I am glad you are including the story of two Jewish teachers attempting to tear down the golden eagle from the Jerusalem Temple, and you could hardly omit the fall of Jerusalem to the Romans in 70 CE, but what about those dead people who came back to life around 30 CE, wasn't that the most spectacular thing you've ever heard of, Josephus?' Josephus might then reply tiresomely, 'No no, it isn't *that* exciting and I think they'll find my witty accounts of the political wranglings in Jerusalem more than stimulating.'

There is only one serious conclusion to be drawn from all this: the story in Matthew 27.52–53 simply did not happen. More to the point, with Matthew 27.52–53 we now have a very good piece of evidence that the first Christians were inventing stories about bodily resurrection.

That alone should warn us that the resurrection stories could involve substantial rewriting of history. And we can now look at what we find in Matthew, Luke and John. After Mark emphatically telling us that the women told no one about such things, and in what looks like a deliberate rewriting of Mark, Matthew has the disciples suddenly being told by the women what happened, and there is an extra emphasis on going to Galilee. The angel says to the woman:

> 'Then go quickly and tell his disciples, "He has been raised from the dead, and indeed he is going ahead of you to Galilee; there you will see him." This is my message for you.' So they left the tomb quickly with fear and great joy, and ran to tell his disciples. Suddenly Jesus met them and said, 'Greetings!' And they came to him, took hold of his feet, and worshipped him. Then Jesus said to them, 'Do not be afraid; go and tell my brothers to go to Galilee; there they will see me.' (Matthew 28.7–10)

Is that not reason to be suspicious? Luke's Gospel and John's Gospel also add Peter present at the empty tomb (Luke 24.11–12; John 20.6–8). Is adding such a major authority not just a *little* suspicious? Then what do we make of Matthew's Gospel ending with a story about the resurrected Jesus talking on a mountain about a *mission* to Gentiles/non-Jews (Matt. 28.16–20)? The historical Jesus did not have any concern for a *mission* to Gentiles and was only really concerned with Jews (see my chapter on the historical Jesus [pages 1–17 and 33–7]) but we know for a fact that the early Church had an interest in a *mission* to Gentiles/non-Jews and so I would suspect that the obvious conclusion for a historian would be that the resurrected Jesus talking of the gentile mission is an invention by the early Church.

Remember that in Mark the angelic man tells the women that Jesus is going ahead to Galilee (Mark 16.7). In Luke the appearance in Galilee is virtually eliminated. Luke's Jesus does not *return* to Galilee but instead two – not one – yes two, angelic men (where did this second one come from?) refer to what Jesus *said* in Galilee. Compare the two passages:

> But go, tell his disciples and Peter that he is going ahead of you to Galilee; there you will see him, just as he told you. (Mark 16.7)

> He is not here, but has risen. Remember how he told you, while he was still in Galilee, that the Son of Man must be handed over to sinners, and be crucified and on the third day rise again. (Luke 24.6–7)

No surprise then that in Luke the resurrection appearances and the resurrected Jesus' ascension to heaven take place around Jerusalem, and *not* Galilee. What is going on here other than creative invention and a clear rewriting of Mark's Gospel?

John's resurrection stories have all sorts of what can only be called invention. So, for example, this passage:

> Thomas answered him, 'My Lord and my God!' Jesus said to him, 'Have you believed because you have seen me? Blessed are those who have not seen and yet have come to believe.' (John 20.28–29)

This story occurs only in John's Gospel. There is little chance that any other Gospel would have omitted something so staggeringly dramatic if such a thing were *really* said. In fact John's Gospel is the *only* Gospel that has anything like the full equation of Jesus and God (see further my chapter on the Gospels [pages 116–32]). Again, this is all well within the boundaries of ancient storytelling and should not be confused with modern notions of lying. But he is making it up.

In sum, *something* happened after the death of Jesus, and the closest we get to eyewitness accounts suggest that various people had visionary experiences. There is not serious evidence for there historically being an empty tomb. Yes, the first Christians *believed* that Jesus had been bodily raised but belief does not prove anything happened, anymore than lots of people believing in God proves God exists. If something like the resurrection stories were from some other religion in the ancient world, ancient historians would rightly be judging the resurrection stories for what they more or less are: creative retellings of the past, or what we might call fiction.

Some common evangelical arguments

There are plenty of well-known arguments given in support of there being an empty tomb and the bodily resurrection being the best explanation for the empty tomb. It is to some of these that we now turn.

Women were not regarded as reliable witnesses

The ace-up-the-sleeve for those wanting to argue for the historical probability of the empty tomb is frequently thought to be women as the first witnesses. Women, the argument usually goes, were regarded as exceptionally poor witnesses so that no one would have made up a story about the women being the first witnesses and therefore the empty tomb story is most probably historically accurate. Bird, as we saw, uses this kind of argument.

Against this, it might be pointed out that women were given a relatively prominent role in Jesus' ministry and that this could have made their testimony more acceptable for some. Mark says at the crucifixion, just before the empty tomb story:

> There were also women looking on from a distance; among them were Mary Magdalene, and Mary the mother of James the younger and of Joses, and Salome. These used to follow him and provided for him when he was in Galilee; and there were many other women who had come up with him to Jerusalem. (15.40–41)

Also, the socio-economic upheaval, along with the 'utopian' ideals that tend to accompany such upheaval, which provided the context for the emergence of the Jesus movement in Galilee (see my chapter on the historical Jesus [pages 1–17 and 33–7]) was conducive to a temporary shift in the understanding of gender relations as well as other social relations, a point noted in the cross-cultural study of social upheaval.[22] We even have one Jewish revolutionary at the time of the Jewish revolt against Rome called Simon bar Giora who had a culturally unusual following of women (Josephus, *J.W.* 4.505).

Celsus, the second-century CE opponent of Christianity, also noted the relatively prominent role of women in Christian history:

> For such was the charm of Jesus' words, that not only were men willing to follow Him to the wilderness, but women also, forgetting the weakness of their sex and a regard for outward propriety in thus following their Teacher into desert places . . . By which words, acknowledging that such

---

[22] E.g. M. A. Tétreault, 'Women and Revolution: A Framework for Analysis', in *Women and Revolution in Africa, Asia, and the New World*, ed. M. A. Tétreault (Columbia: University of South Carolina Press, 1994), 3–30.

individuals are worthy of their God, they manifestly show that they desire and are able to gain over only the silly, and the mean, and the stupid, with women and children.   (Origen *Cels.* 3.10, 44)

This passage is sometimes used to show how unlikely it would have been for the female witnesses to be invented, but it can also be used to support alternative arguments: women at the tomb, who were said to be capable of supporting the Jesus movement, may well have been culturally acceptable for Christians to use as witnesses to Jesus or to be given a prominent role in the story.

Another possible counter-argument might mention that Jews could and did write stories of women, such as Esther and Judith, who played much more prominent roles than some might expect in certain contexts. So could Christians not do the same and write stories about heroic women in a given context? What such a counter-argument shows is that, as ever, we do not have to resort to explanations that point to the supernatural. There might be another perfectly naturalistic explanation.

Let's try another hypothetical explanation. After Jesus' arrest, clearly as a political threat from the perspective of the Romans, Jesus' male disciples scattered out of fear. This was perfectly understandable because the group would also have been deemed worthy of killing. So it is quite believable that when Jesus got led away with bandits to be crucified there would have been a big armed presence (Mark 15.16) and no male disciples around. At the same time it is also quite believable that a group of supportive female disciples would have been around: hence Mark says the women watched at a distance. Now think what Mark has left: a story where men had fled but women remained. The narrative almost requires the women to be the first witnesses.[23]

So, yet again, we have a perfectly logical explanation for the fact that someone somewhere in earliest Christianity could use women to do things of high importance in the narrative and without us having to resort to supernatural implications. Furthermore, the man dressed in white, presumably an angel, may have provided all the authority Mark's audience required.[24] In narrative terms, the *angel* is really the first witness to the

---

[23] In a helpful critique of various positions on the resurrection (including mine), Dale C. Allison ('Explaining the Resurrection: Conflicting Convictions', *Journal for the Study of the Historical Jesus* 2 (2005), 117–33 [125]), claims that I credit this view to Goulder even though Bultmann had previously made it. However, against Allison, I did not attribute the claim to Goulder at all and I also made reference to Bultmann. As I said in the relevant footnote: 'I owe the following point to a discussion with Maurice Casey. Compare also R. Bultmann, *The History of the Synoptic Tradition . . .*' (Crossley, 'Historical Plausibility', 184, n. 50).

[24] Crossley, 'Historical Plausibility', 184.

empty tomb and not the women. Bird claims that 'if Mark was trying to "cover-up" lack of knowledge of the empty tomb then he would probably have had the news of the empty tomb on the lips of the angel himself' (see page 43). But isn't putting the news on the lips of the angel effectively what Mark did?

Jews were not expecting a suffering Messiah

It is sometimes argued that the earliest Christians believed that Jesus was the Messiah despite no Jewish belief in a suffering and dying Messiah. Therefore the only real justification for a suffering Messiah would be a bodily raised Jesus, otherwise the first Christians were faced with damning evidence that Jesus was a failed Messiah.

It seems to me that history does not work in such compartmentalized and neat ways and is full of particularities. In the case of Jesus, there are some notable particularities. Leaving aside the question of whether the concept of 'the Messiah' was crystallized by the time of Jesus, there is a strong case to be made that Jesus knew he would die: John the Baptist had been killed and Jesus must have been aware that by doing something dramatic in the temple – which he did – then he was risking his life (see my chapter on the historical Jesus [1–17]). So this changes everything. Jesus was deemed to be a prominent figure in Jewish history by his followers and no doubt by himself *but* he actually thought/knew he was going to die. That required some new thinking and so this historical particularity means that an argument appealing to a non-suffering Messiah has little bearing on the arguments for or against the bodily resurrection.

Tombs and pilgrims

Another popular evangelical argument suggests that as there is no evidence of anyone venerating Jesus' tomb, it was almost certainly empty. But this is not a strong argument and it can be explained in different ways. If there were visions of Jesus interpreted as a bodily figure of Jesus then it would have been assumed that the tomb was empty, an argument that would gain further strength if no one knew where Jesus was buried, as I suggested above in relation to Mark 16.8. Alternatively, with religious sentiment being what it is, would someone not have started up a shrine to Jesus' tomb even if it was empty? In fact, it is just possible that the fact that there are no known details of pilgrimage to a shrine could also be interpreted to mean that no one actually knew where the tomb was. But, ultimately, explanations based on shrines and pilgrimages that we know nothing about either way are far too speculative to be of any serious use. They certainly do not mean we should go all supernatural on the evidence.

A cautionary tale

Finally, I would like to end this section on some of the common evangelical arguments with a slightly over-the-top but what I think is a potentially useful parallel. In *The Last Vampyre*, the TV adaptation of Arthur Conan Doyle's story, *The Sussex Vampyre*, Sherlock Holmes was reluctant to take up a case supposedly involving vampires because it was all too superstitious for his this-worldly rational mind, with all the allegations levelled at the so-called vampire Stockton able to be explained in a this-worldly manner.

Now such an analogy with the historical study of Christian origins may seem a touch far-fetched. But it seems to me that there may be a regrettable need for people to keep showing that there are perfectly normal explanations for the resurrection in order to prevent the supernatural explanations hindering more conventional explanations for Christian origins. In historical terms we have at the very least seen that the evidence for the bodily resurrection hardly demands that it really did happen with God intervening in history. Among the many things that worry me about certain evangelical arguments (e.g. those of N. T. Wright) is that when alternative arguments ultimately grounded in naturalistic explanations (such as those given here) are supposedly shown to be unlikely, then the argument effectively has to go straight to the supernatural![25]

So instead of finding a range of *possible* this-worldly historical explanations, the divine – something we do not know, something we cannot

---

[25] Wright has attempted to respond to some of my criticisms of his work but most of his claims either invent what I say or rely on argument-free polemic. See N. T. Wright, 'Resurrecting Old Arguments: Responding to Four Essays', *Journal for the Study of the Historical Jesus* 3 (2005), 209–31. One example should highlight this. Wright claims that my reference to Jewish storytelling refers to 'legends about figures in the distant past, written to justify a belief in the present, are in fact very significantly different to the resurrection narratives. The latter . . . concern a figure of very recent memory, not Moses or Abraham or someone else from long ago . . .' (Wright, 'Resurrecting', 219–220). Compare this with what I said, which absolutely explicitly talks not only of figures of long ago but also of figures from the recent present. Not once does Wright mention this despite quoting the final sentence immediately after the key points. As I said: 'While it is true that much of the rewriting of history concerns distant figures, this alone does not prove that creative storytelling could not be done in the case of more recent historical figures. In fact historically inaccurate storytelling was done for fairly recent historical figures. Stories of rabbis are one example. Another notable parallel is the rapid emergence of miraculous and legendary traditions surrounding pagan figures such as Alexander or Augustus, even within their own life times. It is regrettable that these points still need to be made.' (Crossley, 'Historical Plausibility' 181). Sadly, Wright's response is typical. In the absence of serious argument and accurate representation there seems little point in spending too much time here on the subject. For a more detailed response see <http://earliestchristianhistory.blogspot.com/2007/07/resurrection-and-scholarly-rhetoric.html> (accessed 28 March 2008).

see – is somehow a superior explanation. This is a poor way to proceed. If some this-worldly arguments explaining the empty tomb are necessarily speculative, how speculative are arguments that push instead for the supernatural?

So we should remember Sherlock Holmes: he was involved in a case where the local villagers think that all the evidence points toward Stockton being a real vampire from an old family of vampires and there is even the unusual instance of Sherlock Holmes having a vision/hallucination. But thankfully our hero does not give in to supernatural explanations and is sure there are rational this-worldly explanations (and keeps providing a range of them). Eventually all is explained even when everyone else thought otherwise.[26] So whose example do you want to follow: the supreme rationalist or the deluded villagers believing in vampires without *seriously* trying to seek alternative explanations?

Conclusions

My guess is that few committed believers would really be persuaded not to believe in the bodily resurrection just because I give historical arguments against its historical plausibility. And this is fine. But if people want to come to this *as historians*, there is no serious evidence in favour of the bodily resurrection of Jesus really happening. If there were a similar story in the ancient world and if we were applying the conventional standards of historical research to this story, no one would take it seriously as a historical account of what actually happened. Arguments suggesting that we cannot explain Christian origins if the resurrection did not happen are staggeringly naïve and only work if some basic historical trends and evidence are ignored. Some of the trends we have already seen, and we will turn to more in due course.

But the kinds of issues discussed here have wider implications than the historical study of Christian origins. What a debate over the historical accuracy of the resurrection often boils down to is two different approaches to history that are close to being irreconcilable. To give this a contemporary slant, do we want to find whatever naturalistic causes are possible in historical explanation, leaving questions of the divine completely to one side, or do we want to take the pseudo-scientific route of Intelligent Design or Creationism and say that the supernatural can be shown to be directly intervening in historical change in the study of history?

---

[26] Most entertainingly – and forgive me for teasing a little – Holmes suggests to the local vicar that the reason why word about vampires got around was because of 'the church, the fount of all gossip'!

Response from Michael F. Bird

This is the juncture where Crossley and I cross swords the most violently. Let me deal with several big picture issues about how we approach the historical task and then quibble about details with Crossley on the empty tomb and resurrection appearances.

Worldview and historical explanations

To begin with let's talk about worldview, evidence and history. Crossley acknowledges his secular presuppositions but he never defends them. Why do we have to start with a priori atheism in order to be truly historical in our approach? If it is at least possible that God exists, is it not possible that this God can choose to intervene in our world? That means that 'resurrection' is one explanation that must remain on the table until Crossley convincingly establishes that this option is metaphysically impossible, not merely different from how the fields of geology and linguistics work, but metaphysically kaput. I'm doing history with a full deck of cards but I feel that Crossley has cut the cards in his favour. On a similar tack, is invocation of the supernatural really so absurd? Crossley insists that in other academic disciplines invocation of the supernatural is not a respectable option for explaining empirical events. To that I say, go and talk to some scientists about what caused the *Big Bang* and the word 'God' is at least one option that some scientists are willing to contemplate even if it is in a vague sense about what 'God' means.

For that matter what is an 'explanation'? Crossley seems to imply that an explanation is one that conforms to standards of evidence and proof that would be accepted by other disciplines, but I say unto you, an explanation is a hypothesis that has the power to account for all of the existing data and variables given our present knowledge. In the history of ideas there have been multiple cases where certain proposals or hypotheses were put forward and they did not conform to the received rationality of the day and were not immediately verifiable. For example, Einstein's theory of general relativity was controversial and not provable until a solar eclipse took place, to see if space was really distorted by gravity. Heisenberg's uncertainty principle is not paralleled in other disciplines to my knowledge; does that make it false? When British botanists arrived in Australia they reported the existence of a mammal that laid eggs, had fur like a rabbit, a bill like a duck, and webbed feet. When the report reached Britain it was ridiculed as a hoax. Even when the botanists in Australia sent back the hide of this animal, it was still jeered as an elaborate joke. Little did they know that such a creature does exist and is called a platypus.[27] My point is that evidence does not always conform to scientific expectations, so I am reticent to let anyone place limits on what is possible in a space–time universe which might co-exist with a divine being. That is not religious dogma, it is simply being open to a range of possibilities.

Crossley is adamant that we must find explanations for the seismic shifts in early Christianity apart from purely theological ideas and the postulation of supernatural events like the resurrection. Here I am actually sympathetic to Crossley and readily admit that the history of ideas (especially theological ideas) has been given too much air time in explaining the early Christian movement at the expense of historical, economic, cultural and social factors. But things are on the mend and the work of Christian scholars such as Gerd Theissen, Howard Kee, Philip Esler and Stephen Barton are drawing attention to the importance of sociological issues in describing early Christianity – and I wholeheartedly endorse their aims. Still, something extraordinary happened to the disciples to convince them that Jesus' death was not a defeat but in fact a glorious victory. Their own explanation as to what happened is that God raised Jesus from the dead. Crossley of course rejects that explanation. But let us say that Jesus did rise from the dead. What kind of historical impact or imprint would we expect it to have? Would it be violently different from what Christianity actually became? Crossley does not even entertain this problem. If he could demonstrate that had Jesus actually risen from the dead that the result would have been exceedingly different from what Christianity became, then he would have a stronger case, but he does not go that route.

On the limitations of evidence, in one sense I have to agree with Crossley, as the very most we can say is that the disciples believed that Jesus rose from the dead but the mere fact of their belief does not necessitate or prove in the absolute sense that he did rise from the grave. Moving from their belief to the supernatural is indeed an inference, but it is an inference that the witnesses are begging us to make! We can either (a) accept their testimony, or (b) reject their testimony and seek an alternative explanation. What separates me from Crossley is that my theistic worldview leaves me open to option (a) and none of the arguments from option (b) seems particularly persuasive. Thus, I am not convinced that Crossley has shown how the emergence of belief in Jesus' resurrection

---

[27] I owe this last example to Ross Clifford, Principal of Morling Theological College in Sydney, Australia.

arose without an actual resurrection. That is not to say his conclusion is false, it merely shows that the evidence he adduces creates more problems than it solves and it does not adequately account for the materials before him.

The empty tomb

On the empty tomb, Crossley maintains that Paul mentions no eyewitnesses to the empty tomb. But as I said before Paul doesn't mention Pontius Pilate, Jerusalem or the crucifixion either – are we to doubt these events too? What Paul does say is that Christ 'died' was 'buried' and 'rose'. Now if Paul had merely said that Jesus 'died' and 'rose' then I think Crossley would have a genuinely good point. But burial means that Jesus was interred in a place for corpses and thus we have to assume that the place of burial was vacated by the physical transformation of Jesus' body into its immortal and glorious state. In other words, burial plus resurrection has to imply an empty tomb.

As for Mark inventing the story of the empty tomb, I confess that I do not understand why Mark would do it to begin with. If one can believe in resurrection without a physical appearance, as Crossley proposes, why is an empty tomb needed to prove a physical appearance? Other forms of Christianity did not need an empty tomb to find a living voice for Jesus in their own day (e.g. that form of Christianity represented by the *Gospel of Thomas*). If Mark was so into a form of creative storytelling that takes liberty with historical facts, then why would he feel it necessary to develop a story that squares up the historical incongruity of belief in the empty tomb with the fact that no one knew of its whereabouts? If the other Evangelists could create stories of the resurrection that are purportedly contradictory and live with them (as Crossley alleges), why not Mark? I think Crossley is also mistaken as to what the women failed to report. According to Crossley, what the women failed to report to others was the whereabouts of the empty tomb. However, what they 'said nothing to anyone about' was not just the empty tomb, but also the angel, the angelic news of resurrection, and the coming appearances of Jesus in Galilee. Why does Crossley only regard the empty tomb as a Marcan invention? Why does he not regard the resurrection itself as an invention of Mark too? Crossley is being grossly selective with the evidence. If we push the logic of his conclusion it would mean that Mark invented the story of the empty tomb and the news of the resurrection.

In summary, Crossley's proposal that Mark 16.1–8 is an invention by Mark is unreasonable because:

1 the empty tomb is already presupposed by Paul which (contra Crossley)[28] is earlier than Mark;

2 Crossley does not establish why Mark would need to invent the story of the empty tomb in the first place when it was possible to believe in a resurrection without an empty tomb;

3 the early Christians did not try to reconcile conflicting historical evidence in such a rationalistic manner, as Crossley himself acknowledges;

4 what the women failed to report was not only the whereabouts of the empty tomb but also the fact of the empty tomb, the angelic visit and the report of a forthcoming appearance of Jesus in Galilee;

5 the group to whom the women failed to report the news to, on account of fear, were probably members of the wider public, and they did mean to tell the disciples, which is exactly how the other Evangelists understood the story (Matt. 28.8; Luke 24.9; John 20.2, 18); and

6 the tradition seems distinctly non-Marcan and not just early.

Resurrection appearances

Every time Crossley says the word 'resurrection' I feel like quoting what Inigo says to Vizzini in the movie the *Princess Bride*: 'You keep using that word, but I do not think it means what you think it means.'[29] The word 'resurrection' does not mean that I have a warm fuzzy feeling that our dear and departed friend Moshe is still somehow with us (to be fair that is not what Crossley exactly says but it is in the same ball park). There was a holy host of options in Jewish literature that could be used to describe

---

[28] While it is true that a minority of scholars date the Gospel of Mark to the 40s they are such a minority that if they ever got together for a meeting it could probably be held in a Volkswagen. Let me add that Christianity was not a big movement and by the end of the 40s CE there might have been as few as a couple of thousand Christians worldwide. If Mark did invent a story about the empty tomb one has to consider the possibility that many of the eyewitnesses or people known to the eyewitnesses would have taken him to task rather quickly.

[29] The central issue here is what counts as a 'resurrection' and what language would be appropriate to describe it. We cannot assume that any post-mortem appearance of someone can automatically pass as a resurrection. Does resurrection have any singular and recognizable meaning? Part of the difficulty is that scholars debate exactly how physical the resurrection body is according to New Testament witnesses. Did Jesus rise spiritually to appear luminously? Was his new post-mortem existence immaterial except when he wanted to appear in physical form? Does Paul regard Jesus' resurrected body as made of spirit or animated by the Spirit (1 Cor. 15.44–45). For the view that the New Testament portrays a fairly consistent picture of Jesus' resurrection body as physical see Robert H. Gundry, 'The Essential Physicality of Jesus' Resurrection according to the New Testament', in *The Old is Better* (WUNT 178; Tubingen: Mohr-Siebeck, 2005), 171–94.

a hero entering the afterlife: becoming an angel, becoming a star, assumption into heaven, etc. But resurrection was something programmed to occur at the millennium or eschaton. It was usually corporate, with everyone or at least the righteous/wise raised up. It was also physical. This physicality is quite clear in the accompanying descriptions: resurrection *from the dead* or resurrection *of the flesh*. While some authors in Graeco-Roman literature might describe a soul in quasi-somatic terms (i.e. almost bodily), we are still a long way off resurrection in the Jewish sense of the term. A vision of Jesus ascending to heaven on a fiery chariot or reclining in the bosom of Abraham would not have led to descriptions of Jesus as 'raised from the dead'. To give another example, in an extra-canonical writing called *The Testament of Job*, the story is given of how some children killed in the collapse of a house are translated into heaven. The children are killed when a house collapses upon them, but Job urges the rescuers not to bother clearing away the debris because the bodies are nowhere to be found. Job urges the mother to look heavenward, where she sees a vision of the two children in heaven, translated there by God and now crowned in splendour (*T. Job* 39.8—40.6). The absence of the dead bodies and the account of a vision did not necessitate belief in the children's resurrection, but only of their translation into the abode of heaven. Why didn't Jesus' disciples interpret the Easter events in similar fashion (empty tomb + visions = translation)? Why resurrection over a heavenly translation? I suspect that resurrection was a better way of describing what they actually believed that they had seen, heard and experienced.

Now Crossley argues that the content of visions of deceased persons is provided by culturally specific ways of understanding the vision itself. He also asserts that visionary experiences can be interpreted in any number of ways in different cultures. Let us grant as much. So what were the options for interpreting a vision: meeting a ghost, an angel, a spirit, an astral being, appearance of a person from heaven, etc.? Why didn't the disciples and the Evangelists regard the appearance of Jesus in one of these categories? Why resurrection? Crossley states that resurrection was one of the culturally specific ways of interpreting a vision and he cites 2 Maccabees 7 as an example. But therein lies the problem. In 2 Maccabees the event envisaged is physical (i.e. receiving back maimed limbs), it is corporate and involves 'all' martyrs, and it happens at the end of history. Yet Crossley tells us that what happened to Jesus was non-physical, it happened to an individual and in the middle of history. While there are culturally specific ways of interpreting a vision surely there has to be some correlation between the event and its accompanying description. To avoid this incongruity the disciples could have used other categories to describe what happened to Jesus, but they did not do so. What I want to know is why? Why is the tradition unanimous in affirming resurrection? One answer that I think remains plausible is that the disciples really believed that they had seen Jesus in physical form after his death.[30]

Further reading

Allison, D. C., *Resurrecting Jesus: The Earliest Christian Tradition and Its Interpreters* (London: T&T Clark, 2005).

Copan, P. and R. K. Tacelli (eds), *Jesus' Resurrection: Fact or Figment: A Debate between William Lane Craig and Gerd Lüdemann* (Downers Grove: IVP, 2000).

Craig, William Lane, *The Son Rises: Historical Evidence for the Resurrection of Jesus* (Eugene, OR: Wipf & Stock, 2001).

Davis, Stephen T., *Risen Indeed: Making Sense of the Resurrection* (Grand Rapids, MI: Eerdmans, 1993).

Goulder, M., 'The Baseless Fabric of a Vision', in G. D'Costa (ed.), *Resurrection Reconsidered* (Oxford: Oneworld, 1996), 48–61.

Habermas, Gary, and Michael R. Licona, *The Case for the Resurrection of Jesus* (Grand Rapids, MI: Kregel, 2004).

Harris, Murray J., *Raised Immortal: Resurrection and Immortality in the New Testament* (United Kingdom: Marshall Morgan & Scott, 1983).

Journal for the Study of the Historical Jesus 3 (2005) – this issue is on the theme of the resurrection, including reactions to N. T. Wright's arguments.

Longenecker, Richard, (ed.), *Life in the Face of Death: The Resurrection Message of the New Testament* (Grand Rapids, MI: Eerdmans, 1998).

Lüdemann, G., *What Really Happened to Jesus: A Historical Approach to the Resurrection* (Louisville: Westminster John Knox, 1995).

---

[30] While Crossley alludes to the story of Jesus walking on the water in Mark 6.46–53, this is really a red herring. The disciples do not think that Jesus was a ghost despite the fact that he had physical form. Rather, they think that he was a ghost because he was walking on the water in the middle of a storm. The physicality of ghosts is just not an issue with which the Evangelists were concerned. Matthew 27.51–53 is an interesting story and Crossley raises some genuinely good points. My understanding of this text is that it is not historical and it blends the present and the future together, so that Matthew provides a cameo of the future resurrection at the point of Jesus' death to underscore its living-giving power.

3

The apostle Paul

James G. Crossley

I have stressed that three of the key features that were to distinguish Christianity as a religion in its own right were its general abandonment of the Law, its major inclusion of Gentiles in the salvation history of Israel, and its full deification of Jesus in a system that believed in one God. We saw that Jesus did little to contribute to these major developments. In sharp contrast, but facing a very different situation from Jesus, Paul makes and/or reflects some of the most significant steps in these directions and provided the intellectual foundations for subsequent Christian theology. We may turn first to the issue of the Law, arguably Paul's most important contribution to Christian theology and distinctiveness.

Paul and the Law

It is sometimes argued that Paul's call or conversion almost immediately led to his view that practising at least some parts of the Law was not required from the believer. This argument often suggests that Paul realized God's grace had now saved him aside from Law-based Judaism, which had much more time for salvation through the Law than salvation through grace. This view, however, seems to read Christian theology back into texts where there are no such explicit sentiments. In Galatians, Paul says,

> But when God, who had set me apart before I was born and called me through his grace, was pleased to reveal his Son to me, so that I might proclaim him among the Gentiles, I did not confer with any human being, nor did I go up to Jerusalem to those who were already apostles before me, but I went away at once into Arabia, and afterwards I returned to Damascus.
>
> (Gal. 1.15–17)

There is no indication that this grace sets Paul apart from a Law-based religion that had little concern for God's grace. In fact, the idea that Law and grace were not compatible may well be a misunderstanding of Judaism. We might note a scholarly argument that a more accurate translation of John 1.16 is, 'grace *instead of* grace' (NRSV: 'grace *upon* grace'). In terms of John's theology this would be referring to the new system of grace, revolving round Jesus, replacing a different system of grace associated with Judaism. Back to Paul's account of his call or conversion: he mentioned what God wants him to do (go to the Gentiles) and in the context of Galatians this sets up Paul's authority to defend his theology, which involves inclusion in the Christian community without having to observe key parts of the Law. Given this, it is particularly striking that Paul does not mention the issue of Law observance.

Moreover, it seems that during Paul's early years as a member of the movement that would become Christianity, this movement was largely Law-observant, just as the historical Jesus was. The earliest clear indications that Christianity included people who were not observing the Law suggest dates in the 40s CE. At the Jerusalem council of the late 40s, recorded in Acts 15 and Galatians 2.1–10, we get attempted solutions to people's no longer observing the Law. In Acts 13.38–39 we have Paul apparently preaching sometime in the 40s, saying,

> Let it be known to you therefore, my brothers, that through this man forgiveness of sins is proclaimed to you; by this Jesus everyone who believes is set free from all those sins from which you could not be freed by the law of Moses. (Acts 13.38–39)

This does not quite say that Law observance was not being practised but the aftermath (13.44–52) suggests that something dramatic regarding the Law is being implied. Prior to this in the narrative of Acts is Peter's vision (Acts 10.1—11.18), placed sometime in the 40s, though it is clear that Luke does not know precisely when this was supposed to have happened. In this vision, Peter was said to have been told by God that he could drop one of the most notable aspects of the Law: the food laws.

Whether or not all of this is historically accurate, this is the best evidence for the first rumblings of non-observance; if there were evidence of earlier non-observance then Acts or Paul would have used it. Of course, it has been claimed that there is indeed earlier evidence and that Paul accepted ideas surrounding non-observance in the immediate aftermath of his vision of Christ. While the accounts of Paul's vision do consistently tell us that he was to evangelize Gentiles, they do not say that non-observance began after his vision. Naturally, Paul may ground his authority to make decisions in his vision (e.g. Gal. 1—2; Phil. 3), but this does not mean that decisions he made (e.g. on circumcision and the Law in Galatians) were already openly made just after his vision.

Another argument made in favour of early (30s CE) non-observance is that in Acts 6—7 the group close to Stephen, usually labelled 'the Hellenists', was persecuted by a pre-conversion Paul, presumably because of non-observance of at least some biblical commandments. Arguably, Stephen was killed because of a radical take on the Law. After all, he was accused of speaking 'blasphemous words against Moses and God' (Acts 6.11). However, it is important to remember that Acts not only regards these people as 'false witnesses' (Acts 6.13) but also adds that,

> They set up false witnesses who said, 'This man never stops saying things against this holy place and the law; for we have heard him say that this Jesus of Nazareth will destroy this place and will change the customs that Moses handed on to us.' (Acts 6.13–14)

This is the language of *expanded* or *interpreted* Law I discussed in my chapter on the historical Jesus (see pages 1–17 and 33–7) and we know that many Jews were attributing their legal interpretations to Moses or even God (e.g. *Jubilees*; 11QT; Mishnah *Pe'ah* 2.6). Acts also tells us that Stephen, in a lengthy speech (Acts 7.2–53), was critical of the Temple system, a system that was grounded in the Law, especially in Acts 7.45–50:

> And it was there until the time of David, who found favour with God and asked that he might find a dwelling-place for the house of Jacob. But it was Solomon who built a house for him. Yet the Most High does not dwell in houses made by human hands; as the prophet [Isa. 66.1–2] says . . .

First, we should note the not unimportant fact that Moses the Law-giver and the Law itself are portrayed very positively in Stephen's speech (e.g. 7.20, 22, 38, 53). Moreover, the key verse 7.47 could equally be translated, '*And* it was Solomon who built a house for him', implying a continuation rather than a contrast. But the problems arise in 7.48 when Stephen says, 'Yet the Most High does not dwell in houses made by human hands'. This refers to the Temple system, grounded in the Law, but this does necessarily imply that the Temple was a bad thing. After all, Stephen's speech actually quotes a scriptural passage (Isa. 66.1–2) and, in the context of Scripture, the Temple was, ideally, a good thing.

Yet we cannot overlook the fact that Stephen does say that God does not dwell in houses 'made by human hands' (7.48), a phrase usually associated with idolatry. This might be deemed as an attack on the present Temple system as being corrupt, similar to Jesus' attack on the present Temple (cf. Mark 14.58). To support this, there are some closely related scriptural traditions (e.g. 2 Chron. 6.16; 7.19–20) that contain conditional threats at Solomon's dedication of the Temple, where abusing the commandments would lead to an end of God's relationship with the Temple. And it is at the time of Solomon that Stephen's history of Israel ends. He continues by criticizing the Temple authorities for not observing the Law. Then

Stephen is attacked and put to death. The evidence here therefore favours an internal Jewish dispute over the correct interpretation of the Law. Consequently, this does not provide an immediate context for Paul rejecting observance of at least some parts of the Law after his call/ conversion.

It is sometimes suggested that Paul himself refers to Christians whom he persecuted partly because of their apparent rejection of parts of the Law. The big problem is that Paul never says this. Here is what Paul says:

> I was violently persecuting the church of God and was trying to destroy it. I advanced in Judaism beyond many among my people of the same age, for I was far more zealous for the traditions of my ancestors.
>
> (Gal. 1.13–14)

> . . . as to zeal, a persecutor of the church . . . (Phil. 3.6)

But once again, this could simply reflect a dispute over the interpretation of the Law, and Paul never makes clear mention of a supposed group who were not observing the Law so soon after Jesus' death. Note also that Paul says he was 'far more zealous for the traditions of my ancestors' (Gal. 1.14), language typical of the interpretation of the expansion of the Law (cf. Mark 7.5; Josephus, *Ant.* 13.297). It is again difficult to see how Paul's persecution of the earliest Christians was because they were dropping parts of the Law. Consequently, we simply have no serious evidence that anyone, Paul included, was advocating non-observance of the Law in the years prior to the early 40s CE.

Paul and the emergence of the non-observance of the Law

But as we have seen, things changed in tandem with the emergence of Gentiles in earliest Christianity. This is where some of the decisions made by the historical Jesus become important. Jesus' controversial association with (Jewish) sinners provided a strong ideological justification for further association with non-Jewish sinners: both Jewish and gentile sinners are strongly overlapping categories. After Jesus' death followers of Jesus went into synagogues and associations which would have involved consistent interactions between Jews and Gentiles. The impetus given by association with people deemed beyond the Law and covenant (as gentile and Jewish sinners both were) meant that the Jesus movement could begin to spread outside Judaism.

In the light of what we have seen, it initially seems that the first Gentiles were Law-observant, so how do we explain the rise of non-observance?

Building on the work of Rodney Stark on conversion through social networks and various sociologists on studies of shifting commitment levels among converts, I have argued that conversion of individuals and conversion of households interested in Law-observant Christianity involved contacts with, and inclusion of, people with little interest in key aspects of the Law, such as food and Sabbath laws, not to mention circumcision.[1] As early Jewish literature would suggest, it does not follow that the conversion of households would lead to a wholly heartfelt conversion of individuals within the household. Logic alone suggests that some would have been more dedicated than others: Paul's letter to Philemon is a useful analogy here. We could also envisage the situation of one partner being converted whereas the other was not: 1 Corinthians 7 is a useful analogy here. Involvement in groups other than the Christian movement led to a whole host of different counter-influences: 1 Corinthians 8.10 might be a useful analogy here. So with this greater connection with Gentiles, there are already serious pre-existing counter-influences. In this context earliest Christianity was faced with the problem of more and more people associated in differing degrees with the Christian movement and not necessarily observing biblical laws.

So what do you do with all these non-observant people? A major attempt to deal with this issue was the Jerusalem council (Acts 15; Gal. 2.1–10) in the mid-first century CE. Here there were different suggestions put forward but it seems that there was some general agreement and compromise. Galatians 2.1–10 appears to show that Paul gained permission for a mission to Gentiles that did not require full observance. The parallel in Acts suggests that there were certain restrictions on Gentiles (Acts 15.20, 29). But this was not enough to stop the almost inevitable pressures from all these non-observant people, as the incident at Antioch shortly after the Jerusalem council shows:

> But when Cephas [Peter] came to Antioch, I opposed him to his face, because he stood self-condemned; for until certain people came from James, he used to eat with the Gentiles. But after they came, he drew back and kept himself separate for fear of the circumcision faction. And the other Jews joined him in this hypocrisy, so that even Barnabas was led astray by their hypocrisy. But when I saw that they were not acting consistently with the truth of the gospel, I said to Cephas before them all, 'If you, though a Jew, live like a Gentile and not like a Jew, how can you compel the Gentiles to live like Jews?' (Gal. 2.11–14)

---

[1] For a full discussion, see, J. G. Crossley, *Why Christianity Happened: A Sociohistorical Account of Christian Origins 26–50 CE* (Louisville: Westminster John Knox, 2006).

There are different views of the Antioch controversy mentioned in Galatians 2.11–14.[2] Traditionally it was generally thought that the issue at stake among Peter, Paul and those from James was whether the biblical food laws ought to be observed. More recently there have been suggestions that the issues might have involved one or more of the following:

- Expansions or interpretations of biblical purity and food-related laws.
- Jewish Christians simply refusing to eat with gentile Christians unless male gentile Christians were circumcised.
- Jewish Christians would not associate with gentile Christians because Gentiles were unclean.
- There were two distinct groups within early Christianity – Law-observant Jewish Christians and non-observant gentile Christians – and if these two groups overlapped significantly then problems would arise because Jewish views on association with Gentiles ranged from suspicion to open co-existence, with the ranges represented in this dispute and poor old Peter caught in the middle.
- James was anxious that too much association with gentile Christians could lead to idolatry or transgression and so Peter's mission to Jews could have been seriously discredited.

It's unlikely that expansion of the Law was the issue because Jesus was emphatically critical of such expansions, and expansions of purity law and food-related laws were not developed in any known strand of earliest Christianity. In contrast we do know from Paul's letters (see below) that the issue of observing at least some aspects of biblical Law was a major issue within first-century Christianity.

Circumcision was probably not the issue because when the language of compelling converts to live like Jews is used in Jewish literature (literally, 'to Judaize') it implies taking on Jewish practices, with circumcision being a *different* and final practice in the process of becoming a Jew (e.g. LXX Esth. 8.17; Josephus, *J.W.* 2.454, 462–63).[3] It is sometimes added that as the general context of Paul's letter to the Galatians is more concerned with circumcision so Paul's use of the Antioch incident must also concern circumcision. But this does not necessarily follow. A recent issue involving another problematic biblical law would have highlighted Paul's point nicely and so we should not assume that circumcision must have

---

[2] For a more detailed discussion of different perspectives, see J. G. Crossley, *The Date of Mark's Gospel: Insight from the Law in Earliest Christianity* (London and New York: Continuum/T&T Clark, 2004), chapter 5.

[3] See e.g. J. D. G. Dunn, *Jesus, Paul and the Law: Studies in Mark and Galatians* (London: SPCK, 1990), 129–82.

to be in mind when Paul cited previous examples. Moreover, observance of biblical Law without reference to circumcision was also an issue in Galatians (Gal. 4.10).

Whether or not Gentiles were unclean would not have been an issue. Again, a notable stress for Jesus was the non-observance of the expanded view of the Law whereby Jews should keep clean all the time, particularly in the context of meals (and, incidentally, this is not against any biblical commandment). To stress, there is no serious evidence that Christians were disputing the role of expanded laws about clean and unclean. Moreover, there have been some powerful arguments made by scholars of early Jewish purity law that there was no such thing as 'gentile uncleanness' at the time of Jesus: the real problem with Gentiles is that they stray too much toward idolatry and bad behaviour (e.g. Lev. 18.24–30; Deut. 7.2–4, 16; 20; Tobit 14.6; *Jub.* 9.15; *Ep. Arist.* 152; Philo, *Spec. Laws* 1.51; *Sib. Or.* 3.492, 496–500; 5.168).[4]

The idea of there being two distinct movements of observant Jewish Christians and non-observant gentile Christians within earliest Christianity is a problem because the Jewish Peter was remembered as accepting that he could, in principle at least, eat food prohibited in biblical Law (Acts 10.1–11.18) and the Jewish Paul implies that he himself behaved differently when among Gentiles (1 Cor. 9.19–23).

The final point listed above seems to me to be most convincing but it should be tied in with the traditional view that the biblical food laws were at stake. The problem may have been subtle: if increasing numbers of Gentiles were eating food banned in biblical Law (e.g. pork) then the movement at Antioch starts looking like a gentile movement and not a Jewish movement.[5] This might account for the attitude of those who came from James worried about the loss of Jewish identity, even if Jewish Christians present at Antioch were not necessarily eating banned food such as pork. People like James may have agreed at first with a non-observant mission but once it starts looking like a gentile movement, and possibly discrediting Peter's mission to the Jews, then it is no surprise that Law-observant Jewish Christians were worried.

That argument is too general and requires further evidence to show that food was the issue. There are numerous pagan texts that talk of Jews not

---

[4] J. Klawans, *Impurity and Sin in Ancient Judaism* (Oxford: Oxford University Press, 2000), 43–60, 134–5; C. E. Hayes, *Gentile Impurities and Jewish Identities: Intermarriage and Conversion from the Bible to the Talmud* (Oxford: Oxford University Press, 2002), 107–44, 199–221.

[5] Cf. E. P. Sanders, *Jewish Law from Jesus to the Mishnah: Five Studies* (London: SCM Press, 1990), 383–8.

associating with Gentiles because they were, apparently, unsociable and looked down on others. But we should not take the views of these texts too seriously because they did not give the details of *why* there was a lack of association. That said, occasionally they do give clues away. So, for example, in a view recorded in *Life of Apollonius* 5.33, Jews do not join in with pagan 'libations or prayers or sacrifices'. This is hardly surprising and is reflected in Jewish sources where the reasons for association or non-association with Gentiles are consistently given.

Throughout Jewish literature from roughly around the time of Christian origins two issues recur as a problem when eating with Gentiles: food and idolatry. In retellings of the story of Esther, for example, Esther avoided the wine of libation at the royal table (Rest of Esther C 14.17). In the story of Judith, Judith ate different food from the Gentiles when dining (Judith 12.17–19). By this logic, if there was no idolatry and no banned foods present at the table, then there would have been no problem with Jews and Gentiles eating together. In fact, this is precisely the case in one Jewish text which talks of a gentile Egyptian king preparing a banquet with Jews:

> 'Everything of which you partake,' he [the Egyptian king] said, 'will be served in compliance with your habits; it will be served to me as well as to you.' They expressed their pleasure and the king ordered the finest apartments to be given to them near the citadel, and the preparations for the banquet were made. (*Ep. Arist.* 181)

The above text shows that table fellowship was possible if the circumstances were right. In terms of the Antioch controversy we can probably eliminate idolatry as a problem for the Christians: it is difficult to see them worshipping a pagan god! The issue must have been food, at least in the light of Jewish discussions of table fellowship with Gentiles. It is for these reasons that I would argue the following: if Christians at Antioch were notably eating banned (non-kosher) food then it would be no surprise that certain Jewish Christians felt that Jewish identity focused on the Law was seriously under threat. Peter was certainly remembered as being accepting of non-observance of biblical food laws (Acts 10.1—11.18), and so something like this could underlie the fierce allegations that Paul levelled at him.

The Law in Paul's theology

This debate over the relevancy of the Law for Christians now leads us neatly into the heart of a major debate in Pauline studies. Since the 1970s there have been some of the most intensive debates over whether or not

Judaism was a religion of salvation through good works or whether there was a concept of grace, with the results being determinative for how we view Paul's theology. A traditional view in Pauline scholarship, influenced by strands of Protestant thought, was, put crudely, that Judaism was a religion where salvation was gained through merit, especially through strict observance of the Law. Paul then came along, so the argument went and sometimes still goes, and argued that salvation comes through God's grace and not through merit and strict observance of the Law.

This view was challenged in the late 1970s by E. P. Sanders, who argued that Judaism was a religion that had a strong concept of grace.[6] Israel's covenant with God was not owing to Israel's good deeds but to God's graceful election of Israel ('getting in'). Jews would then continue this relationship with God by obeying the commandments ('staying in'). People were not infallible, however, so God also provided means of atoning for sin and was merciful towards his people, so, ultimately, Judaism has a strong concept of grace. This system was labelled 'covenantal nomism'. Since Sanders, there have been numerous attempts to reconcile this understanding of Judaism with Pauline theology (usually called 'the New Perspective'), and plenty of reactions against Sanders' view of Judaism.

My own view is that Sanders offered a massively important critique of scholarly caricatures of early Judaism, arguably *the* most important critique in the history of modern scholarship. But attempts to view Judaism in such systematic terms are problematic, even if he got the broad details right. It seems to me that, from all sides of the debate, categories from Christian systematic theology have been imposed on texts that are neither Christian nor systematic in their treatment of the relevant topics. Furthermore, there are texts where works/Law observance are stressed very heavily with reference to the salvation of the person and where grace does not seem to play a part.[7]

But whatever view we take on Sanders, the issue of observance of the commandments in relation to salvation and God's grace becomes sharply focused in the context of earliest Christianity when Paul is faced with significant numbers of Gentiles in the movement who are no longer observing the Law. What is to be done with them? And what is to be done with Jews prepared not to observe the Law? For Paul, these people were here to stay but were here without observing major commandments and

---

[6] E. P. Sanders, *Paul and Palestinian Judaism: A Comparison of Patterns of Religion* (Philadelphia: Fortress; London: SCM Press, 1977).

[7] Cf. S. J. Gathercole, *Where Is Boasting? Early Jewish Soteriology and Paul's Response in Romans 1—5* (Grand Rapids: Eerdmans, 2002).

in many cases without being circumcised. The Jewish tradition stressing the importance of works and the Law was of very limited use. In contrast, the Jewish tradition of grace would clearly have been a very useful way of justifying all those who were non-observant. In this context, Paul emerged as a serious thinker in Western history and for the development of Christianity as a religion in its own right. And it is the theological justifications of the events on the ground that need some further discussion.

Paul did not think that observance of Sabbath and festivals was necessary for members of the Christian community (Rom. 14.3–6; Gal. 4.10; cf. Col. 2.16). We have seen in the discussion of the incident at Antioch (Gal. 2.11–14) that he did not think that food laws should be *imposed* on the believer either. When writing Galatians, Paul was faced with the problem of people wanting to impose circumcision on believers and he stressed in no uncertain terms what he thought of such a thing: 'I wish those who unsettle you would castrate themselves!' (Gal. 5.12).

It is worth stressing the significance of *imposing* the Law in this context. In Romans 14.1–8, it is clear that there are people linked to the Christian community intent on keeping practices relating to food and holy days. So Paul says that if such things are done, then they ought to be done in praise of the Lord. For Paul such people are weaker members of the community, in contrast to the stronger who do not need to practise such things. It could be argued that a passage such as Romans 14.1–8 is in contradiction with the more ferocious attitude toward the Law in Galatians, but social context helps explain this apparent contradiction. In Galatians, Paul was dealing with a problem of people imposing the Law (notably circumcision) whereas in Romans this was not a pressing issue. The crux of the matter is whether the Law is *imposed* on the believer. If not, then it was not a major problem for Paul; if so, then it was. Seen in this light, is a passage like Romans 14.1–8 all that different in meaning from the following in ferocious Galatians?

> For neither circumcision nor uncircumcision is anything; but a new creation is everything! (Gal. 6.15)

We have now seen some specific examples of biblical Law that Paul no longer required. But once key aspects of the Law went, then one logical path would be for the Law as a whole to start becoming ineffective for the believer. This is also implied when Paul says, 'Once again I testify to every man who lets himself be circumcised that he is obliged to obey the entire law' (Gal. 5.3). This does not mean that entire Law observance is possible from a Pauline perspective. In Galatians, Paul makes it clear that a real problem with the Law is that it is, well, just far too good for mere humans to be able to keep (cf. Gal. 3.21–25)! And so the Law is impossible to keep effectively and consequently Law observance will lead to sin. Those who now claim an ability to keep the Law are more or less deluded (Gal. 6.13). In the early chapters of Romans this pessimistic view of humanity is elaborated further with a string of scriptural 'proofs', and note the broad scope of humanity as a whole:[8]

> What then? Are we any better off? No, not at all; for we have already charged that all, both Jews and Greeks, are under the power of sin, as it is written: 'There is no one who is righteous, not even one; there is no one who has understanding, there is no one who seeks God.' (Rom. 3.9–11)

This lack of ability to observe the Law is grounded in a pre-existing social problem: Gentiles not observing the Law. But Paul now extends this to everyone – Jew and Gentile – and this may well reflect a possible fact on the ground: that some Jews associated with the Christian movement were not observing the Law. And if Paul can make the argument that it is impossible for the Law to save the individual, then something else is required: faith and Christ (e.g. Rom. 3—4; Gal. 3.24; 5.6). With this intellectual shift, Paul makes a significant major decision that would establish Christian distinctiveness over against Judaism, and the world at large, thereby making major strides toward Christianity becoming a religion in its own right.

Of course, Paul was no fan of what he deemed bad behaviour (cf. 1 Cor. 6), so he had to find a way of preventing people from taking the idea that no one could really observe the Law to the logical conclusion: that each person can behave as they see fit! As Paul says, 'What then? Should we sin because we are not under law but under grace? By no means!' (Rom. 6.15). More specifically, to solve the problem, Paul invokes the Spirit to guide people because the Spirit will make sure the individual behaves:

> But you are not in the flesh; you are in the Spirit, since the Spirit of God dwells in you. Anyone who does not have the Spirit of Christ does not belong to him. But if Christ is in you, though the body is dead because of sin, the Spirit is life because of righteousness. If the Spirit of him who raised Jesus from the dead dwells in you, he who raised Christ from the dead will give life to your mortal bodies also through his Spirit that dwells in you.
> (Rom. 8.9–11; cf. Gal. 5.13–26)

In Romans 6, Paul grounds the new life of the believer, no longer a slave to sin, in baptism and the death and resurrection of Jesus. Paul is unsur-

---

[8] Cf. R. H. Bell, *No-one Seeks for God: An Exegetical and Theological Study of Romans 1.18— 3.20* (Tübingen: Mohr Siebeck, 1998).

prisingly keen to stress negatives, what believers should *not* do in their new lives. They should *not* be involved in fornication, idolatry, anger, drunkenness and so on and those who do these 'works of the flesh' will not inherit the kingdom (Gal. 5.19–21). But Paul also stresses positives, namely, that believers can now show the 'fruit of the spirit', such as love, joy, peace, faithfulness, goodness and so on (Gal. 5.22–23). The Law too can now be summarized in a single commandment, 'You shall love your neighbour as yourself' (Gal. 5.14). In early Judaism and in the teaching of Jesus this commandment could be used in summaries of the Law (cf. Matt. 7.12; Mark 12.28–34) with the understanding that the whole Law still had to be observed. Paul clearly takes this one step further by dropping more widespread observance.

Paul and the figure of Christ

As I repeatedly stress, another key feature that would be used by insiders and outsiders to distinguish Christianity from its Jewish roots was its take on the divine and the incorporation of Jesus into the figure of God. Paul also had an important role to play in this development. It is clear that he had an extremely elevated view of Jesus and that, contrary to what Bird believes (see pages 94–6), it was far more developed than the ways Jesus perceived himself and the ways Jesus' original audiences perceived him. Paul's vision of the raised Jesus virtually assumes that Jesus has now to be a significantly elevated figure, a figure who is not like an average human being, a figure perhaps more comparable to those deemed supernatural (e.g. angels). According to Acts 9.3, Paul saw Jesus accompanied by a dazzling light, while in Galatians 1.16 Paul talks of God revealing 'his Son to me'.

But we can be more precise about Paul's view of Jesus. 'Christ', for instance, is a common and important term given to Jesus in Paul's letters where it seems to become part of Jesus' name. We saw in the chapter on the historical Jesus that 'Christ' is the Greek term for 'Messiah' or 'anointed' and that the earliest Christians developed this term to have Jesus as *the* Messiah or *the* person anointed by God at the expense of any other Jewish contenders (see pages 1–17). Paul's view of the significance of the death of Jesus goes beyond what the historical Jesus may have thought about the significance of his own impending death. Paul explicitly sets Jesus' death at the heart of human history, with the dominance of sin being introduced with Adam's sin and with Jesus' death ending this dominance (Rom. 5.12–21). More specifically, Christ 'died for *our* sins' (1 Cor. 15.3; cf. Rom. 3.21–26; 5.10), which in the context of Paul's letters and their recipients must include at least the Jewish and gentile members of earliest Christianity, and may even have a broader application for humanity as a whole. This is significantly wider than the recipients of atonement in Jesus' teaching. But while Christ/Messiah and Christ's atoning function are undoubtedly dramatic uses of language, they are not as dramatic as some of the other language applied to Jesus in Paul's letters.

'Lord' is a common and important (1 Cor. 12.3) title given to Jesus in Paul's letters. The phrase 'Lord' has a variety of meanings in the ancient world, ranging from a polite form of address (like the English 'sir') right up to a title for God. Paul appears to use the title in an extremely strong sense in Philippians 2.9–11, where the title for God can be used of Jesus. Jesus as 'Son' or 'Son of God' is another title used by Paul and found in the synoptic tradition. Although it might not be the most common title found in Paul it does reflect some significant Christological developments. Paul would certainly have known of the range of meanings the phrase Son/son of God had in early Judaism, and the view recorded in Romans 1.3–4 shows signs that it was already being used in a more elevated sense than we saw in the life of the historical Jesus. With Paul, Son/son of God becomes a term that shows the distinctiveness and uniqueness of Jesus in the role of salvation (Rom. 5.10; 8.3; Gal. 4.4–5).

What is significant about this Pauline material is that for all the dramatic developments of the figure of Jesus, it does not quite make Jesus fully equated with God, or worshipped in a sense that fully equates Jesus with God.[9] Paul's use of Son/son of God may make Jesus a figure of stunningly high importance in the cosmic hierarchy (the sole way to God) but when it comes to the Son's relationship to the Father, as it were, Paul only mentions *distinction* from the Father (e.g. Rom. 5.10, '... we were reconciled to God through the death of his Son'). In contrast with what we will see when we look at John 5 in the chapter on the Gospels, there is nothing in Paul's letters to indicate that there were conflicts over Jesus as 'the Son'.

Paul's use of the word 'Lord' and the implication of the pre-existence of Jesus in Philippians 2.6–11 are the major pieces of evidence for Paul equating Jesus with God in the strongest sense. This passage has several key points relating to the elevated status of Jesus which need some brief comments. The phrase, 'who, though he was in the form of God, did not regard equality with God as something to be exploited' (Phil. 2.6), does not necessarily mean that Jesus was God in the strongest sense. This

---

[9] M. Casey, *From Jewish Prophet to Gentile God: The Origins and Development of New Testament Christology* (Louisville: Westminster John Knox, Cambridge: James Clarke, 1991), 110–40.

passage is often read in the context of the figure of Adam and we should recall that Adam was also *like* God but clearly not God:

> . . . for God knows that when you eat of it your eyes will be opened, and you will be like God, knowing good and evil.   (Gen. 3.5)

> Then the LORD God said, 'See, the man has become like one of us, knowing good and evil; and now, he might reach out his hand and take also from the tree of life, and eat, and live for ever'.   (Gen. 3.22)

Stronger still is this: 'Therefore God also highly exalted him and gave him the name that is above every name, so that at the name of Jesus every knee should bend, in heaven and on earth and under the earth' (Phil. 2.9–10). This is certainly dramatic but not unparalleled in early Judaism. We have already seen that calling Jesus 'Lord' does not necessarily have to imply he is God. Compare now these early Jewish passages where other figures are given some exceptionally elevated names yet in each case the author(s) hold the idea that God is above all:

> I am going to send an angel in front of you, to guard you on the way and to bring you to the place that I have prepared. Be attentive to him and listen to his voice; do not rebel against him, for he will not pardon your transgression; for my name is in him.   (Exod. 23.20–21)

> For nothing mortal can be made in the likeness of the Most High One and Father of the universe but only that of the second God, who is his Logos/Word.   (Philo, *QG* 2.62)

> And even if there be not as yet any one who is worthy to be called a son of God, nevertheless let him labour earnestly to be adorned according to his first-born word, the eldest of his angels, as the great archangel of many names; for he is called, the authority, and the name of God, and the Word, and man according to God's image, and he who sees Israel.
>   (Philo, *Confusion* 146)

> I am Iloil (or Jaol, or Aol), so named by him who shakes what is with me on the seventh expanse above the vault of heaven, a power by the ineffable name that dwells in me.   (*Apoc. Ab.* 10.9)

> The holy One, blessed be he . . . fashioned me a kingly crown . . . He set it upon my head and he called me, 'The lesser YHWH' in the presence of his whole household in the height, as it is written, 'My name is in him' [Exod. 23.21].   (*3 En* 12.2–5)

In addition to these important parallels, we should also recall that in Philippians 2.11, God the Father remains *distinct* ('every tongue should confess that Jesus Christ is Lord, to the glory of God the Father') and the passage, while getting closer to the views we will see in John's Gospel, still does not quite say Jesus was made God.[10]

As is commonly noted by scholars, Paul believed that Christ was, in some way, a pre-existent figure in Philippians 2.6–11 and elsewhere believed Christ was involved in creation (1 Cor. 8.6; cf. Col. 1.15–23). While pre-existence may imply a highly elevated status it does not necessarily mean Jesus was made God. Various other figures in early Judaism could be classed as pre-existent. In later Judaism, the Messiah was regarded as pre-existent (e.g. *Gen. Rab.* 2.4; cf. 4Q521), while, in Judaism roughly contemporary with Paul, Enoch was regarded as pre-existent (e.g. *1 Enoch* 48.3, 6; 62.7). An important comparison with the elevated figure of Jesus was Wisdom because developments in the figure of Wisdom were used by Christians and applied to Jesus. Wisdom was also said to be involved in the creation of the world (e.g. Prov. 8.22–31; Jer. 10.12; Ecclus. 24) but Wisdom remains not quite God, no matter how close to God writers made her: 'she is a breath of the power of God, and a pure emanation of the glory of the Almighty . . . she is a reflection of eternal light, a spotless mirror of the working of God, and an image of his goodness' (Wisd. 7.25–26).

It is therefore clear that Paul views Jesus in an extremely elevated way, more elevated than any other figure. But the evidence does not quite let us go the full way and say that Jesus was worshipped in a way that made him equal with God. In the abstract, the evidence *could* be read this way but there is a more general argument that would suggest that it should not be, namely, that it is clear Paul does not come into conflict with Jews over making God a human, something that would have been blasphemous for many, as we will see when we look at John's Gospel (John 5). In sharp contrast to John's Gospel, we saw that Paul was involved in some extremely harsh debates with people over the role of the Law. If he had made Jesus God surely there would also be evidence of Christological conflicts in his writings. That such conflict is not found indicates that Paul does not quite go beyond anything already done in early Judaism.

The problem is, of course, that we cannot directly ask Paul what he thought about the full deification of Jesus. If really pushed he *may* have said that Jesus was fully equal with God. But the full equation of Jesus with God was not something that became a point of friction with Jews as

---

[10] We might also mention the strongest possible translation of the difficult Romans 9.5 in this context: 'Messiah/Christ, who is God over all, blessed for ever'. Even if this is the correct translation, its use of the term 'God' echoes other Jewish uses of the term 'God' to refer to figures such as Moses and angels. As Paul lacks the serious conflicts and explanations surrounding Jesus-as-God in John's Gospel, we should not read this into Pauline theology.

such a shocking development almost certainly would have done. But it leaves the development of Jesus teetering on the edge and only requires a new context to make the shift quite explicit. And we shall see this as we turn to the Gospels in the next chapter.

Michael F. Bird

Paul was probably executed by Nero in Rome sometime during the mid-60s of the first century. This was indicative of the hostility between Christians and the Roman Empire, a hostility that was to last another 250 years. But when Roman soldiers started putting the insignia of the cross on their shields during the time of Constantine it signalled the triumph of Paul's God and Paul's Messiah over the might of Rome's armies and the madness of Rome's emperors. Christ and Caesar met in the arena of history, and Christ won hands down. And yet who would have ever thought at the time that the old eccentric Jew who heralded the Lordship of a victim of Roman violence, and was himself put to death by a megalomaniac emperor, would play such a crucial part in the victory of Christianity over pagan Rome. But that is precisely the legacy of Paul. It is entirely fitting then that we have a whole chapter dedicated to Paul and examine several of the controversial contours of his life, ministry and thought.

The road to Damascus

Sometime around 31–4 CE, Paul experienced his Damascus road Christophany (i.e. the appearance of the risen Christ), which turned his world upside down and left him for ever changed. The zealous *persecutor* of the Church became one of its most ardent *proclaimers*. In order to understand the great reversal in Paul's thinking, values and allegiances we must contrast who Paul was prior to the Damascus road Christophany with who he was afterwards.

There are several scant references to Paul's pre-Christian past in his letters. In Galatians, Paul states: 'You have heard, no doubt, of my earlier life in Judaism. I was violently persecuting the church of God and was trying to destroy it. I advanced in Judaism beyond many among my people of the same age, for I was far more zealous for the traditions of my ancestors' (Gal. 1.13–14). In Philippians, Paul says that he was: 'a Hebrew born of Hebrews; as to the Law, a Pharisee; as to zeal, a persecutor of the church; as to righteousness under the Law, blameless' (Phil. 3.5–6). Elsewhere, Paul regards himself as the least of the Apostles because he formerly persecuted the Church (1 Cor. 15.9). From this we can make several observations.

First, Paul (or Saul as he was named then) was a good Jew who sought to live his life according to the will of God set out in the Law or Torah and he followed the Pharisaic pattern for living that life as directed by the traditions of the elders. Saul was not a Jew with a guilt-strained conscience waiting for a God-Man to take his burden of guilt away; on the contrary, Saul considered himself 'blameless' under the Law.

Second, Saul was zealous for Torah, which means far more than possessing an unbridled enthusiasm. To be zealous meant a willingness to use violence against other Jews who threatened the sanctity of Israel's separation from Gentiles. For instance, during Israel's wilderness wanderings the priest Phinehas manifested a great 'zeal' and killed an Israelite man who intermarried with a foreign Midianite woman (Num. 25.11). During the forced Hellenization of Judea during the Greek period (167–64 BCE), Jews were being forced to give up their national customs and made to adopt the Greek way of life. When a certain Jew went to offer a sacrifice to a pagan God, an old priest named Mattathias burned with zeal and killed the Jew (1 Macc. 2.24–26, 50, 58). This was not an isolated instance as Philo reports of 'thousands of vigilantes, full of zeal for the laws, strictest guardians of the ancestral traditions, merciless to those who try to abolish them' (Philo, *Spec. Laws* 2.253). Thus, Paul's 'zeal' was aimed against Christians who were, in his mind, threatening the sanctity of the boundaries separating Jews from Gentiles and endangering the ethnic integrity of the Jewish people. The catalyst for Saul's persecution was probably the Greek-speaking Jewish Christians who had begun proclaiming Jesus to Gentiles and were welcoming them into the people of God without having to come via the route of proselytism or conversion to Judaism (Acts 11.19–21). To insinuate that Gentiles can stand before God as if they were Jews was to lower the currency of Israel's election; it devalued the covenant marker of circumcision and would lead to Jews excessively fraternizing with Gentiles. What is more, this was all in the name of a crucified pseudo-messiah whom some Jews were incorporating into patterns of devotion normally reserved for Yahweh.

Third, Paul never repudiated Judaism nor did he anathematize the Jewish people for being Jews, but he did renounce his former way of being Jewish; he rejected both his inherited privileges as a Jew and the way that he expressed that Jewish heritage as a militant Pharisee: neither were a path to true righteousness. In fact, Paul says in Philippians 3.8 that compared to Christ he considers his former way of life as *skubala*, or what I would translate as 'human filth'.

Nowhere in his letters does Paul relate the exact circumstances of his encounter with Christ, but he does drop some hints along the way. In

Galatians 1.15–16 he writes: 'But when God, who had set me apart before I was born and called me through his grace, was pleased to reveal his Son *in me*'. In 1 Corinthians 9.1, he reports that he has 'seen Jesus our Lord'. Then in 1 Corinthians 15.8–9, Paul catalogues the list of witnesses to the resurrection and includes himself: 'Last of all, as to someone untimely born, he appeared also to me. For I am the least of the apostles, unfit to be called an apostle, because I persecuted the church of God.' That phrase 'someone untimely born' is the same word used for an abortion or miscarriage (*ektrōma*). Paul arguably likens his conversion to an infant being ripped out of the womb and being brought into the light. More vivid and detailed accounts of Paul's conversion are found in the Acts of the Apostles where Luke presents Paul's conversion-story no fewer than three times (9.1–21; 22.1–21; 26.2–23). The repetition shows how important this episode of Paul's life was to Luke in his early Christian historiography. There are also variations in all three retellings in Acts and critics have had a field day with the differences. What did Jesus actually say? When did Paul get his commission to go to the Gentiles? Do the differences imply different sources and if so which one is more authentic? Although we have the same basic story in the three Lucan accounts, different elements are emphasized. Acts 9 highlights Paul's persecution of the Church, Acts 22 portrays Paul as a learned and devout Jew, and Acts 26 emphasizes Paul's obedience to his missionary call. All three accounts are compatible but they do not say the same thing. That is because Luke wants to show the role of Paul in the spread of Christianity from Bethlehem to Rome.

Others have speculated that Paul had an epileptic seizure or that his conscience was so ravaged with guilt by his violent persecutions that it led him into some kind of ecstatic state that caused him to have a vision of Jesus. But these explanations about what 'really' happened to Paul are fanciful and imaginative. All we can say is that something happened to Paul on the Damascus road and Paul himself described it as the moment when God revealed his Son in him. Paul and Luke both recount that, sometime during his career as a zealous Pharisee, Paul was seized by a spiritual power that gripped him and turned the persecutor into a proclaimer of the faith that he once tried to destroy. The only evidence we have about what happened is from Paul and Luke. We either believe Paul or we don't. Either we accept his interpretation of what happened or else we shrug our shoulders and confess that what happened to Paul is simply a mystery of a religious phenomenon that is beyond our grasp. Given that Paul seems intelligent and honest, at least that's how he appears to me in his letters, I see no reason not to believe him. We cannot demonstrate that it happened just like Paul states or how Luke narrates, but neither can we disprove it.

Was Paul converted then? Paul's 180-degree turnaround means that he was indeed converted in some sense, but it was not a conversion from one religion to another. Paul was converted from the Pharisaic sect to a messianic sect *within Judaism*. We can add that Paul was not only converted but was also called to a specific mission, namely, to be the apostle to the Gentiles. Paul and Luke imply that Paul's commission to go to the Gentiles was given during his Christophany (Acts 26.17–18; Gal. 1.16). We should also consider Acts 22.15, 21 which suggest that the mission to the Gentiles was based on a revelation that Paul received sometime afterwards in Jerusalem and that it was an aspect of his calling that only became apparent to him later. I am more inclined to think that the revelation to go to the Gentiles was part of the Damascus road experience since Paul's first period of ministry was in Damascus and Arabia/Nabatea (Acts 9.19b–25; 2 Cor. 11.32; Gal. 1.17), which was a region that comprised non-Jews. This call is formulated in language indicative of the Old Testament prophets (e.g. Isa. 42.1–7; 49.1–7; Jer. 1.4–5) since it parallels the arresting nature of the prophetic call and the summons to service to be a light to the Gentiles (Acts 13.47/Isa. 49.6; Rom. 15.21/Isa. 52.15).

Did Paul receive his gospel at his Christophany? That is what he claims in Galatians 1.11–12: that his gospel is not of human origin but was a direct revelation from Jesus Christ. It is important to realize that this observation can be pushed too far, and we should not suppose that, after regaining his sight in Damascus, Paul suddenly had an entire theological package worked out in every detail as if God had magically downloaded it to his brain. There is no doubt in my mind that Paul's theology developed or matured over time as he had to think, work and pray through the issues that emerged in the course of his ministry. Paul's view of the Law as it relates to fellowship between gentile Christians and Jewish Christians is a good example of how he was able to apply his thinking to different situations between his writing of Galatians (49 CE) and Romans (55 CE). It must be borne in mind though that, after his Damascus road experience, Paul would have been completely disorientated, personally, spiritually and theologically. In the following days, weeks and months he had to figure out what had happened and what it meant. We cannot underestimate the theological shockwaves that now echoed throughout Paul's mind. In terms of *Christology* (the study of the person and work of Christ) Paul had to come to grips with the realization that Jesus was not a false prophet and a messianic pretender but, on the contrary, was the risen and exalted Son of God (e.g. Rom. 1.4; 2 Cor. 1.19; Gal. 2.20). It impacted on his view of *soteriology* (the study of salvation) because Jesus was hung on a cross and Deuteronomy says that anyone hung on a tree is under God's curse (Deut.

21.23). But if Jesus was cursed then he must have been cursed by God the Father who must have cursed him for a reason. The reason was that 'Christ redeemed us from the curse of the law by becoming a curse for us' (Gal. 3.13). Regarding *eschatology* (the study of the last things), Paul formerly believed as a Pharisee that God would resurrect all men and women at the end of history and vindicate those who remained faithful to the covenant. Instead, God had raised up one man in the middle of history and vindicated him. That is why Christ is the one through whom 'the ends of ages have come' (1 Cor. 10.11) as his resurrection and the bequeathing of the Spirit marks the partial arrival of the future age and highlights things soon to come. On the topic of *ecclesiology* (the study of the Church), Paul had persecuted Christians and yet the risen Lord could ask Saul, 'why do you persecute me?' The implication is that by persecuting Christians Paul was persecuting Christ. That suggested that Christians are in some sense the 'body of Christ' (e.g. Rom. 12.5; 1 Cor. 10.16; 12.12–13, 27; Eph. 5.23). Thus, the Damascus road experience gave Paul a new theological framework and the rest of his ministry was concerned with how to fill that frame with bricks and mortar.

Law and righteousness

All five accounts of Paul's conversion occur in contexts where the relationship between Judaism and Christianity is an issue.[11] More specifically, the problem revolved around the application of the Law or Torah to Paul's gentile converts. The question was: do Gentiles have to become Jews in order to become Christians? For Paul the answer was an emphatic 'No!' since Gentiles are saved *as Gentiles* and they do not have to become proselytes to Judaism. Faith in Christ is sufficient to incorporate Gentiles into the messianic community and to incorporate them into Christ who is the locus of salvation. That is why Paul can say on several occasions that no one shall be justified by 'works of the law' (Rom. 3.20, 27, 28; Gal. 2.16; 3.2, 5, 10). What does that mean?

To begin with 'works of the law' simply means the works that the Law requires and it refers to the entire legislation of the Mosaic code, all 613 commandments. The Law was not given as a stepladder to salvation as if the Israelites had to earn their salvation. The Law was given after God's miraculous deliverance of the Israelites out of Egypt. In other words, the Law was given to *redeemed* people not to *redeem* the people. The Law was

---

[11] J. M. Everts, 'Conversion and Call of Paul,' in *Dictionary of Paul and His Letters*, Gerald F. Hawthorne, Ralph P. Martin and Daniel G. Reid (eds) (Downers Grove, IL: IVP, 1993), 156–63 (159).

Israel's covenant charter and it defined the promises and expectation of God's relationship with Israel, that he would be their God and they would be his people. The Law included provision for the atonement for sins and the very giving of the Law itself was an act of grace. Another function of the Law was to keep Israel separate from the nations so as to protract Israel's capacity to serve God and to enable her to enact her covenantal vocation to be a kingdom of priests.

During the Greek period many Jews felt the attraction of Greek culture and began to abandon their religion and laws in order to follow the Greek way of life. Eventually the Greek king Antiochus IV Epiphanes sought to force all the Jews of Judea to renounce their ancestral customs and monotheistic religion and to adopt the Greek lifestyle (*c.* 167–64 BCE). During this period obedience to the Law was a sign of fidelity to God and his covenant and it served to keep Jews separate from Gentiles. Certain laws such as circumcision, Sabbath keeping and adhering to the food laws were obvious emblems of resistance to the trend of apostasy. It also raised the question of what would happen to those Jews who, unlike others, remained faithful and steadfast in their obedience to the Law. The answer was that God would vindicate them, judge in their favour and resurrect them if they had been martyred for their faith. Thus we see that doing the works of the Law took on a twofold function: it was a boundary marker that delineated faithful Jews from apostate Jews and Jews from Gentiles. It also constituted the basis upon which God would vindicate believers in the age to come. In this framework, Jewish authors themselves differed on details such as the balance between the grace of election and the merit of works, and different groups could emphasize one over the other. The question of what would happen to the Gentiles was also handled differently, and answers included their salvation as Gentiles, their conversion to Judaism, their subjugation under a Jewish king or even their destruction by a coalition of angelic beings and Jewish warriors (contrast 1QM; *Pss. Sol.* 17; Tobit 13—14).

What then did Paul find wrong with the Law and what was the solution? First, no one fulfils the Law since the permeation of sin in the human condition and the existence of the 'Adamic self' prevents anyone from performing the Law sufficiently to attain salvation (Rom. 1.18—3.20). Second, the Mosaic covenant was an interim arrangement between the covenant with Abraham and the arrival of the new covenant with the advent of the Messiah (Gal. 3.15–25). The birth of Israel and the giving of the Law did not annul God's promises to Abraham. Third, the Law temporarily cocooned God's promises around Israel but those promises were also meant for the nations (Rom. 9—11; Gal. 3—4). Fourth, since the Law had been fulfilled the basis of upright living was no longer to be found in its precepts. Instead, the basis of ethics was the teaching of Christ, the example of Christ and life in the Spirit, and when Christians did such things they fulfilled the Law (Rom. 12—15; Gal. 5; Col. 3). Paul certainly could echo elements of the Decalogue and make it part of the moral life of the Christian, but it no longer comprised the definitive structure of his ethics. For Paul, then, the Law no longer defined the boundaries of God's people, it was not the means to vindication at the final assize, it did not make anyone a child of Abraham, and it was not the standard of righteous behaviour – these had been replaced by Christ. That is why Paul can say that Christ is the 'end of the law so that there may be righteousness for everyone who believes' (Rom. 10.4). The Law is not a bad thing that has been done away with, rather, it is a good thing that has been fulfilled by Christ.

On the subject of justification we might describe this as God's act of vindication or even his rectification of those who believe in Jesus. What is significant here for the eventual Christian split is that God justifies Jews and Gentiles without Law observance. In other words, obedience to the Law is not the basis upon which God will save his people and the Law no longer marks out who his people really are. For Paul these things have been replaced by faith in Jesus. Justification means that one has been put in a right relationship with God and is vindicated from a verdict of condemnation associated with personal sin and identification with the sin of Adam. Justification by faith is Paul's most concise theological explication of the gospel in categories that are drawn from the world of jurisprudence and the language of 'righteousness' in the Old Testament. Justification is *forensic* in that it refers to one's status before God and not one's state of moral righteousness. To be justified is the opposite of being condemned (Deut. 25.1; Rom. 8.1–3, 33–34; 2 Cor. 3.9). God does not justify the righteous because all have sinned and none are truly righteous (Rom. 3.20–23). Instead, he justifies sinners and the ungodly through the provision of setting forth Christ (Rom. 3.21–25; 4.5; 5.6). Justification is not a fictitious verdict rendered by God, but Jesus' death satisfies God's justice. In fact God himself is justified as Judge and Saviour in the event (Rom. 3.26). Justification is also *covenantal* and it answers the question: 'who are the people of God?' The answer is, those who believe in the Messiah (Rom. 3.27—4.25; Gal. 4.31; Eph. 2.11—3.6). Those whom God has justified are constituted as full and equal members of the new covenant community and they all belong at the one communion table (Gal. 2.11–21). That explains why Paul's references to justification occur predominantly in contexts that address the relationship between Christian Jews and Christian Gentiles and endeavour to argue that Gentiles do not have to convert to Judaism. Justification is *eschatological* as the verdict that was anticipated on judgment day has been declared in the present (Rom. 2.13–16; 8.31–34; Gal. 5.5). Indeed, the future verdicts are enacted in Jesus' death and resurrection where God prosecutes his contention against believers by handing over Jesus to atone for their sins, and he enacts their justification by raising his Son from the dead (Rom. 4.25). In his resurrection, Jesus is vindicated by God and since believers are united with Jesus through faith they participate in his vindication too. What was theirs (sin) becomes his, and what is his (righteousness) becomes theirs. Justification is *effective* in that God's transforming power to free believers from the power of sin is the logical outcome of his verdict of vindication (Rom. 6.7, 18). Thus, justification is the act whereby God creates a new people, with a new status, in a new covenant, as a foretaste of the new age. The revealing of God's righteousness in the gospel, his saving power so to speak, delivers believers from the nexus of law–sin–death and shows that God has not limited his kindness and compassion to one ethnic race. Martin Hengel relates justification by faith to Paul's biography in this way:

> For the most part Pauline theology rests on the radical reversal of former values and aims which came about through the encounter with the crucified and risen Jesus of Nazareth. The Jewish teacher becomes the missionary to the Gentiles; the 'zeal for the law' is replaced by the proclamation of the gospel without the law; justification of the righteous on the basis of their 'works of the law' is replaced by justification of the 'godless' through faith alone; the free will is replaced by the faith which is given by grace alone as the creation of the word; and hatred of the crucified and accursed pseudo-messiah is replaced by a theology of the cross which grounds the salvation of all men and women in the representative accursed death of the messiah on the cross.[12]

Let me contrast this with Crossley's approach to the Law and early Christianity. In my mind Crossley treats the Law like tables at a restaurant and it comes down to the issue of 'smoking' or 'non-smoking' or 'Law-observant' or 'non-Law-observant'. Things are a bit more complex than this since there was in early Christianity a constellation of views and practices about the Law, and such sharp bifurcations are all too simplistic. For instance, some Christian Jews could affirm salvation in Christ and hold to the Law for social and familial reasons; other Christian Jews held to the Law because they associated it with holiness; again other Christian Jews

---

[12] Martin Hengel in collaboration with Roland Deines, *Pre-Christian Paul* (London: SCM Press, 1991), 86.

saw Christ as merely complementing rather than completing the Mosaic dispensation; or again there were others who held that Law obedience was necessary for salvation and membership in God's people.[13]

What is more, some Gentiles with varying levels of attachment to Judaism and Jewish practices may also have held similar views. One cannot assume that Christian Gentiles were non-Law-observant while Christians Jews were Law-observant. Paul himself is a Jew and yet he numbers himself among the 'strong' in Romans 14. In Romans, 1 Corinthians, Galatians and Colossians we find traces of Gentiles who adhere or feel the need to adhere to Jewish customs, which is plausible if some of them had a former history as God-fearers, proselytes or sympathizers to Judaism. I would also point out that one piece of continuity between Jesus and his brother James the Just is that both were accused of being Law-breakers by the Judean leadership (cf. Mark 2.24; 3.4; Luke 13.14; 14.1–6; and Josephus, *Ant.* 20.200).[14]

While the Hellenists were not a branch of liberal Jews who had dispensed with the Law, the circle associated with Stephen had begun to emphasize those aspects of Jesus' teachings that questioned the purported monopoly that the Temple had in containing the divine presence and the role of the Law in marking out covenant identity in light of the dawning new age. In Acts 6.13–14, what is false is not the accusation of the witnesses against Stephen but the character of the witnesses themselves. The same phenomenon occurs in relation to the charge made against Jesus by the false witnesses in Mark 14.58, that he spoke of the destruction and rebuilding of the Temple.

Another problem I have is that Crossley never explains why Paul persecuted the Church. If the early Church was Law-obedient until the 40s and if its members were not worshipping Jesus in any unprecedented way, then why on earth was Paul (or Saul) willing to travel as far as Damascus to throw them in jail? Crossley might say that he was persecuting them for failing to obey the Pharisaic *halakhah* or legal teachings. But would the Sadducean priestly class sanction a Pharisee to do that and, what is more, why would Paul restrict his persecution to Christians? Why not persecute Philo of Alexandria, the Teacher of Righteousness at Qumran,

---

[13] See Peter Stuhlmacher, 'The Law as a Topic of Biblical Theology', in *Reconciliation, Law, and Righteousness* (Philadelphia: Fortress, 1986), 110–33; Raymond Brown and John P. Meier, *Antioch and Rome* (New York/Ramsey: Paulist, 1983), 1–9.

[14] Cf. Michael F. Bird, 'Jesus the Law-Breaker,' in *Who Do My Opponents Say That I Am? Investigating the Accusations against Jesus*, eds Joseph B. Modica and Scot McKnight (LHJS; T&T Clark/Continuum, 2008), 3–26.

persons like Banus the Ascetic whom Josephus mentions, or Jewish peasants who were generally lax in their adherence to the Law? While Crossley succeeds in making Paul and the early Church thoroughly Jewish, their abrasive relationship with certain Jewish parties and factions is not sufficiently explained.

The revelation that Paul received was not that the Law was a bad thing that should no longer be obeyed by anyone, but that there was an instantaneous awareness that Christ eclipsed the Law as the locus of God's salvation, wisdom, righteousness and glory (see 1 Cor. 1.30; 2 Cor. 4.4; Phil. 3.6–9). And I concur with Crossley that the bee in Paul's bonnet was primarily his objection to those who wanted to impose Law-observance on Gentiles. In places such as Galatians 2.11–14 (which I date before the Jerusalem council of Acts 15) we have Paul protecting the integrity of Gentiles *as Gentiles* against those who would force them to take on the visible emblems of Jewish identity. Crossley thinks that the problem was Gentiles eating banned food and too much fraternizing with Gentiles by Christian Jews. I am not convinced by this. All this problem would need is a change of menu, and not necessarily a segregation of groups. What is more, in the Graeco-Roman world Jews could freely associate with Gentiles in the social, political and economic sphere so long as they did not transgress precepts relating to the Mosaic Law. Keep in mind that Paul cites this episode in his efforts to prevent the Galatians from being circumcised (e.g. Gal. 5.2–3; 6.12–13) and the preceding context of Titus not being circumcised confirms that point as well (Gal. 2.3). In Antioch, Paul's opponents were not called the 'food faction' but the 'circumcision faction'. What would be so bad about asking Gentiles to observe Jewish food laws if they were the guests and in the minority? Paul seems willing to grant as much in Romans: 'it is good not to eat meat or drink wine or do anything that makes your brother stumble' (Rom. 14.21). The real problem for the 'certain men from James' was that the meals at Antioch made Gentiles equal with Jews without requiring Gentiles to be circumcised.[15]

Did Paul think that Jesus was God?

On the person of Christ, Crossley allows for the notion that Paul saw Jesus in elevated categories and even regarded him as pre-existent and active in creation (see page 81). But Crossley does not think that Paul put Jesus on a par with God in any strong sense. To be frank, all that Crossley has proved is that Paul was not a modalist. Modalism is the view that Jesus is

[15] Cf. Michael F. Bird, *The Saving Righteousness of God: Studies on Paul, Justification and the New Perspective* (Carlisle: Paternoster, 2007), 124–34.

merely a personified expression of the Father, and it was denounced as a heresy by later Christian theologians.

There are several places where Paul intimates that Jesus participates in the identity of God or, put more simply, to talk of God requires Paul to talk also of Jesus but without actually compromising monotheism.[16] Let me give a couple of examples. In 1 Corinthians Paul makes reference to the *Shema* of Deuteronomy 6.4 which was the basic confession of Israel's monotheistic faith. Interestingly enough, in 1 Corinthians 8.6 Paul echoes the *Shema* in his teaching about different 'Lords' in the marketplace of Corinth and applies it in relation to Jesus Christ.

Deuteronomy 6.4 Hear O Israel
              The Lord our **God**,
              the **Lord** is **one**.

1 Corinthians 8.6 Yet for us there is
              one God, the Father, from whom are all things and
                for whom we live
              one Lord Jesus Christ, through whom are all
                things and through whom we live. (Author's
                translation)

Paul does not say that 'Jesus is the Father', but he locates the identity of Jesus within the matrix of the *Shema* so that the titles 'Lord' and 'God' can equally describe Jesus as much as they describe the Father.

Towards the end of 1 Corinthians, Paul closes the epistle with a short exhortation: 'Let anyone be accursed who has no love for the Lord. *Our Lord, come!*' (1 Cor. 16.22). That final phrase 'Our Lord, come!' is transliterated from the Aramaic *marana tha* where *mara* stands for 'Lord' or 'Yahweh'. Paul rehearses a praise or prayer from the Aramaic-speaking Church that in effect regarded the future coming of Jesus as the eschatological coming of God and used a designation for Jesus that was ordinarily used of Israel's God.

I am unable to concur with Crossley's reading of Philippians 2.5–11, which he interprets in terms of an alleged 'Adam Christology' (see page 83). On the contrary, I see here a strong case for Jesus being placed in the orbit of the divine identity. Crossley acknowledges that pre-existence is implied here and he rightly points out that pre-existence does not on

---

[16] Cf. Larry Hurtado, *Lord Jesus Christ: Devotion to Jesus in Earliest Christianity* (Grand Rapids, MI: Eerdmans, 2003); and Richard Bauckham, *God Crucified: Monotheism and Christology in the New Testament* (Carlisle: Paternoster, 1998).

its own necessarily amount to deity, though we should admit that in this context it is at least suggestive of deity. That suggestion is legitimized by the phrases 'form of God' and 'equality with God', which relate Jesus to the being of God and the authority of God. The fact that Jesus 'emptied himself' shows that he did not regard his divine prerogatives as a means to self-aggrandizement but for the purpose of self-abasement. Equality with God did not excuse him from the task of redemptive suffering. On the contrary, it uniquely qualified him for it. Nowhere in extant ancient literature is Adam ever called 'equal with God' and the phrase appears elsewhere in a pejorative sense to describe the vain efforts of human beings to attain divine status for themselves (e.g. 2 Macc. 9.12; John 5.18; Philo, *Legat.* 1.49).[17] Philippians 2.5–11 is about a pre-existent one who is equal with God and voluntarily takes on human form and is finally acknowledged as 'Lord' at the end of his redemptive mission. Out of all the parallels that Crossley cites he never mentions Isaiah 45.23 and its relationship to Philippians 2.9–11. Note the similarities:

Philippians 2.9–11	Isaiah 45.23
Therefore, God exalted him and graciously gave him the name that is above every name in order that at the name of Jesus **every knee should bow** in heaven, on the earth, and under the earth and **every tongue confess** that Jesus Christ is Lord to the glory of God the Father.	By myself I have sworn; from my mouth has gone out in righteousness a word that shall not return: 'To me **every knee shall bow, every tongue shall swear allegiance.**'

This is a fairly obvious case of, once more, Paul taking language normally reserved for Israel's God and applying it to Jesus. What is more, if Philippians 2.5–11 is a pre-Pauline hymn then this Christological move was already being made by persons prior to Paul's conversion![18] That substantiates my claim that the highest Christology is among the earliest.

Conclusions

The primary legacy of Paul is that he addressed the key questions that enabled the Church to relate the coming of the Messiah to God's dealings with Israel and Abraham. He also maintained that Christ is not an add-on to the Mosaic covenant and the coming of Christ has inaugurated a whole new epoch of redemptive history. As such, Gentiles do not have to

---

[17] Hurtado, *Lord Jesus Christ*, 122–3.
[18] See further Michael F. Bird, *A Bird's-Eye View of Paul: The Man, his Mission, and his Message* (Nottingham: IVP, 2008), chapter 8.

become Jews in order to become Christians because God, through Christ, accepts Gentiles *as* Gentiles. Paul did not repudiate Israel's Law, but he strenuously rejected its imposition on Gentiles and so laid the groundwork for Christianity to be embraced by large numbers of Gentiles. Raymond Brown spells out the significance of Paul in this way:

> Next to Jesus Paul has been the most influential figure in the history of Christianity. Although all the NT writers are working out the implications of Jesus for particular communities of believers, Paul in his numerous letters does this on the widest scale of all. That range, plus the depth of this thought and the passion of his involvement, have meant that since his letters became part of the NT, no Christian has been unaffected by what he has written. Whether or not they know Paul's words well, through what they have been taught about doctrine and piety, all Christians have become Paul's children in the faith.[19]

Response from James G. Crossley

Strange as it may seem, I actually agree with a great deal of what Bird has to say about Paul, though I perhaps would be more reluctant to use the elaborate theological language. I see no significant difference on the general issue of Paul and the Law when it comes to those letters that are genuinely Pauline (i.e. those that are accepted by most scholars as having been written by Paul himself in the 40s and 50s as opposed to the deutero-Pauline letters, i.e. those written at a later date and considered by most scholars – although not by certain conservative evangelicals – to have been written by someone else using Paul's name). One reason for this, I suspect, is that when dealing with texts directly in front of us in their so-called 'final form', and without having to reconstruct earlier history (especially the miraculous), evangelical scholars, and Christian scholars in general, really come into their own. This is, presumably, because they are dealing with the core books of their sacred text and so it is no surprise to see their care and attention to detail at work, something particularly helpful for non-believers such as myself.

Law and conflict

It was a surprise, though, to find that I am misrepresented on an issue about which I actually agree with Bird. Bird claims that I treat the Law in earliest Christianity merely in terms of 'Law-observant' and 'non-Law-

---

[19] Raymond E. Brown, *An Introduction to the New Testament* (ABRL; New York: Doubleday, 1997), 422.

observant' before informing/lecturing me/you that 'Things are a bit more complex than this since there was in early Christianity a constellation of views and practices about the Law, and such sharp bifurcations are all too simplistic' (see page 92). He then gives examples: 'some Christian Jews could affirm salvation in Christ and hold to the Law for social and familial reasons; other Christian Jews held to the Law because they associated it with holiness; again other Christian Jews saw Christ as merely complementing rather than completing the Mosaic dispensation; or again there were others who held that Law obedience was necessary for salvation and membership in God's people . . . One cannot assume that Christian Gentiles were non-Law-observant while Christian Jews were Law-observant' (see page 93). Notice, however, that he cites no argument from me to back up his claims and implications about me. If he tried, he would find nothing. I have never claimed that the situation was like that which Bird rightly opposes. To be sure I have been accused of something similar before, but I must admit I do not understand where such an allegation has come from. All I can do here is re-stress my position: I simply argue a case for when non-observance became an issue in earliest Christianity (*c.* early 40s CE). I do not argue that everything suddenly changed and all became non-observant; I do not argue that there became two camps of observant and non-observant; and I do not argue that there was widespread uniformity over such issues. In fact I have even written a book attempting to explain the differences in Law observance in earliest Christianity and I have quite explicitly made detailed points (e.g. Jewish-Christian non-observance) which Bird rightly claims reflect the realities of the first century![20]

Aside from basic misrepresentations, there are some important differences, however, and they may have something to do with confessional/non-confessional issues. First, Bird wants to push the idea of non-observance emerging as early as possible. A 'problem' Bird has is 'that Crossley never explains why Paul persecuted the Church' (see page 93). Against Bird, however, I did speak of evidence that 'favours an internal Jewish dispute over the correct interpretation of the Law' (see page 73). But then Bird seems to recognize this and argues that 'Crossley might say that he was persecuting them for failing to obey the Pharisaic *halakhah* or legal teachings. But would the Sadducean priestly class sanction a Pharisee to do that and, what is more, why would Paul restrict his persecution to Christians? Why not persecute Philo of Alexandria, the Teacher of Righteousness at Qumran, persons like Banus the Ascetic whom Josephus

---

[20] Crossley, *Date of Mark's Gospel*, esp. chs 5—7; Crossley, *Why Christianity Happened*.

mentions, or Jewish peasants who were generally lax in their adherence to the Law?' (see page 94).

These are problems of Bird's own making. Why on earth would the 'pre-Christian Paul' persecute Philo of Alexandria? Bird does not let us know. On the issue of the Law, the 'pre-Christian Paul' and Philo may have in fact agreed. For instance, Philo talks about not picking fruit on the Sabbath (Philo, *Mos.* 2:22), a view that is echoed in Jesus' Pharisaic opponents in the Gospels (Mark 2.23–28) and in rabbinic tradition (e.g. *m. Pesaḥ.* 4.8). Besides, what chances would Paul really have had of persecuting such an elite figure as Philo anyway, assuming for the moment that they would have disagreed on Law observance? Bird's questioning can be taken to strange logical conclusions. We know that the Qumran group (with whom the Teacher of Righteousness was associated) were attacked by opponents (e.g. 4Q171 4), so by Bird's logic (namely, that Paul would have criticized others if the conflicts were internal Jewish legal disputes) it would have to be extremely puzzling as to why these opponents are not mentioned persecuting others! Josephus speaks of Sadducees having serious differences with Pharisees (Josephus, *Ant.* 13.297–98), so by Bird's logic Josephus would have to mention other groups and individuals in order to be deemed plausible! On the general level, groups fall out with one another and do not necessarily attack everyone else who might be in disagreement. On the more empirical level, Jesus seriously fell out with Pharisees over legal issues (Mark 2.28—3.6), so much so that the Gospels say that the Pharisees wanted him dead (Mark 3.6). If this is in anyway accurate (as I suspect evangelicals like Bird would believe it is) I fail to see why Bird thinks it implausible for those acting in Jesus' name immediately after Jesus' death to be engaged in similar disputes. Unless of course, Bird approaches the text *wanting* the disputes to be over what would become orthodox Christian doctrine (i.e. non-observance and the incarnation).

The incident at Antioch

Bird also takes issue with my argument that the problem at Antioch was over Gentiles eating food banned in the Bible and too much association with Gentiles by Christian Jews. Bird flippantly claims that if this were the case all that was needed was 'a change of menu' (see page 94). Bird presumably does not appreciate how problematic the issue of food was at the time of Christian origins. We know that there were Gentiles who simply could not understand why Jews avoided pork (e.g. Juvenal, *Sat.* 14.96–106; Philo, *Legat.* 361–362). We also know that issues of food and association between those who observe food laws and those who do not was an issue in Rome, as Paul reveals (Rom. 14). By Bird's logic,

Paul should simply have solved the problem by telling everyone to have a menu change. Moreover, as I showed, whenever early Jewish sources speak of the issues surrounding association with Gentiles at the meal table, the problematic issues are food and idolatry (not circumcision). As idolatry can be ruled out, food is the obvious contender for Antioch. As Bird did not engage with this argument or the ancient sources, I will say no more.

Moreover, as Bird points out, plenty of Jews certainly did associate with Gentiles in the ancient world and could still have observed the food laws should they have wished to do so. But, if at a meeting of a group that emerged, or was emerging, from Judaism, if more and more people were eating banned food then this becomes a very serious identity problem: is this a Jewish movement or not?

Bird, however, favours the idea of circumcision. Certainly the problems in *Galatia* involved circumcision but it hardly follows that this must necessarily have been the problem in *Antioch*. Paul may have cited the Antioch incident to the Galatians but he could easily have done so to attack the idea of *imposing* Law observance, an important issue for Paul as both of us accept.

Bird also asks, 'What would be so bad about asking Gentiles to observe Jewish food laws if they were the guests and in the minority? Paul seems willing to grant as much in Romans [14.21]' (see page 94). Well, what if Gentiles were neither guests nor in a minority? Indeed, what if they were? The point is not necessarily important because Paul was concerned with the unity of the Christian movement, something that may be fairly said to be close to the heart of Paul's message. Paul, as both of us have pointed out, was a pragmatist when it came to keeping unity.

Paul and the divinity of Christ

On issues of Jesus' divinity, Bird starts his criticisms of me on the wrong footing. He claims that all 'Crossley has proved is that Paul was not a modalist. Modalism is the view that Jesus is merely a personified expression of the Father and this was denounced as a heresy by later Christian theologians' (see page 95). As Bird knows, I placed Jesus in the context of various figures in earliest Judaism and how they could be described in relation to God and monotheism. I did not use such categories from Christian theology. I did not describe Jesus in anything like the terms he suggests. Bird has let polemic get in the way of proper argument here.

Bird says he is unable to agree with my alleged interpretation of Philippians 2.5–11 in terms of an 'alleged "Adam Christology"' (see page 95). Against Bird, I did not quite argue for an 'Adam Christology'. All I claimed was that we have similar language applied to Adam as we do in Philippians 2.5–11 and Adam cannot be described as God. Therefore in using such language about Jesus in Philippians 2.5–11 cannot necessarily imply divinity in the strongest sense. This is an important nuance.

Bird also uses language that is too vague if he wants to describe Jesus as the Jewish God in the strongest possible sense. Language such as the 'orbit of the divine identity' and 'suggestive of deity' could apply, as I pointed out, to a number of elevated figures in early Judaism without implying that they were fully co-equal with God. This is also an important point to keep in mind when Bird points out that I do not mention Isaiah 45.23 and its relationship to Philippians 2.9–11. Indeed, I could have mentioned this parallel and I have no issue with the idea that Paul is directly alluding to Isaiah 45.23. But, contrary to Bird's implication, this does not necessarily mean that Jesus is to be directly equated with God in the strongest sense of orthodox Christian theology. The Dead Sea Scrolls can use biblical verses that talk about God (Ps. 7.8–9; 82.1) and apply them to an elevated individual such as Melchizedek (11Q13 2.10–11; cf. Gen. 14.18–20). The Dead Sea Scrolls do not contain arguments that Melchizedek was co-equal with God in the sense that orthodox Christian theology believes Jesus is. We should not, therefore, automatically impose arguments made by Bird on Paul.

Of course, this is not to deny that Paul thought of Jesus in extremely elevated terms, nor that Paul would have an important influence on Christology. But, as I argued above, Paul certainly comes into conflict with Jewish figures over issues such as the Law although he never comes into conflict over Jesus' nature. In direct contrast, when John's Gospel makes dramatic claims that Jesus is equal with God, there are severe conflicts with Jewish opponents (John 5; 9). John, not Paul, is the earliest evidence of something like the full divinity of Christ.

Finally, let's go on the offensive. Bird claims that 'when Roman soldiers started putting the insignia of the cross on their shields during the time of Constantine it signalled the triumph of Paul's God and Paul's Messiah over the might of Rome's armies and the madness of Rome's emperors. Christ and Caesar met in the arena of history, and Christ won hands down' (see page 85). Well maybe. We may write this vague and fluffy theological history another way, however. Christ may have won but at what cost? Christianity now *becomes* the might of Rome's armies, or even the progenitor of the Crusades, the Inquisition and the New American Empire. Christianity must now be feared, just as Rome was always feared, just as the New American Empire also must now be feared. Maybe Christianity needed to adapt to survive, maybe not, but on the elite level at least, it did survive by becoming Rome. Is this really such a glorious history or one that is worth boasting about?

Further reading

Bird, Michael F., *A Bird's-Eye View of Paul: The Man, his Mission, and his Message* (Nottingham: IVP, 2008).

Bird, Michael F., *The Saving Righteousness of God: Studies on Paul, Justification and the New Perspective* (Carlisle: Paternoster, 2007).

Boyarin, D., *A Radical Jew: Paul and the Politics of Identity* (Berkeley and Los Angeles: University of California Press, 1994).

Casey, M., *From Jewish Prophet to Gentile God: The Origins and Development of New Testament Christology* (Louisville: Westminster John Knox; Cambridge: James Clarke, 1991).

Gathercole, S. J., *Where Is Boasting? Early Jewish Soteriology and Paul's Response in Romans 1—5* (Grand Rapids: Eerdmans, 2002).

Horrell, D. G., *An Introduction to the Study of Paul* (2nd edn; London and New York: Continuum, 2006).

Longenecker, Richard, (ed.), *The Road from Damascus: The Impact of Paul's Conversion on His Life, Thought, and Ministry* (Grand Rapids, MI: Eerdmans, 1997).

Sanders, E. P., *Paul and Palestinian Judaism: A Comparison of Patterns of Religion* (Philadelphia: Fortress; London: SCM Press, 1977).

Stowers, S. K., *A Rereading of Romans: Justice, Jews and Gentiles* (London: Yale University Press, 1994).

Thielman, Frank, *Paul and the Law: A Contextual Approach* (Downers Grove, IL: IVP, 1994).

Wenham, David, *Paul: Follower of Jesus or Founder of Christianity* (Grand Rapids, MI: Eerdmans, 1995).

4

The Gospels

Michael F. Bird

I remember once hearing the American scholar D. A. Carson tell the story of a missionary in Thailand who gave a copy of the four Gospels to a Buddhist monk. About a month later the missionary approached the monk to see if he had read them and to find out what he thought of them. When he questioned the monk about the Gospels the monk's face lit up with excitement. The monk said with delight, 'You know this Jesus, he is God, and he is greater than Buddha!' The missionary was most encouraged by this response and asked what led him to that conclusion. 'Well,' said the monk, 'Jesus is born and then he dies, he is born and then he dies, he is born and then he dies, he is born and then he dies, and then he becomes a god. It took Jesus only four lifetimes to become god and yet it took the Buddha a thousand lifetimes to become god.' If one approaches the four canonical Gospels with an ingrained belief about reincarnation and reads the four narratives as four consecutive life cycles of Jesus then one can easily understand how the monk reached this conclusion. At the end of the Gospel of John, Jesus is addressed by Thomas as 'my Lord and my God' (John 20.28). But that was obviously not how the Evangelists intended their Jesus stories to be read.

Even for those of us who do not read the Gospels through the lens of Buddhism, the Gospels can be equally confusing at times. There are details that do not always appear to agree (e.g. whether Jesus entered Jerusalem on a donkey or a colt: compare Mark 11.1–10; Luke 19.28–38; John 12.14–15 with Matt. 21.1–9), the genre of the Gospels is perplexing, there is a question of how reliable the traditions in the Gospels are, given the mix of history and theology, how to account for the different mood and motifs of the Fourth Gospel, and whether the Gospels give us four different Jesuses or four independent testimonies to the one Jesus. Furthermore, when the Evangelists wrote their Jesus stories, what did they think they were doing? What does their literary achievement tell us about the Evangelists themselves, their audiences and the life and faith of the early Church? It is these questions that I'd like to explore in this chapter because they relate to several issues concerning the birth of Christianity.

The beginnings of the Gospels

What type of literary artefact or what kind of genre is a Gospel? This is not an academic matter, as understanding the genre of a document helps us to grasp what the author was trying to achieve and what the audience would expect to find in the story. Genre provides a fixed framework for meaning which is understood and accepted by an audience. If the librarian at the ancient university of Alexandria were given a Gospel where would he put it in the library? Would it be among biographies, tragedies, comedies, histories, letters or sacred-writings? There have been many suggestions for the genre of the canonical Gospels. Some find parallels with Jewish *Haggadah* or Jewish storytelling about legendary figures, such as the renowned miracle-worker Honi the Circle-Drawer. In the Graeco-Roman sphere there are comparisons made with aretologies, which are stories of the miraculous deeds of godlike heroes, Greek epics where the hero of the story dies in order to make a moral point and tragedies and novels which narrate dramatic accounts often involving the gods. There are other approaches that find in the Gospels a compendium of Christian proclamation. Still others regard the Gospels as sui generis or an unprecedented literary genre.

My own approach takes on a threefold direction. First, the second-century Apologist Justin Martyr called the Gospels the 'memoirs' (*aponmēmoneumata*) of the Apostles (*1 Apol.* 66). This designation has obvious affinities with the various 'Lives' written about ancient figures, including Xenophon's *Memorabilia*, which is a biographical account of the life of Socrates, Philo's *Life of Moses*, Tacitus' biographical account about his father-in-law, *Agricola*, and Lucian's *Life of Demonax*. The most analogous genre to the Gospels then is the *Bios* or *Vita*, which is essentially a biographical narrative about a particular individual.[1] Like the *Bios/Vita* the Gospels portray the significant elements of the protagonist's life, but unlike them the Gospels are formally anonymous and they do more than commend the virtues of the protagonist since they seek to evoke faith and call for patterns of discipleship. Nonetheless, the *Bios/Vita* was a relatively broad category and could encompass works of considerable diversity.

---

[1] See further Richard Burridge, *What Are the Gospels? A Comparison with Graeco-Roman Biography* (Cambridge: Cambridge University Press, 1992).

Second, the Gospels are also theological biographies. They are concerned with the significance of Jesus for multiple Christian communities in the Graeco-Roman world. The decision to write a gospel about Jesus constitutes an effort to say something about God and what God has done and is continuing to do in the world of the authors and audience. While it is true that Jesus is the central character of the Gospels we cannot lose sight of the theocentric reality that pervades the narratives. The Gospels are about *God's* Son doing *God's* will to achieve *God's* purposes upon the earth. M. Eugene Boring says this about Mark's Gospel:

> What is this story about? The obvious answer: it is about Jesus, who appears in almost every scene and is the subject of most of the verbs in Mark. One could also say: it is about the disciples, who are called in the first chapter and accompany Jesus and are taught by him throughout until they abandon him in chapters 14 and 15; they are the goal of the final revelation pointed to in 16:7. The real answer, however: the story is about God, who only rarely becomes an explicit character, but who is the hidden actor in the whole drama, whose reality spans its whole narrative world from creation to eschaton, and who is not an alternative or competitor to the view that regards Jesus as the principle subject. To tell the story of Jesus is to tell the self-defining story of God.[2]

Third, the Gospels represent a continuation of the Old Testament story and they consciously connect the early Church to Israel via the history of Jesus. This is evident in all four Gospels. Matthew's Gospel opens with the 'scroll of the genealogy of Jesus the Messiah, the son of David, the son of Abraham'. Matthew's genealogy that follows is an annotated list that contains the story of Israel in a nutshell – creation, patriarchs, exodus, exile – and leaves the story waiting for resolution. Mark's Gospel commences with quotations from Isaiah 40.3 and Malachi 3.1 which associate the ministries of Jesus and John the Baptist with the dawning of a new exodus as foretold by Isaiah. Luke writes for his patron Theophilus about 'the events that have been fulfilled among us' (Luke 1.1), harking back to Israel's sacred scriptures. The prologue to John's Gospel overflows with Old Testament themes and the opening words, 'In the beginning was the Word' (John 1.1), clearly relate back to Genesis 1.1 and the beginning of creation. Whereas the Law came through Moses, in Jesus Christ there is 'grace upon grace' (John 1.17).

We can discern a number of broad purposes for the composition of the Gospels, including:

---

[2] M. Eugene Boring, *Mark: A Commentary* (NTL; Louisville, KY: Westminster John Knox, 2006), 3.

1 the desire to teach the story of Jesus to Christians so that they might know more about his person and imitate his behaviour;
2 to defend Christians against certain allegations made against the founder of their movement (e.g. Mark's Gospel is probably an apology for believing in a crucified Messiah);
3 the Gospels are evangelistic to some degree and this is quite evident in John 20.31;
4 the Gospels lend themselves to liturgical use in Christian worship; and
5 they also assist in the self-definition of Christians and serve to forge a community's identity in view of the identity of Jesus and so establish their claim to be the people of God over and against Jewish competitors and pagan detractors.

The Gospels were probably written at a time when the first generation of eyewitnesses to Jesus has died or is dying off and the Gospels were penned in order to preserve and disseminate the members' accounts of his life for others. Luke evidently writes as a second-generation Christian (Luke 1.2) and John's Gospel deals with the explicit problem of the death of the 'Beloved Disciple' prior to the *parousia* and so secures the testimony of this disciple for others to hear (John 21.22–23). Dating the Gospels is notoriously difficult and it depends on how one understands the web of literary relationships between the Gospels, how one appreciates the sociology of writing stories and external attestation of the various Gospels among second-century sources. I follow the consensus in dating Mark *c.* 60–70 CE, Luke and Matthew *c.* 75–90 CE, and John *c.* 90–100 CE. These dates are contestable (e.g. Crossley dates Mark in the early 40s), but they seem the most plausible if we identify the impetus for writing principally in the passing away of the first generation of Christians, the portentous events of 66–72 CE with the Judean revolt against Rome, and the struggles faced by Christians in the Graeco-Roman world in 65–100 CE, including persecution by Roman authorities, missionary expansion among Gentiles, the spasmodic expulsion of Christians from some Jewish synagogues, and the emergence of Christian defectors/apostates.

How reliable are the Gospel traditions?

The Gospels are often treated with scepticism about their historical value since there is a perception that the oral tradition embedded beneath the Gospels was fluid and vulnerable to unsupervised alteration. There are also questions about the theological creativity of the Evangelists in refashioning the traditions to suit their own agendas, along with misgivings as to whether or not the Evangelists even intended to write history at all. It is legitimate to ask, then: how reliable are the Gospels?[3]

When we say that the Gospels are biographies we do not mean that in the sense of modern biographies where we are accustomed to inverted commas for marking out exact quotes, footnotes for sources, pictures, charts and bibliographies – our Gospels contain nothing like that. The Gospels are written up in a form very similar to the *Bios* as I've just argued above but they also contain the *memory of Jesus* and the *testimony to Jesus* as preserved by the earliest Christian communities.[4] Those who want to play off history against theology ignore the fact that there is no such thing as uninterpreted history. We do not have to choose between theology and history because what the Gospels produce is not the Christ of faith superimposed on to the historical Jesus; rather, they offer a dramatic representation, much like a docu-drama, of Jesus' actions in the past and his voice for the present available through the public memory of Jesus. Consequently, the memory of Jesus deposited in the Gospels bequeaths to us both authenticity and artistry, fact and faith, history and hermeneutic. The objective of the Evangelists is not to write a life of Jesus to satisfy modernist demands for detail, nor is it to offer an image of Jesus concocted out of thin air to be used in a war of conflicting ideologies. The Gospels intend to narrate a story and evoke the significance of one called Jesus, Israel's Messiah and the world's rightful Lord.

Even with this overarching concern for the enduring significance of the risen and exalted Jesus, the Evangelists are consciously interested in the past of Jesus, a past different from their own time. The reason for this interest is that Jesus' earthly life was properly basic to faith, his teachings had practical value, his stories comprised the rubric of Christian self-definition, individuals and communities sought to imitate his actions, and his words and deeds were likely to be recalled as the deposit of a movement founder. Furthermore, the continued use of the name 'Jesus' and the absence (with a few exceptions) of the titles 'Christ' and 'Son of God' as terms of address for Jesus in the Gospels underscore the continued awareness of the pre-Easter history of Jesus.[5]

---

[3] For a more thorough treatment, see Michael F. Bird, 'The Formation of the Gospels in the Setting of Early Christianity: The Jesus Tradition as Corporate Memory', *WTJ* 67 (2005), 113–34; Bird, 'The Purpose and Preservation of the Jesus Tradition: Moderate Evidence for a Conserving Force in its Transmission', *BBR* 15 (2005), 161–85; and also Craig Blomberg, *The Historical Reliability of the Gospels* (2nd edn; Downers Grove, IL: IVP, 2007).

[4] Cf. James D. G. Dunn, *Jesus Remembered* (Grand Rapids, MI: Eerdmans, 2002); and Richard Bauckham, *Jesus and the Eyewitnesses* (Grand Rapids, MI: Eerdmans, 2006).

[5] Michael F. Bird, *Jesus and the Origins of the Gentile Mission* (LNTS 331; London: T&T Clark, 2006), 23–24.

A good test case to demonstrate the historical value of the Gospels is the discourse on the Mount of Olives in Mark 13 (cf. Matthew 24—25 and Luke 21). Since Mark is the earliest of the Gospels on which Matthew and Luke are partly dependent, I will focus on Mark 13. The discourse begins with Jesus' disciples admiring the adornments of the Temple and Jesus responding that the great religious monument will be thrown down. The disciples ask what will be the sign that such things are about to happen and the subsequent speech is an exposition of that point, namely, the destruction of Jerusalem. The contents of vv. 5–23 concern the tumultuous event leading up to the sacking of Jerusalem, including rumours of war, messianic pretenders, persecution by authorities, familial discord and the desecration of the Temple. The focus of vv. 24–28 is the coming of the Son of Man. The accompanying language about the stars falling and so forth invests a socio-political disaster with cosmic imagery in order to underscore its catastrophic significance. It may be possible to take vv. 32–37 as referring to Jesus' *parousia* or to detect a merging of historical and eschatological events throughout the speech, but this is far from certain. The most obvious point of reference is that the entire speech refers to the destruction of Jerusalem, which is a vindication of Jesus as the prophet who opposed the Temple: that is, the coming of the Son of Man.[6]

With regards to authenticity, the discourse of Mark 13 plausibly derives from an anti-Temple address given by Jesus in Jerusalem during his final days. Jesus was not the first prophet to speak against the Temple (Jeremiah and Ezekiel)[7] nor was he the last to do so (Josephus notes that Jesus ben Ananias predicted the Temple's destruction on the eve of Jewish revolt against Rome in 66 CE).[8] The overall plausibility of the discourse is enhanced when we bear in mind that many other Palestinian Jews harboured suspicions and even animosity towards the Temple and its hierarchy, and there is no reason why Jesus could not have thought similarly (1QpHab 12.8–9; CD 5.6–8; 4Q390 1.8–10; *1 En.* 89.73–74; *Jub.* 23.21; *Liv. Pro.* 10.10–11; 12.10–11; *Pss. Sol.* 2.3; 8.11–13; *T. Levi* 14.5–8; 16.1–5; *T. Mos.* 5.3—6.1). Furthermore, one cannot lay this speech at the feet of some Hellenistic Christianity far removed from Palestine that was somehow indifferent towards the Jerusalem cultus when we have ample evidence that Jews, God-fearers and Proselytes of the Diaspora revered the Temple and made

---

[6] See further Michael F. Bird, 'Parousia', in *Encyclopedia of the Historical Jesus*, ed. Craig A. Evans (New York: Routledge, 2008), 438–42.

[7] Jeremiah 7.1–15; 19.14–15; Ezek. 10.1–19; 24.15–23.

[8] Josephus, *J.W.* 6.300–9.

pilgrimages to it annually (Josephus, *J.W.* 5.223; *Ep. Arist.* 83–104; Philo, *Spec. Laws* 1.67–77; *Sib. Or.* 3.657–60). Second, the speech is simultaneously similar to and different from views of the Temple in the early Church, a key index to its probable authenticity. Jesus' critique of the Temple was probably carried over into the Church by some Jewish Christians, including Stephen (Acts 6.13–14) and the Ebionites (*Gos. Eb.* § 6) in contrast to others in the early Church who were exceptionally devout in their attendance of the Temple in an effort to reach their fellow Jews with the good news that Jesus was the Messiah (see Acts 2.46; 3.1; 5.21; 21.26). Third, elements of the discourse also deviate from the actual events of 70 CE when the Temple was razed, as there were 'stones left upon another' in the surviving foundations (the current Wailing Wall), which were not completely destroyed. If someone has written up this speech after the event itself then they have done a poor job of it. Fourth, that Jesus did criticize and speak against the operation of the Temple is multiply attested in the Gospel tradition (Luke 13.34–35/Matt. 23.37–39; Mark 13.2; 14.58; 15.29; Matt. 26.61; Luke 19.41–44; 21.20–24; 23.27–31; John 2.19; *Gos. Eb.* § 6; *Gos. Pet.* 7.25–26; *Gos. Thom.* 71). Jesus' speech is cross-referenced with his short, sharp protest in the Temple as narrated in Mark 11.15–17. If Jesus did find something wrong with the Temple, a tool of economic exploitation and fostering a nationalistic anti-Gentile ethos, then the discourse of Mark 13 tells us what he thinks will happen to it as a result. That he would refer to Jerusalem and the Temple was inevitable since in Jewish reckoning Zion was the epicentre of the cosmos and what happens there will affect the entire world. The sacking of Jerusalem and the destruction of the Temple marks the coming of a new social, political and religious order and heralds the beginning of the final judgment as well. To this we can add the woefully neglected study of David Wenham, who meticulously combs through the apocalyptic material in the synoptic tradition and its New Testament parallels and presents a robust case for a pre-synoptic eschatological tradition that goes back to Jesus.[9] In light of this I concur with the words of Bruce Vawter:

> That Jesus actually made such a prophecy, in view of his consistent eschatological teaching on the soonness of a divine visitation on Jerusalem and Judea, his conviction of the decisiveness of his own role in the workings of salvation history, and his reading of the temper of the times, there

---

[9] David Wenham, *The Rediscovery of Jesus' Eschatological Discourse* (Gospel Perspectives 4; Sheffield: JSOT Press, 1984); and, more recently, Alistair I. Wilson, *When Will These Things Happen? A Study of Jesus as Judge in Matthew 21—25* (Milton Keynes: Paternoster, 2005).

is absolutely no reason to question. His words are in the tradition of Israel's prophecy (cf. Jer. 7:1–15; Ezek. 24:15–23) and have not been simply made up by Christian writers in light of later events.[10]

History and theology in the Fourth Gospel

How does the Gospel of John relate to the history of Jesus? The fact is that John is different from the Synoptic Gospels in many regards. John possesses different contents, vocabulary, narrative sequence, geographical focus and major themes. John has no parables, exorcisms, tax-collectors, temptation account, Transfiguration story, and no institution of the Lord's Supper. The unique material in John includes the 'I am' sayings, dialogues with Nicodemus and the Samaritan woman, stories of female disciples, the foot-washing episode, the promise of the coming of the *Paraclete* or 'comforter', and Jesus' high-priestly prayer. The Johannine Jesus is far more aware of his own divinity than in the Synoptics. The disciples in John are far more enlightened and agreeable with Jesus as compared to their often naïve, immature and faithless behaviour in the Synoptics. There is much about 'eternal life' but relatively little about the 'kingdom' in contrast to Mark, Luke and Matthew. There are distinctive themes such as truth, witness, world, love, abiding, faith, light/darkness and the Father–Son relationship. John prefers the reference to 'signs' (*sēmeia*) over 'miracles' (*dynameis*). In the Fourth Gospel, Jesus cleanses the Temple at the start of his ministry, while in the Synoptics it is during his last days in Jerusalem. In the Synoptics, Jesus eats a Passover meal on the night before his death, whereas John presents Jesus as dying on the same day when the lambs are slain for the Passover meal.

These differences and apparent conflicts in details are not a recent discovery. Interpreters of the Gospels have long noted John's distinctive character in relation to the Synoptics. Clement of Alexandria labelled John as a 'spiritual gospel' (Eusebius, *Hist. Eccl.* 6.14.7). Another Church Father, Origen, compared John with the Synoptics on Jesus' action in the Temple and said: 'I conceive it to be impossible for those who admit nothing more than history in their interpretation to show that these discrepant statements are in harmony with each other' (*Comm. Jo.* 10.15). For many scholars John's historical value is negligible and John is regarded as an early 'systematic theology'.[11] Modern commentators have continued to debate whether John is dependent on or independent of the Synoptic Gospels and

---

[10] Bruce Vawter, *The Four Gospels: An Introduction* (New York: Doubleday, 1967), 322.
[11] John P. Meier, 'The Present State of the "Third Quest" for the Historical Jesus: Loss and Gain', *Bib* 80 (1999), 459–87 (465).

dispute over the historical utility of John.[12] Some might say that John aced theology but flunked history. And yet even John's theology has been subject to debate. It has been suggested that the theology of the Fourth Gospel is on a path to the heresies of Docetism and Gnosticism. The first-known commentary on John, or its prologue at least, was by a second-century gnostic teacher, Ptolemy, a disciple of Valentinius (Irenaeus, *Haer.* 1.8.5–6). A late-second-century presbyter of the church in Rome named Gaius is said to have found elements of the Fourth Gospel difficult to reconcile with the Synoptics and he attributed the Gospel to the heretic Cerinthus (Epiphanius, *Pan.* 51.4.5).[13]

On John and history, the tradition in John seems mostly independent of the Synoptics although John has probably read or heard Mark at some point. Some of the differences between John and the Synoptics are not quite as sharp as is often supposed. For instance, the 'I am' sayings cohere with the 'I have come' sayings of Mark 1.38; 2.17; Matthew 5.17; 9.13; 10.34–35; Luke 12.49 that imply pre-existence. Similarly the 'I am the good shepherd' discourse of John 10.1–21 comports with the picture of Jesus as a shepherd in Matthew 18.12–14/Luke 15.3–7 and his sympathy for the masses who have no shepherd-leader in Mark 6.34. In John 12.25 the threat of losing and keeping one's life correlates with similar warnings in the Synoptics (e.g. Mark 8.35; Matt. 10.39; Luke 9.24). The divide between John's purportedly high Christology and the apparent low Christology of Mark is an exaggeration. The truth is that Mark has a rather high view of Jesus' person that clearly edges towards divinized categories.[14] The Father–Son theme that dominates the Fourth Gospel can also be found in the Synoptics (e.g. Matt. 10.32; Luke 23.34; Luke 10.21–22/Matt. 11.25–27). The Fourth Gospel concentrates on the theme of 'eternal life' rather than the 'kingdom of God', but in Mark 10.24, 30, eternal life could function as a synonym for the kingdom of God. John retains 'kingdom' in his repertoire (e.g. John 3.3–8) even if it is not his primary motif. Even the notion of Jesus as the Son in the sense of being a divine emissary is not limited to John but emerges in the Parable of the Tenants (Mark 12.1–12). There is the 'Johannine Thunderbolt' in Luke 10.21–22/Matt. 11.25–27 that sounds like a quote from John in the middle of Matthew and Luke: 'I thank you, Father, Lord of heaven and earth, because you have hidden these things

---

[12] Contrast Craig L. Blomberg, *The Historical Reliability of John's Gospel* (Leicester: IVP, 2001) with Maurice Casey, *Is John's Gospel True?* (London: Routledge, 1996).

[13] Martin Hengel, *The Johannine Question* (trans. John Bowden: London: SCM Press, 1989), 5–8.

[14] Cf. M. Eugene Boring, 'Markan Christology: God-Language for Jesus?', *NTS* 45 (1999), 451–71.

from the wise and the intelligent and have revealed them to infants; yes, Father, for such was your gracious will.'[15] The Johannine discourses are plausible if understood as Jesus' self-disclosure and explanation of his teachings to his disciples away from the crowds, analogous to Jesus' private teachings to the disciples in the Synoptics (Mark 4.10–12; 7.17; Luke 10.23–24). With regard to the speeches and sayings, John's Gospel evidently contains much more of the *ipsissima vox* (exact voice) than the *ipsissima verba* (exact words) of Jesus. The present form of the discourses could be an exposition or midrash of such sayings. John has no doubt moulded and cast his presentation of Jesus along the lines of Jewish wisdom traditions, but such a framework can be traced back to Jesus himself (cf. Matt. 8.20; 11.28–30; Luke 7.35/Matt. 11.19; Luke 11.31/Matt. 12.42). John may be more theologically pronounced than the Synoptics, but he plots an interpretative trajectory from similar traditions that parallel the Synoptics. In sum, there are several reasons why the Fourth Gospel is different from the Synoptics:

1 John writes with a largely missionary purpose and parades a variety of figures in his Gospel, including Samaritans, Jewish officials and Gentiles;
2 John drew on traditions not available to the Synoptic writers or else not in accordance with their outlines (e.g. raising of Lazarus); and
3 John's mode of presentation is more dramatic than that of the Synoptics.[16]

The Fourth Gospel also possesses several historiographical characteristics.[17] The author exhibits an intimate awareness of Palestinian topography, including the Pool of Siloam (9.7), the Kidron Valley (18.1), the Pool of Bethesda (5.2) and Gabbatha (19.13). John provides some chronological markers concerning Jesus' movements to and from Jerusalem for the various feasts. The narration is marked by selectivity, parenthetical remarks and appeal to eyewitness testimony that were traits of historiography. The dialogues and discourses are probably elaborations undertaken with fidelity to sources and verisimilitude with respect to the content that was congruent with the depiction of speeches in antiquity.

---

[15] According to Simon Gathercole (*The Preexistent Son: Recovering the Christologies of Matthew, Mark, and Luke* [Grand Rapids, MI: Eerdmans, 2006], 79): 'a heavenly christology is not a distinctively Johannine phenomenon: there are plenty of thunderbolts through Matthew, Mark, and Luke as well'.

[16] Ben Witherington, *John's Wisdom* (Louisville: Westminster John Knox, 1995), 36–7.

[17] Richard Bauckham, 'Historiographical Characteristics of the Gospel of John', *NTS* 53 (2007), 17–36.

The fact that there are several places where the 'beloved disciple' is invoked as the source and authenticator of material (19.35; 20.2–9; 21.24) indicates that at some point in the tradition eyewitness testimony was involved. Although the beloved disciple is, narratively speaking, an ideal disciple, he is not purely a symbolic character, but is regarded as a real person who validates the historical message of the Gospel. At a bare minimum we could argue that the Fourth Gospel was indebted to the teaching of a Judean disciple of Jesus, who was an eyewitness to Jesus' miracles and death, and later led a Christian community in Asia Minor.[18] In later Christian tradition this person is identified as the apostle John.

The Evangelist has thoroughly reworked his traditions in accordance with his own theological design and purpose. Yet there is sufficient reason to warrant the conclusion that the Fourth Gospel contains a genuine deposit of information about Jesus. The main burden of this Gospel, however, is not merely historical testimony but a striving to identify Jesus the Nazarene with the eternal Word of God and call others to faith or to a deeper faith in that person (John 20.31).

Four Gospels and one Jesus?

Why are there four Gospels? It might have been much easier if the early Church had just picked a single Gospel and authorized it for collective usage. We would not have to try to reconcile the Synoptics with John and there would be no need for desperate harmonizations between alternative versions of the same event. In fact, many Christians in the second century took this exact view. The disciples of Marcion argued that Paul's reference to 'my gospel' in Romans 2.16 was evidence that there was only one Gospel and not a plurality, so they opted for a heavily edited version of Luke (Origen, *Comm. Jo.* 5.4). Similarly, other groups restricted their usage to one Gospel, such as the enthusiastic Montanists with John's Gospel and the Docetists who often preferred Mark. Hence some groups venerated the Gospel which they found most conducive to their spiritual interests. Tatian decided to put all of the Gospels together into one hybrid account that was subsequently called the *Diatessaron* ('through the four'). Some groups did not like the four that were available and decided to write their own Jesus stories including works such as the *Gospel of Thomas*, *Gospel of Judas*, *Gospel of Philip*, *Gospel of Truth*, *Gospel of Mary Magdalene*, *Gospel of the Ebionites*, the *Gospel according to the Nazarenes* and *Gospel of Peter*, etc. Most Christians got around this problem by acknowledging the

---

[18] Cf. Hengel, *Johannine Question*, 124–35.

validity of all four Gospels but by using Matthew as their preferred Gospel text.

In the third book of Irenaeus' *Against Heresies* written about 180 CE, the view is set forth that the four Gospels are 'Scripture' and they constitute the sacred literature of Christians. According to Irenaeus, there is one Gospel in fourfold form, held together by one Spirit (*Haer.* 3.11.8–9). Irenaeus justifies the existence of specifically four Gospels with several allegories about the quality of the number four such as four points of the compass, four winds, the four-faced cherubim of Ezekiel 1.10, the four living creatures of Revelation 4.7 and the four covenants God has with humankind. He wrote: 'while the Church is scattered throughout all the world, and the "pillar and ground" of the Church is the Gospel and the spirit of life; it is fitting that she should have four pillars, breathing out immortality on every side, and vivifying men afresh'. Other Christian writers drew on the image of Genesis 2.10–14 with the four rivers of Paradise which flowed from the Garden of Eden into the whole world (Hippolytus, Cyprian, Victorinius of Pettau). Before one accuses the Church Fathers of some crass allegorizing, it is important to orientate the discussion to the wider context of the acceptance of the four Gospels in the early Church. It was not the magical quality of the number 'four' that led Christians to accept them as authoritative, but the four Gospels that we call canonical were the ones that were handed on in the earliest days of the Church (unlike, for example, the *Gospel of Thomas*, which probably dates to the beginning of the second century). They were theological witnesses to Jesus Christ in narrative form, they were widely read and accepted, and they corresponded to the apostolic preaching about Jesus. In light of such criteria the developing Church of the second and third centuries was within its rights to accept them and reject others. The Church bravely accepted them rather than opting for the solutions of Tatian or Marcion, and did so in the face of pagan critics like Celsus who lampooned the differences between the four. This was attributable to the conviction that these four Gospels are the pillars of the Church, are bounded together by one Spirit and are narrative testimonies to Jesus the Messiah.

Despite all the differences in the narratives and theologies of each Gospel we can identify a whole array of commonalities and shared characteristics between them. Luke Timothy Johnson lists them as follows:[19]

---

[19] Luke Timothy Johnson, 'Does a Theology of the Canonical Gospels Make Sense?', in *The Nature of New Testament Theology*, eds Christopher Rowland and Christopher Tuckett (Oxford: Blackwell, 2006), 93–108 (103–5).

1 All four Gospels are realistic narratives.
2 All four Gospels have specific historical roots in first-century Palestine.
3 All four Gospels explicitly connect the story of Jesus to that of Israel, using the texts and stories of the Torah and Prophets to express the identity and role of Jesus.
4 All four Gospels emphasize the way that humans respond to Jesus.
5 All the Gospels climax in the passion of Jesus.
6 All the Gospels share an understanding of the resurrection of Jesus that is continuous with his human existence and sustaining of the relationships formed in his human ministry.
7 The Gospels, despite their manifold differences, agree in their portrayal of Jesus as a human sent from God for the sake of other humans, who speaks and acts as God's representative, even as he is also radically committed to obedience to God.
8 In all of the Gospels, God is at once the father of Jesus and the God of Israel.
9 In the all of the Gospels, God's triumph is still in the future.
10 In all of the Gospels, despite their divergent portrait of the disciples, they agree that discipleship means walking the path of radical obedience to God and living in service to Jesus Christ.

One should not overplay the diversity card too much as there are more similarities than differences between the four Gospels and what differences do exist are usually incidental (e.g. like two versions of the Lord's prayer). I want to add that the plurality of Gospels gives us four portraits of Jesus and not four Jesuses. The central person in each Gospel is recognizable as the same character. Comparing the Gospels may be like comparing four portraits of Elizabeth II or Abraham Lincoln; the backgrounds and foregrounds may vary with each canvas, different emphases are apparent with each colourful depiction, some artists paint with a thick brush and others with a small brush, one portrait is perhaps more impressionistic while others are more life-like. Nonetheless, the person in all four portraits is readily identifiable – it is Jesus.

Conclusions

The Gospels are the interpretation and the application of the memory of Jesus for readers in the Graeco-Roman world. They are theological biographies that connect the story of Jesus to the story of Israel and invite the identification of the risen and exalted Jesus with the historical figure of Jesus. The Evangelists were not intending to write theological responses to new situations, devising their stories out of thin air; but the stories are rooted in the historical reminisces, eyewitness testimony, communal memory, theological reflection, and evangelistic proclamation of the early Church. They can be taken as history in much the same way as one understands 'history' written by Thucydides, Tacitus, Suetonius and Arian. Even John's Gospel, where the theological colouring is brighter than that of the Synoptics, still contains a genuine deposit of information about Jesus and fills in many gaps in our knowledge.

Where is all this taking us? The Gospels are not simply a collection of traditions about Jesus that have been strung together by the Evangelists. Neither are the Gospels a deposit of the beliefs about Jesus held by certain isolated and introspective Christian communities. Essential to understanding the purpose and setting of the Gospels, then, is the fact that the intentionality of the texts is to tell the story of Jesus for readers spread throughout the Graeco-Roman world. The reason they want to tell this story is because:

1 they believed that both Jesus and themselves were bringing the story of Israel to its great climax and pointing towards the end of all things;
2 they regarded the time of Jesus as a special or unique period of human history into which God had broken into in order to do something amazing through his Son, Israel's Messiah;
3 they provided second and third generations of Christians with vital information about the life history of Jesus, assuming that such persons were indeed interested in his pre-Easter history;
4 they show that Christians saw their own identity and purpose as being bound up with Jesus, God and the hope of Israel;
5 finally, they are evidence of the struggles that christians had among themselves, with the Jewish communities, and with the culture and politics of pagan cites in how to live a life centred on the stories, symbols and praxis of Jesus in the wider Graeco-Roman world.

In short, the Gospels explain to converts and critics alike who Jesus is, why there are Jesus people, who the Jesus people are and how the Jesus people are to follow their master.

James G. Crossley

There has been much recent debate about privileging the New Testament Gospels over those gospels (e.g. *Gospel of Thomas*) that did not make it into what we now know as the New Testament. The format of this book has effectively made me retain this prejudice, though inclusion of texts such as the *Gospel of Thomas* does not always have much impact in terms of a secular–evangelical/Christian debate and it makes little difference to my overall concerns in this book, namely, to explain some of the key developments in the emergence of a new religion. While I am very much in favour of alternative histories and explanations of history's 'losers' (e.g. the people behind some of the non-canonical gospels), my overall concern here is to explain history's 'winners', and it just so happens that one of the canonical Gospels (John) reflects the trump card. Moreover, the canonical Gospels can be of further interest for a secular–evangelical/Christian debate because, as I shall show, the Synoptic Gospels (Matthew, Mark and Luke) do not have the developed view of Jesus that we find in mainstream Christian doctrine, and John's Gospel took some of the most important steps in the creation of Jesus as God. With this in mind, a comparison between the Synoptic Gospels, on the one hand, and John's Gospel, on the other, on the big issues of Law, Gentiles and Christology should be enough to begin to show the dramatic contribution of John's Gospel to Christian history.

Mark's Gospel, the Law and Gentiles

There are some scholars, myself included, who have argued that the Gospel of Mark did nothing to promote non-observance of the Law and still saw the Jesus movement as within Judaism. Those who reject such suggestions of a more Law-observant Gospel of Mark have not, as far as I am aware, replied with convincing arguments, or sometimes with *any* arguments, but rather fall back on established opinion about, for example, what biblical Sabbath law Jesus breached and without exploring what contemporary Jewish purity practices might underlie debates on purity. This failure to engage with sometimes complex ancient views is not helpful historical practice and I suspect it may stem from a feeling of religious and/or cultural superiority. Against such criticisms, I will now lay out some of the key arguments.

Some of the passages key to my argument have already been outlined in my chapter on Jesus. In the Sabbath disputes in Mark 2.23—3.6, Mark does not record anything that runs contrary to any biblical commandment. Yet there is one controversial passage in relation to the Law where Mark does make a significant addition, namely, his famous words, 'Thus he declared all foods clean' (Mark 7.19). For some, after nearly 2,000 years of Christianity largely not observing the food laws, this passage conclusively shows that Mark's Jesus rejected the food laws. But, when Mark was first written down, there were other readings of this text. For a start, Mark 7.18–19 ('He said to them . . . Thus he declared all foods clean') does not make very good grammatical sense, as scholars have occasionally pointed out.[20] Grammatically speaking, the Greek underlying 'declaring . . . clean' (or, literally, 'cleansing') simply does not match up with the Greek underlying 'he said'. To get the conventional meaning and translation 'he declared all foods clean' these non-matching verses ought to match. Scholars have generally argued that this does *really* mean all foods were declared clean, but this is not an obvious reading of the Greek. Nor indeed was it the obvious reading for the early transmitters of the manuscripts. One Syriac (a dialect of Aramaic, the language in which Jesus spoke) manuscript makes a closer connection with the immediately preceding words, going for, 'all the food being cast out and purged away'. So why should *we* read Mark 7.18–19 as overriding the biblical food laws? Because Christian tradition (which, of course, largely abandoned food laws) has said so? I think not.

There are other cultural reasons that show the conventional reading of Mark 7.19 to be problematic, namely, early Jewish purity laws. Mark 7.19 is set in the context of a debate over hand-washing before ordinary, every-day, regular meals eaten outside the Temple. This is an *interpretation* or *expansion* of the biblical laws of the variety we saw in my chapter on Jesus because biblical texts do not mention that ordinary meals should be protected from impurity by washing hands. The logic of the transmission of purity laws is extremely complex and quite alien to gentile and Christian readers. Consequently it is no surprise that the purity system underlying hand-washing before ordinary meals is often not discussed. To simplify, the transmission of impurity in the Pharisaic system would be from impure/unclean hands to the food – via a liquid (e.g. water, wine, blood, oil, honey) – to the insides, thereby making the insides impure. What hand-washing did was to stop the transmission of impurity. There were other things done to become and stay pure. One important one was the immersion of the body in an immersion pool. One of the interesting decisions made was that hands could become impure as distinct from the rest of the body, even after the whole body had been immersed.

Mark 7.1–23 can clearly be read in light of this logic. Jesus' disciples did not wash their hands before a meal. Mark explains that the Pharisees do wash their hands before meals along with other things related to table purity (cups, pots, bronze kettles and dining couches). There is also

---

[20] Cf. M. Black, *An Aramaic Approach to the Gospels and Acts* (3rd edn; Oxford: Oxford University Press, 1967), 217–18; D. A. J. Cohen, 'The Gentiles of Mark's Gospel: A Jewish Reading' (PhD Thesis, Australian National University, 2006), 150–71; Mark Goodacre, 'Did Jesus Declare All Foods Clean?', <http://ntgateway.com/weblog/2006/01/did-jesus-declare-all-foods-clean.html> (accessed 28 March 2008).

mention of bodily immersion (the alternative translation of immersing food, mentioned in some English Bibles, is problematic because there was no known practice and the translation of immersing bodies reflects more conventional Greek grammar). The key verse 15 ('there is nothing outside a person that by going in can defile, but the things that come out are what defile') would make perfectly good sense in terms of a rejection of hand-washing and the need to keep the insides pure. Verse 19 ('he declared all foods clean') could also be viewed in this way: hand-washing to prevent food from becoming unclean is no longer required. If the debate is framed this way, then this would also imply that the food was food acceptable for Jews to eat and would have nothing to say on the issue of foods like pork prohibited in biblical law.[21] I would suggest that Matthew was interpreting Mark accurately when he concludes, 'but to eat with unwashed hands does not defile' (Matt. 15.20).

There are further arguments suggesting that this is a debate over the *interpretation* of biblical commandments. Read through Mark 7.1–13 and see how the theme of 'tradition' versus God's commandments is heavily stressed by Mark. If Mark's Jesus is firing at the interpretation of biblical commandments, or 'tradition', and contrasting this with biblical commandments throughout Mark 7.1–23, then the reading that Jesus rejects a key biblical commandment in 7.19 is problematic. Why outline all that detail lambasting opponents over their failure to keep God's commandments when Mark's Jesus does exactly the same? Is Mark's Jesus simply outrageously self-contradictory? More generally, if Mark does not have Jesus contradict biblical commandments elsewhere, why does he suddenly do so here?

If I am right with this reading of Mark 7.19, then this verse has something to say concerning Mark's view of Gentiles (cf. Mark 7.3; 13.10; 14.9), as it is at the heart of a section of Mark (chapters 6—8) that is usually regarded as a narrative about inclusion of Gentiles. After Mark 7.1–23, Jesus goes well out of his way into territory associated with Gentiles, including the notoriously/stereotypically anti-Jewish town of Tyre (Josephus, *Ag. Ap.* 1.70; *Ant.* 14.313–21; cf. Josephus, *J.W.* 2.478; Isa. 23; Jer. 25.17–22; 47.4; Ezek. 26—28; Joel 3.4–8; Amos 1.9–10; Zech. 9.2–4; Acts 21.3–4). More immediately, Jesus has contact with a gentile woman and heals her daughter (Mark 7.24–30). Consequently, it is usually argued, Mark sandwiches the material in chapter 7 between two feeding miracles, one for

---

[21] See further J. G. Crossley, *The Date of Mark's Gospel: Insight from the Law in Earliest Christianity* (London and New York: T&T Clark/Continuum, 2004), 183–205; D. Instone-Brewer, 'Review of J. G. Crossley, *The Date of Mark's Gospel*', *JTS* 57 (2006), 647–50 (649–50).

Jews in Mark 6.30–44 and one for Gentiles in Mark 8.1–10. It seems to me that many Gentiles reading or hearing this section of Mark could potentially have read themselves into the story and seen gentile inclusion in Mark 8.1–10. But this inclusion clearly is limited and Gentiles should firmly know their place. In the story of the gentile Syro-Phoenician woman, Jesus makes this quite clear as we saw in the chapter on the historical Jesus:

> Let the children [Jews] be fed first, for it is not fair to take the children's food and throw it to the dogs [Gentiles].' But she answered him, 'Sir, even the dogs under the table eat the children's crumbs.'   (Mark 7.27–28)

The standard reading of Mark, based on the food laws supposedly abandoned in Mark 7.19, can then have Mark narrate a shift toward Gentiles. But if the reading that Mark 7.19 does not override food laws is correct then Mark 6—8 can be re-read in a different light. Here we can note that Mark 7.1–23 ends with a big stress on ethical behaviour (7.21–23). Such 'vice-lists' as Mark 7.21–23 were common enough in distinguishing Jew from Gentile, and find their way into earliest Christianity (1 Cor. 6.9–11; Gal. 5.19–21; 1 Pet. 4.3–6; Rev. 9.20–21). In fact, it was morality that was *the* key way that Jews distinguished themselves from Gentiles in early Jewish literature (e.g. Exod. 34.15–16; Lev. 18.24–30; Deut. 7.2–4, 16; 20.18; Tobit 14.6; *Jub.* 9.15; *Aristeas* 152; Philo, *Spec. Laws* 1.51; *Sib. Or.* 3.492, 496–500; 5.168). Notice that in Mark the vice list comes immediately before Jesus' contact with the gentile woman (7.21–23), so highlighting the concerns some Jews would have had with gentile behaviour. Once that is recognized, Mark can move on to discuss Gentiles in his narrative.[22]

Matthew's Gospel, the Law and Gentiles

Matthew quite explicitly portrays Jesus as Law-observant. For a start, if there is any ambiguity with Mark 7.19, Matthew makes sure it is ironed out by stressing that Jesus was firing at hand-washing (Matt. 15.20). In fact, Matthew 5—7, along with chapter 23, may well be a manifesto for the particular view of the Law for Matthean Christians. Here we should also note the famous Christology based on Moses. Matthew develops Jewish retellings of the Moses story. For example, he uses Moses-as-Law-giver traditions in early Judaism to show Jesus as the ultimate legal interpreter (e.g. Matt. 5—7; 23; cf. e.g. *4 Ezra* 14.1–3, 42; *b. Sanh.* 11a).

But perhaps the one area where people claim Matthew may override the Law is in the so-called 'antitheses' (Matt. 5.21–47). It is popularly believed

---

[22] See further J. G. Crossley, *Why Christianity Happened: A Sociohistorical Account of Christian Origins* (Louisville: Westminster John Knox, 2006), 127–40.

that the repeated saying 'you have heard it said . . . *but* I say to you' always implies a strong contrast. In some of the sayings this contrast is clear (Matt. 5.33–36, 43–44). However, the Greek does not *automatically* imply a strong contrast and in some places it could equally be translated 'and I say to you'; rather than a contrast there is a continuation (e.g. Matt. 5.27–30). We have already seen how Jesus' interpretation of an eye for an eye is a continuation (Matt. 5.38–42), an interpretation of the biblical passage, and not a contrast as is usually thought. In Matthew 5.33–37 it is usually suggested that Jesus is contradicting biblical law on saying oaths. But there is no *biblical* commandment that oaths must be spoken and there are implications in biblical law that it is better to avoid saying oaths (Deut. 23.22). Indeed, in the descriptions of the strict Law-observant Jewish sect called the Essenes, the groups are said to avoid oaths (Philo, *Good Person* 84; Josephus, *J.W.* 2.135). Likewise, with the love enemies saying (Matt. 5.43–44), there is no biblical commandment to hate enemies, even if there are some highly unsavoury attitudes toward enemies. Jesus may well be contrasting his teachings with groups in early Judaism that were strongly hostile toward enemies (cf. 1QS 1.4, 10–11; 9.21–23; Josephus *J.W.* 2.139), rather than with biblical commandments.[23]

Matthew intensifies the conflicts over the Law. This is clear in Matthew 23 where he collects a variety of polemical sayings of Jesus aimed at the scribes and Pharisees: however, none of it comes close to contradicting biblical law. In recording earlier material, Matthew's Jesus says, 'Woe to you, scribes and Pharisees, hypocrites! For you tithe mint, dill, and cummin, and have neglected the weightier matters of the law: justice and mercy and faith. It is these you ought to have practised without neglecting the others' (Matt. 23.23). Here the biblical commandment to tithe is assumed and in fact the Pharisaic view is even acceptable so long as ethics are kept in mind. The deliberate collection of materials in Matthew 23 almost certainly reflects a context of Matthean Christians in conflict with Pharisees or heirs of the Pharisees.

There is one big question here: is Matthew creating a distinctively *Christianized* identity over against Judaism as a whole? Certainly Matthew uses the phrase 'their synagogue(s)' (Matt. 4.23; 5.22, 35, 36, 38; 9.18, 23, 35; 10.17; 12.9; 13.54; cf. Mark 3.1; 6.1–2). There is also the above-mentioned hostility toward the scribes and Pharisees (e.g. Matt. 22.15, 34–36; 23; cf. Mark 12.29–31; Luke 13.31). There is the dangerous anti-Jewish saying: 'Then the people as a whole answered, "His blood be on us

---

[23] For further discussion with bibliography, see e.g. H. D. Betz, *The Sermon on the Mount* (Minneapolis: Fortress, 1995).

and on our children!"' (Matt. 27.25). All this could be taken as internal Jewish polemic, but then Matthew appears to have his own distinctive space, 'the church' (Matt. 16.18; 18.17; 28.19), in contrast to the synagogue. And he then further points to distinctively Christian figures and interpreters (Matt. 10.41; 13.52; 23.34; cf. Matt. 23.6–13).

However, there are other signs that Matthew does not represent a definitive break from Judaism. Matthew's Gospel may represent an internal Jewish dispute such as those between the Dead Sea Scrolls people and their opponents in Jerusalem, or between the Sadducees and Pharisees. We do not see anything like the criticisms of 'the Jews' that we see in John's Gospel. Instead, a lot of Matthew's polemic is aimed at scribes and Pharisees and there is even the implication that the Pharisees have some influence over people associated with Matthew's Gospel: 'do whatever they teach you and follow it; but do not do as they do, for they do not practise what they teach' (Matt. 23.3). This might suggest that there may have been a highly strained relationship with many Jews but Matthew was still thinking in terms of the Christian movement as a *competing* movement within Judaism.

Of course there are some highly distinctive features of Matthew in relation to Judaism as a whole. There is concern for Gentiles in the future (Matt. 10.18; 21.33–43; 24.9–14; cf. Matt. 8.18–21) but Matthew goes further (this concern may or may not come from the historical tradition; what is important is that Matthew saw fit to include such a viewpoint). Jesus may not have inaugurated a gentile mission (Matt. 10.5–6) yet Matthew concludes his Gospel by having the resurrected Jesus say this:

> Go therefore and make disciples of all nations, baptizing them in the name of the Father and of the Son and of the Holy Spirit, and teaching them to obey everything that I have commanded you.   (Matt. 28.19–20)

As we will see with Luke, Matthew's Gospel reflects the idea that the gentile mission is effectively inaugurated *after* the resurrection of Jesus and was of no significant concern during Jesus' life.

This is important because while Matthew may want Christians to observe the Law he does, grudgingly, accept exceptions: 'whoever breaks one of the least of these commandments, and teaches others to do the same, will be called least in the kingdom of heaven' (Matt. 5.19). The 'least' may not be the best but the 'least' is still included in the kingdom. This inclusion of Gentiles, with the problems of Law observance that inclusion of Gentiles brought, provides the potential for a split from Judaism as a whole.

Luke's Gospel, the Law and Gentiles

Luke is very careful to make sure Jesus is portrayed as a Law-observant Jew, despite the fact that when Luke-Acts was written (the writer of Luke is generally believed to have written Acts too), the challenge to the Law was known and was not practised by at least some members of Luke's audience (Luke 16.17; Acts 10.1—11.18; 13.39; 15; 21.28). The way that Luke has edited his Marcan source makes it clear that in Mark Jesus was observing biblical commandments. For example, Luke's retelling of the dispute over the plucking of the grain on the Sabbath makes a notable change (compare Luke 6.1–5 with Mark 2.23–28). While there is nothing against plucking grain on the Sabbath in biblical law there was always the potential to use the grain to do some work on the Sabbath. Luke's addition makes it abundantly clear that Jesus was not allowing anything that could potentially go against biblical law – though of course it may have gone against *interpretations* of the Law – by stressing that the grain would be used there and then for eating: 'his disciples plucked some heads of grain, *rubbed them in their hands and ate them*' (Luke 6.1 cf. Mark 2.23).

Luke has his own additions to the portrayal of Jesus and the Law, such as the Sabbath healing disputes (Luke 13.10–17; 14.1–6), which reflect the idea that Jesus extends the principle of saving life overruling the Sabbath to include his healings. Certainly there is nothing in Luke against *biblical* Sabbath commandments because there is no banning of healing on the Sabbath in biblical law. At the same time, these Sabbath healing disputes run contrary to or engage with some of the expansions of the Law in early Judaism (cf. *m. 'Erub.* 2.1–4; *m. Šhabbat* 5.1–4; CD 11.13–14).

It is, however, sometimes argued that Luke's famous Parable of the Good Samaritan (Luke 10.30–37) runs contrary to even *biblical* purity commandments.[24] As the man left on the side of the road was dead, the priest, scholars often point out, would not be able to come into close contact with him because priests, according to biblical law, are not supposed to defile themselves with corpses, except for those of their close relatives (Lev. 21.1–3). As the implication in the parable is that the priest should have come into close contact with the supposedly dead man, then a biblical commandment was questioned, at least in this instance.

It should be noted that Luke has Jesus' opponent *agreeing* with Jesus on this point so it could not have been that outrageous. Moreover, there

---

[24] For an extreme version of this see e.g. N. T. Wright, *Jesus and the Victory of God* (COQG 2; London: SPCK, 1996), 307. For a more nuanced view see R. J. Bauckham, 'The Scrupulous Priest and the Good Samaritan: Jesus' Parabolic Interpretation of the Law of Moses', *NTS* 44 (1998), 475–89.

is no reason why he should have been outraged because it is not obvious that the priest is contradicting a biblical commandment. Leviticus 21.1 says that a priest is not to become unclean with corpse impurity when he is 'among his people', which he is most definitely not in this parable (cf. Num. 19.16). Luke gives us another important piece of information: the priest was travelling down from Jerusalem to Jericho (Luke 10.31) so Luke shows that the priest was not on his way to serve in the Jerusalem Temple. In this light Luke's Jesus is criticizing the expansion of purity laws where some Jews were keeping Temple-style laws as much as possible beyond the Temple. The priest, according to this logic, had no excuse for not touching the dead man. Indeed, one rabbi – Rabbi Eliezer b. Hyrcanus – went further than Jesus and said that even the High Priest should be prepared to contract corpse uncleanness in the case of an abandoned corpse (Mishnah *Naz.* 7.1)!

While Luke has nothing in the teaching of Jesus that goes against any biblical commandment, it is important to distinguish between Luke's portrayal of Jesus and the Law and what he expected of his audience because it is clear that Luke knew his audience were not expected to observe all the biblical commandments. In the Jerusalem council of Acts 15, Gentiles did not have to observe major parts of the Law. Even the Jewish Peter was no longer expected to observe food laws (Acts 10.1—11.18). Here we can see Luke's own take on history in relation to the Law and Gentiles (cf. Luke 16.16). While there is a minor *possible* concern for Gentiles in Luke (cf. Luke 7.2–10; 13.28–29), the full-blown gentile mission has to wait until Acts, and tied in with this is a change in the role of the Law in Acts. The close connection between the Law and Gentiles in Luke's scheme is highlighted by his 'Great Omission' of Mark 6.45—8.26. Here Luke appears to remove this section of Mark – which could easily be read as a contradiction of a Law-observant Jesus in the context of a gentile 'mission' – and then place these themes in a new context where the themes of Gentiles and Law observance are now related to Peter's vision from God about being able to eat food banned in biblical law (Acts 10.1—11.18). Luke therefore narrates what was a massive theological shift for the early Christians and one grounded in God's authority: from observance to non-observance.

Christology and the Synoptic Gospels

There is nothing in the Synoptic Gospels that pushes Jesus' status beyond the boundaries of Jewish monotheism in the sense that Jesus was made God. It is sometimes believed that miracles, such as the stilling of the storm, the walking on water and the feeding miracles, somehow show Jesus to be 'divine' in the strongest possible sense and that he is to be worshipped as the God of Israel was/is worshipped.[25] The problem with such views is that, in these miracles, Jesus is not portrayed as doing anything unparalleled by figures in early Judaism.

So, for example, we know there were other figures in first-century Judaism who were associated with miraculous practices but were never considered to be God and never considered themselves to be God. A prophetic figure called Theudas, for example, promised the parting of the Jordan, and another, called 'the Egyptian', promised the fall of the walls of Jerusalem (*Ant.* 20.97–98, 167–172; *J.W.* 2.258–263). In fact, there are a host of elevated and not-so-elevated figures in early Judaism who were also believed to have performed miracles similar to those attributed to Jesus. One of the more entertaining characters is the naughty Rabbi Eliezer who could control the elements like the Jesus of the Gospels. Even Eliezer's opponents had no problem thinking he could do acts such as uproot carob trees and turn the flow of a stream (*b. B. Mes.* 59b).

The Eliezer story is much later than the Gospels but it shows how relatively uncontroversial such miraculous deeds remained (see also my chapter on the historical Jesus [pages 1–17 and 33–7]). An earlier example is the first-century Jewish philosopher Philo's description of Moses who, just like Jesus, could control creation:

> For, since God judged him [Moses] worthy to appear as a partner of His own possessions, He gave into his hands the whole world as a portion well fitted for His heir. Therefore, each element obeyed him as its master, changed its natural properties and submitted to his command . . .
>
> (*Mos.* 1.155–156)

We might recall similar language in Mark 4.41: 'Who then is this, that even the wind and the sea obey him?' When read in this context, it is difficult to see how the Synoptic Gospels are doing anything as radical as making Jesus equal with God, or making Jesus worthy of worship as God when they have Jesus stilling the storm.

Similar comments can be made with reference to Jesus' walking on the water. Some people suggest that 'it is I (*egō eimi*)' (Mark 6.50) refers to the language used by God of himself: 'I AM (Greek version: *egō eimi*) WHO

---

[25] L. W. Hurtado, *Lord Jesus Christ: Devotion to Jesus in Earliest Christianity* (Grand Rapids, MI/Cambridge, UK: Eerdmans, 2003); cf. Gathercole, *Preexistent Son*. I have set out my arguments relating to Mark's Christology in more detail in J. G. Crossley, 'Mark's Christology and a Scholarly Creation of a Non-Jewish Christ of Faith', in J. G. Crossley (ed.), *Judaism, Jewish Identities and the Gospel Tradition: Essays in Honour of Maurice Casey* (London: Equinox, forthcoming).

I AM' (Exod. 3.14). But it is well known that ordinary human beings were perfectly capable of using this language too, and in Mark 6.49–50 (cf. Matt. 14.26–28) it is used by Jesus not to identify himself as God but to make the point that he was not a 'ghost'. We might contrast this with John 18.5–6, where it is clear that 'I am' language is used in a dramatic sense because people fall to the ground when Jesus says 'I am (he)'.[26] There is nothing like this in the synoptic versions of the story of Jesus walking on water and, more to the point, the disciples are awestruck in reaction to Jesus' mastery of the elements and *not* because of his use of 'I am' language.

The feeding miracles reflect one of the most elevated figures in Jewish tradition, namely Moses (cf. Exod. 16), and this should warn us that the synoptic versions might not be equating Jesus with God. There are other figures in Jewish tradition who were said to perform similar feeding miracles, such as the biblical character Elisha (2 Kings 4.42–44) and the Jewish holy man Hanina ben Dosa (*b. Ta'an.* 24b–25a).[27] We will come to John's Gospel shortly, where there are clear signs of equating Jesus with God, but for now we might compare the feeding miracles in John 6 because here explicitly controversial claims are made (e.g. John 6.41–42, 52), claims so shocking that John says those among Jesus' own followers had problems (John 6.60–66). There is *nothing* like this in the Synoptic Gospels. More generally, we will see that there are *no* staggering claims made about Jesus being God in the Synoptic Gospels, in sharp contrast to John's Gospel (e.g. John 5.16–18; 20.28). If the writers of the Synoptic Gospels had actually believed such dramatic claims why on earth wouldn't they have made them explicit?

The other major argument made in favour of the synoptic writers believing Jesus was God in the strongest sense is based on Jesus' statement at his trial before the High Priest. Mark's version is as strong as the parallel versions in Matthew and Luke:

> Again the high priest asked him, 'Are you the Messiah, the Son of the Blessed One?' Jesus said, 'I am; and "you will see the Son of Man seated at the right hand of the Power", and "coming with the clouds of heaven." ' Then the high priest tore his clothes and said, 'Why do we still need witnesses? You have heard his blasphemy!'
>
> (Mark 14.61–64; cf. Matt. 26.63–65; Luke 22.67–71)

---

[26] For a comprehensive discussion of the phrase 'I am' with particular reference to John's Gospel but with more wide-ranging relevance, see C. H. Williams, *I Am He* (Tübingen: Mohr-Siebeck, 2000).

[27] See further G. Theissen, *The Miracle Stories of the Early Christian Tradition* (Edinburgh: T&T Clark, 1983), 103–6.

Here there is a charge of blasphemy levelled at Jesus and it is often argued that Jesus defining himself as God's Son in the strongest possible sense is the source of this problem. However, we cannot surmise from the allegation of 'blasphemy' that Jesus was necessarily doing anything as dramatic as making himself equal with God or the like. 'Blasphemy' was broadly defined in early Judaism and could be used in conflict situations between Jews without anyone thinking God's sole authoritative position had been challenged in any way.[28] For example, the first-century Jewish historian Josephus records an old debate over the nature of the position of the High Priest (Josephus, *Ant.* 13.293–295). A Pharisee called Eleazar said that Hyrcanus should give up being the High Priest because his mother was a war captive. He may have had a point (cf. Lev. 21.14) but from the perspective of a Sadducee called Jonathan this was *blasphemy*.

Of course, it still is theoretically possible that Mark 14.64 (cf. Matt. 26.65; Luke 22.71) suggests the blasphemy charge was owing to Jesus implying he was equal with God, equally worthy of worship. But there is a lack of complementary evidence in the Synoptic Gospels that the use of the title 'Son of God' for Jesus implied equality with God. Furthermore, given that in Johns' Gospel there are explicit examples of disputes over the title implying equality with God, it is difficult to see that Mark 14.64 (cf. Matt. 26.65; Luke 22.71) implies something so dramatic.

Of course, this is not to say the Jesus in Matthew, Mark and Luke is not portrayed as the most elevated figure aside from God. On the contrary, the Gospels made some big claims and, as we have seen, developed new ideas about Jesus as *the* Son of Man and *the* Messiah, for instance. And we should not forget that Jesus was a figure who was spectacularly resurrected from the dead. Indeed, the use of the term 'Son' may be strongly elevated by the synoptic writers, even if it does not imply the Second Person of the Trinity, as the following example shows: 'no one knows the Son except the Father, and no one knows the Father except the Son and anyone to whom the Son chooses to reveal him' (Matt. 11.27/Luke 10.22). Clearly, this Jesus-as-Son tradition has Jesus functioning as the unique way to salvation and there are echoes of the elevated figure of Wisdom (cf. Job 28.21–23; Wisd. 9.13, 14, 17; Matt. 11.28–30; Ecclus. 51.23–27; Luke 11.49/Matt. 23.37–39). There is no indication that such a statement was being used in the sense of Jesus being equal with God (the Son *reveals* the Father – nothing more is mentioned) and, in sharp contrast to John's Gospel, there is no evidence of conflict over such claims.

---

[28] Cf. E. P. Sanders, *Jewish Law from the Bible to the Mishnah* (London: SCM Press; Philadelphia: Trinity, 1990), 57–67.

The distinctive contribution of John's Gospel

I have mentioned John's Gospel several times and so some elaboration on the importance of this Gospel is now required. Sometime after 75 CE, John's Gospel takes some of the themes of the preceding decades and makes one of the key presentations of Jesus for Christian theology. The Law is now seriously challenged. John's Gospel talks of 'their [i.e. the Jews'] law' (John 15.25). It has Jesus saying, 'I am the way' (14.6). The reference to Jesus as 'way' probably implies that Jesus is now to be taken as a replacement of Jewish Law, otherwise known as *halakhah*, and more literally translated as 'way'. Moreover, John 14.6 couples this by stressing the only way to salvation, 'No one comes to the Father except through me' (14.6). John takes the earlier Gospel view of Jesus being the only way to the Father (Matt. 11.27/Luke 10.22) but goes one step further in implying that Jesus also takes over the role of the Law.

These general comments are backed up by a specific instance in John's Gospel. In John 5.1–18, Jesus allows an action on the Sabbath that is banned in biblical Law. When Jesus says to the healed man, 'Stand up, take your mat and walk' (5.8), this appears to contradict Jeremiah 17.19–22, which forbids carrying a burden on the Sabbath, and probably underlies the claims of 'the Jews' in John 5.10: 'It is the sabbath; it is not lawful for you to carry your mat.' To hit the point home, John's Jesus says to 'the Jews', 'My father is still working, and I also am working' (John 5.17). We have now moved beyond the debates over the interpretation or expansion of biblical Law to a rejection of putting biblical Law into practice.

John's Gospel attempts to construct Christianity over against Judaism in the story about a leading Jew, teacher of Israel and potential convert, called Nicodemus (John 3). The central idea concerns being 'born again/ from above' (John 3.3). There is some scholarly debate over how we interpret being 'born again/from above' but in general terms we can say it is central to becoming a Christian from the perspective of John's Gospel, and Nicodemus cannot quite bring himself to cross the threshold. It is significant that John's Gospel can contrast this with physical birth, something that is crucial for Jewish ethnicity in particular. In contrast, a more 'spiritual' (re-)birth is not. And so the mistaken Nicodemus cannot understand the idea of being physically reborn for a second time (John 3.4; cf. 3.9). Here we see something like the replacement of Jewish ethnicity as being central to membership of the people of God and replaced with a new Christian idea of being 'born again/from above'.

Bird notes that 'John retains "kingdom" in his repertoire (e.g. John 3.3–8) even if it is not his primary motif' (see page 111) but this use of 'kingdom of God' is nothing like the use in the Synoptic Gospels. Indeed, given John's concern about delays to end times (John 21.21–23), it is highly significant that John's Gospel removes all mention of the future kingdom, a notable feature of the synoptic tradition. This would therefore suggest that we are dealing with Johannine invention, creation and/or a heavy rewriting of the past to deal with burning issues for the Johannine community. The differences with the words and deeds of the historical Jesus and the Synoptic Gospels are just too vast for the Johannine use of 'kingdom' to be considered of historical worth in terms of the life and teachings of Jesus. As this material is so clearly secondary, it is of great use in reconstructing the Johannine Christianity and in this instance its debates with Judaism.

Although John does do away with the practice of at least some aspects of Jewish observance, this does not mean anything goes. First, John's Gospel retains the traditional language of judging people by works or deeds, and this involves accepting Jesus as Son of God (e.g. John 3.19–21; cf. 1.1–18; 3.1–15; 5.19–21). Additionally, the Law is boiled down to the love commandment: 'This is my commandment, that you love one another as I have loved you' (John 15.12). What is interesting about John's use of this commandment is that there is no stress on loving neighbours or loving enemies but it is all about *loving one another* (cf. John 15.13–14). Here we can see the development of an exclusively Christianized identity over against everyone else, a point to which we will shortly return.

More than any other extant work from the first one hundred years of Christian origins, John's Gospel makes the key step toward orthodox Christian monotheism. Precisely what John thought about Jesus is complex and difficult, possibly even contradictory, at least if we were viewing John's Gospel as a systematic Christology, though that would be a bit unfair. We will see that John's Gospel makes some dramatic claims about Jesus being equal with God yet these exist alongside passages where Jesus/the Son appears to be dependent on the Father (John 3.16–17; 5.18–21). It might be possible to reconcile the language of dependency with the language of equality but we need to focus more on the language of equality because here John's Gospel does something dramatic.[29]

Crucially the Gospel opens with a dramatic claim of equality: 'the Word was with God, and the Word was God . . . the Word was made flesh and lived among us' (John 1.1, 14; cf. 1.17). Toward the end of the Gospel, there is another strong hint in the important context of the resurrected

---

[29] See further P. N. Anderson, *The Christology of the Fourth Gospel: Its Unity and Disunity in the Light of John 6* (Tübingen: Mohr-Siebeck, 1996).

Jesus. Here Thomas calls Jesus, 'My Lord and my God' (John 20.28). There are no claims like these in the Synoptic Gospels. But John goes even further in putting such claims in the context of disputes with 'the Jews'.[30] In the Sabbath dispute of John 5, 'the Jews' respond to Jesus' claims by 'seeking all the more to kill him, because he was not only breaking the sabbath, but was also calling God his own Father, thereby making himself equal to God' (John 5.18). The use of the term 'the Jews' is important here because in this passage there have been radical developments made in relation to Jewish thought. We have already seen that in this passage Jesus allows a deliberate breach of the Sabbath, but to add further insult Jesus has made himself equal with God. And from the perspective of John's narrative, it is no surprise that 'the Jews' are portrayed as wanting to kill Jesus for claims that effectively undermine two of the most distinctive features of Judaism.

These controversial claims are found elsewhere in John's narrative. In John 10, Jesus claims, 'The Father and I are one' (10.30). The Jews in John's Gospel react by throwing stones, citing reasons of 'blasphemy because you, though only a human being, are making yourself God' (10.33). The language of 'Son of God' is very important for John's Gospel, and this too goes well beyond what is known within the usual range of the phrase. It is also used in the context of dispute. As 'the Jews' say, 'We have a law, and according to that law he ought to die because he has claimed to be the Son of God' (19.7). Presumably, 'Son of God' is a problem because it is being used in a very 'high' sense (cf. John 19.7). In terms of John's *narrative*, the extremely close association of Jesus with God is a crucial cause of conflict.

There are no Christological disputes like these in the other Gospels. Bird can provide some very general parallels between the Synoptic Gospels and John but runs into serious difficulties when it comes to this really distinctive feature of John's Gospel. His claims that the 'divide between John's purportedly high Christology and the apparent low Christology of Mark is an exaggeration' and that 'The truth [!] is that Mark has a rather high view of Jesus' person that clearly edges towards divinized categories' (see page 111) are so general and rhetorical they effectively function to mask the significant differences between the Synoptic Gospels and John. For a start, we saw in my previous chapter on Paul (see pages 81–85) how categories of the divine can vary, and Bird's analysis lacks this crucial point. We have already commented on Bird's handling of some of the synoptic

---

[30] The precise identity of 'the Jews' in John's Gospel remains controversial. For a recent discussion with bibliography, see W. E. S. North, ' "The Jews" in John's Gospel: Observations and Inferences', in Crossley (ed.), *Judaism, Jewish Identities and the Gospel Tradition*.

material (see also my chapter on the historical Jesus, especially on the so-called 'Johannine thunderbolt' in Matthew and Luke [pages 1–17]).

Further, and I think seriously damaging, comments against Bird's case can be made. Bird says that the 'Father–Son theme that dominates the Fourth Gospel can also be found in the Synoptics' (see page 111) but the Synoptic Gospels simply do not have anything as dramatic as 'The Father and I are one' (John 10.30). This is a serious difference. It is also worth commenting on Bird's far too general comment that 'Even the notion of Jesus as the Son in the sense of being a divine emissary is not limited to John but emerges in the Parable of the Tenants (Mark 12.1–12)' (see page 111). But as I said in the chapter on the historical Jesus, 'In Mark 12.1–12, the language is vague and parabolic, making no claims whatsoever to Jesus' divinity in any strong, or indeed weak, sense' (see page 36). The general Mark 12.1–12 is only similar to the dramatic John 3.17–21 in the sense that there is a son sent, which is not strong enough evidence to suggest much similarity in theological convictions concerning the figure of Jesus.

It is also inconceivable that the Synoptic tradition would have left out passages such as those where Jesus is described as equal with God (John 5.18; 10.33) and where Thomas proclaims Jesus his Lord and God (John 20.28). If John has as much in common with the Synoptic material and contains so much historical material as Bird implies, how on earth did this kind of explicit material about equating Jesus with God pass not one but *three* Gospel writers of roughly the same period? The only plausible solution is that this strong identification of Jesus with God in John's Gospel is a later product unknown to the Synoptic writers.[31]

This would, therefore, suggest that the social situation behind John's Gospel might provide the immediate reasons why the Christians made the fateful step in equating Jesus with God and creating narratives explaining the controversies surrounding this equation. Clearly, there is some problem with 'the Jews' and this is no surprise as making God a human was unheard of in early Judaism. It is worth noting that there is another

---

[31] While I would accept that the Synoptic Gospels give us much more historically useful information about the life and teaching of Jesus, Bird still takes this too far and this is, I think, a direct result of his evangelical worldview. Bird's discussion of Mark 13 (see pages 108–10) is the most problematic non-miraculous example, not least because it does not engage with most of the telling points raised against its historicity. See further Crossley, *Date of Mark's Gospel*, chapter 3. Moreover, Bird effectively says that it is plausible Jesus could have said it in a first-century context. Well, if it is plausible for Jesus then it is plausible for an early follower of Jesus to have invented the story and it is plausible for a Gospel writer to have invented the story. Bird's approach is a problematic way in which to proceed.

related issue of people being cast out of the synagogue for confessing Jesus (John 9.22; 12.42–43; 16.1–2), a conflict that could get deadly (John 16.1–2). In this context we can reasonably suggest that the hugely controversial equation of Jesus with God was a product of conflict with, and identifying against, local Jewish communities.

But we should not forget that for all that John constructs his Christology over against Judaism, John's Gospel emergences from a Jewish context and is relentless in its use of Jewish Scriptures. And John's Gospel would be no fan of idolatry, one of the key defining features of Gentiles from the perspective of Scripture. It is, then, no surprise that Jesus is constructed over against everybody:

> He was in the world, and the world came into being through him; yet the world did not know him. He came to what was his own, and his own people did not accept him. But to all who received him, who believed in his name, he gave power to become children of God, who were born, not of blood or of the will of the flesh or of the will of man, but of God.
>
> (John 1.10–13)

Here we have Christology as a key part of constructing Christian identity. This is well on the way to defining the movement as neither Jewish nor gentile but *Christian*.

Response from Michael F. Bird

Crossley continues to plough the ground in want of sowing his thesis about attitudes towards the Law and Gentiles in early Christianity and about the sharp Christological divergences between John and the Synoptics. It is on these subjects that I shall make my response.

The Jewish Law and the Gospel of Mark

Crossley's dating of the Gospel of Mark to the early 40s CE is a minority view which he maintains largely on the basis that the attitude towards the Law in Mark's Gospel derives from a period when early Christianity was still largely Law-observant. Let me say three things about this.

First, whose standard of Law-observance is he talking about? Does he mean the sectarians from Qumran? Does he mean the Pharisees (if so, which school of the Pharisees: Gamaliel or Shammai)? Does he mean the radical allegorical interpreters that Philo refers to in Alexandria (*Migration* 92)? While there was a diversity of Law-observance and legal interpretation within Judaism, that does not mean that each group thought that each other's interpretation was legitimate and fitted comfortably within the boundaries of a common Judaism. The polemics that Jewish groups vented against each other would suggest otherwise. It would be entirely expected then that a similar context of diversity and debate was inherited by the early Christian movement who had to think through the role of the Law or Torah in regulating their faith and praxis in light of the new eschatological situation that had dawned in the coming of Jesus. In fact the evidence from Acts and Galatians shows that disputes about Torah came to the surface in various debates over food laws, Sabbath keeping and Gentiles. Thus, it is one thing to say that the Gospels make sense as part of intra-Jewish debates about the Torah, but it is quite another thing to suggest that the view of the Torah espoused within the Church during the earliest decades of its existence were regarded *by others* (outsiders or insiders) as exclusively Law-observant. Did the Pharisees who debated with Jesus about hand-washing and purity laws think that he was Law-observant?[32] Would a Jew of the post-70 CE period who read Mark 7.1–23 find nothing objectionable? All of the debates about the Torah in early Christianity can be placed in a Jewish milieu; even Paul's belief that Gentiles do not have to be circumcised has parallels in certain pockets of the Jewish Diaspora (Philo, *QE* 2.2; Josephus, *Ant.* 20.41). Did that stop others from accusing him of anti-nomianism (e.g. Rom. 3.8)? Of course not! If early Christianity was so Law-observant in the 'Jewish' sense that Crossley argues for then why was James the Just (who by all accounts was a righteous, pious and Law-obedient Jewish Christian) put to death on the charge of being a 'Law-breaker' (*Ant.* 20.200)? What is fiercely ironic here is that Crossley in his secular approach is championing the view of taking the sociology, cultural background and history seriously, and yet I would suggest that it is my own evangelical Christian approach that is far more able to engage with the phenomenon of complexity in the origins of the early Church.

Second, I can agree with just about all of Crossley's remarks about purity, Torah and expansive interpretations about hand-washing in Mark 7.1–23; although I think that Mark's editorial comment 'cleansing all food' is a side remark designed for his gentile audience, that is 'for you Gentiles all food is clean'. Crossley has established that the historical Jesus was Law-observant and that Mark portrays him as such. However, using this information to date Mark strikes me as incredibly tenuous. Yes, there were Law-observant Jewish Christians prior to 40 CE and there were also

---

[32] I think it likely that many Pharisees did not think of a hard-and-fast distinction between *Tradition* and *Torah*. While the rabbinic doctrine of 'Two Torahs', one written and one oral, belongs to the second century (*m. 'Abot.* 1.1), a high regard or veneration of the 'traditions of the elders' was known in first-century Pharisaism, as testified by Paul (Gal. 1.14) and Josephus (*Ant.* 13.297, 408).

Law-observant Jewish Christians long after 40 CE in the late first, second, third and fourth centuries. In addition, what was there to stop some followers of Jesus or converts to the Jesus movement adopting views of the Law that were either stricter or laxer than Jesus himself in the 30s–40s CE? Last, the admission of Gentiles into the Church in the mid-40s did not cause a meltdown of Jewish Christian Law-observance and Paul only fought for the freedom of gentile Christians from the Law and not for the freedom of Jewish Christians from the Law. In other words, divergent views of the Law in the early Church probably co-existed side by side from the very beginning and it is incredibly difficult to use Law-observance as a basis for dating Mark.

Third, I think it is worth pointing out the elements of coherence between the Gospel of Mark and the writings of Paul. Mark 7.19c is remarkably similar to Romans 14.14, which reads: 'I know and am persuaded in the Lord Jesus that nothing is unclean in itself; but it is unclean for anyone who thinks it unclean.' So Mark's editorial aside is remarkably similar to Paul's exhortation to Gentiles about food laws. The reference to Jesus as a 'ransom' in Mark 10.45 parallels similar language elsewhere in Paul where he refers to Jesus as providing 'redemption' (e.g. Rom. 3.24; 8.23; 1 Cor. 1.30; Gal. 1.4; Col. 1.14). Mark's use of *euangelion* ('gospel') in Mark 1.1, 14; 13.10; 14.9 is also analogous to Paul's usage (e.g. Rom. 1.1, 16; 1 Cor. 15.1; 1 Thess. 2.2, 4, 8; 3.2). This could be an overlap of a common pool of Christian teaching; it might also indicate that Mark was (at one time or another) within the Pauline circle, and this would have implications for dating Mark and clearly undermine Crossley's thesis.

Christologies of the Gospels

Coming now to the issue of the Christologies of the Gospel of John and the Synoptic Gospels we find here two very different approaches to the Gospels. I think Crossley's argument may be schematized as: (1) John teaches that Jesus is God; (2) the Synoptics are different from John; therefore (3) the Synoptics do not teach that Jesus is God. Let me nuance that by affirming that Crossley is correct when he says that the Synoptic Gospels do not have anything like the material in John which declares Jesus' equality with God (John 5.18), Jesus' oneness with the Father (John 10.30) and Thomas's confession of Jesus as 'my Lord and my God' (John 20.28). But again this does not mean that the Jesus of the Synoptic Gospels is not divine, it only means that they have not expressed his divinity in the categories and language of the Gospel of John.

I shall focus on Mark for the sake of brevity, and I detect here evidence which indicates that Jesus is depicted as intrinsically divine. First, and once again (sigh), in Mark 2.7 the charge of 'blasphemy' and the question 'Who can forgive sins but God alone?' in response to Jesus' forgiveness of the sins of the paralytic still gives Jesus the role of exercising divine prerogatives. What else can possibly be blasphemous about his actions? I still do not find Crossley's explanation in our previous section convincing (see pages 10–11, 36–7). In support of my own position, M. Eugene Boring states:

> The modern 'enlightened' reader cannot understand this story if blasphemy is regarded as only a quaint element of religious paraphernalia of the narrow-minded. It was the most serious of sins, the blurring of the line between Creator and creature, the denial of God's holiness or arrogation of it as one's own . . . The scribes understand themselves as striving on God's behalf and defending the divine prerogative. The uniquely Markan formulation 'the one God' echoes the Shema (Deut 6:4–5) and the monotheistic claim of deutero-Isaiah that God alone forgives sins (Isa 43:25). It reflects the live issue in Mark's own situation of whether devotion to Jesus as Son of God constitutes blasphemy in that it compromises monotheism. While implicit here, the same issue is explicitly developed in John 10:31–39.[33]

Furthermore, the story of Jesus walking on the water in Mark 6.47–52 clearly has an epiphanic flavour. We have Old Testament details of God's power over the sea (Job 9.8; Pss. 77.19; 107.23–32; Isa. 43.16) which cohere with what Jesus is doing here as well as his command to silence the wind and the waves in an earlier passage (Mark 4.36–41). Also, Jesus' reply to the terrified boat crew of disciples, 'Take heart, it is I; do not be afraid' uses the *egō eimi* phrase which is also used as the self-identification of God in the Old Testament (Exod. 3.13–14; Isa. 43.11). Joel Marcus says that 'the overwhelming impact made by our narrative is an impression of Jesus' divinity'.[34]

There are many other examples from the Synoptic Gospels that refer in varying levels of clarity to Jesus' divinity but I do not have space to enter into discussion of them here.[35] Our brief examination of Mark 2.7 and 6.50–51 is enough to show that thinking of Jesus within the sphere of the divine identity was part of the compacted Christology of the Gospel of Mark. Though it may seem self-evident, let me reaffirm that Mark is not John, and Mark does not spell out Jesus' divinity in the same categories or with the same purposes as John. Mark's divine Christology must be judged on its own terms and not according to John's terms. In addition, Crossley

---

[33] Boring, *Mark*, 77.
[34] Joel Marcus, *Mark 1–8* (AB; New York: Doubleday, 2000), 432.
[35] See R. M. Bowman and J. Ed Komoszewski, *Putting Jesus in His Place: The Case for the Deity of Christ* (Grand Rapids, MI: Kregel, 2007).

can dig up as many references and parallels as he likes to show that Jesus might be no more than a semi-divine intermediary figure. The question I have is, which parallels would have been more accessible and able to activate meanings for the author and his audiences? I am all for background studies, but the background I'm reading (especially that derived from the Old Testament) and the actual story-in-the-text itself makes a divine Jesus in the Synoptics not only possible but the most likely explanation of the material before us.

In summary, I think that Crossley has failed to appropriately grasp two elements of the birth of Christianity:

1 Torah observance was a very complicated matter and not everyone would have regarded the Christians as Law-observant (even among themselves).
2 A high Christology did not evolve out of half a century of reflection and debate but belongs to the earliest decades of the early Church.

Further reading

Bauckham, Richard (ed.), *The Gospels for All Christians: Rethinking the Gospel Audiences* (Grand Rapids: Eerdmans, 1996).

Blomberg, Craig, *The Historical Reliability of the Gospels* (2nd edn; Downers Grove, IL: IVP, 2007).

Burridge, Richard, *What are the Gospels? A Comparison with Graeco-Roman Biography* (Cambridge: Cambridge University Press, 1992).

Casey, Maurice, *Is John's Gospel True?* (London: Routledge, 1996).

Davies, W. D. and D. C. Allison, *A Critical and Exegetical Commentary on the Gospel according to Saint Matthew*, 3 volumes (Edinburgh: T&T Clark, 1988–97).

Hengel, Martin, *The Four Gospels and the One Gospel of Jesus Christ* (trans. John Bowden; Harrisburg, PA: Trinity Press, 2000).

Rensberger, D. K., *Overcoming the World: Politics and Community in the Gospel of John* (London: SPCK, 1989).

Stanton, Graham, *Jesus and the Gospel* (Cambridge: Cambridge University Press, 2002).

Theissen, Gerd, *The Gospels in Context: Social and Political History in the Synoptic Tradition* (Edinburgh: T&T Clark, 1992).

Wenham, David, *The Rediscovery of Jesus' Eschatological Discourse* (Gospel Perspectives 4; Sheffield: JSOT Press, 1984).

5

Earliest Christianity

James G. Crossley

With the theology and judgments of Paul and various other figures in the earliest Christian movement, the groundwork for Christianity being a religion that was to define itself aside from the practice of the Law, and was to stress the importance of its highly distinctive Christ-God figure, had been set and would continue to flourish. This did not mean, of course, that Christianity in its many manifestations had suddenly become non-observant of the Law across the board. We know that views associated with Paul had plenty of opposition. Even as late as the late fourth century CE, the theologian John Chrysostom criticized fellow Christians who were observing Jewish festivals. Yet we cannot ignore the fact that non-observance of Jewish practices was one of the key reasons for the spread of Christianity beyond Judaism (indeed, one of the reasons why Chrysostom got so angry). A policy of non-observance was adopted by the orthodox Christians who would come to dominate the Church and set the agendas for the centuries to come.

Similar kinds of comments can be made with reference to Christian forms of monotheism. We have seen that John's Gospel, with some prompting from the Pauline tradition, took the step of distinguishing itself from conventional Jewish monotheism. Again, this does not mean that Christianity in its many manifestations had suddenly adopted the idea that Jesus really was God incarnate. As we will touch upon, trying to establish who Jesus really was in relation to God would become an extremely controversial debate in the first centuries of Christianity.

So far, I have suggested various social reasons (see the sections on Jesus and Paul in particular, pages 1–17, 33–7, 70–85 and 97–102) for the emergence of non-observance in earliest Christianity. I now want to zoom out and look at the broader factors that led to the emergence of Christianity as a major world religion with reference to its distinctive view of God and how the details of previous chapters, including the rise of non-observance, feed into this bigger picture.

Monotheism and empire

Sociologists have argued that a major historical development in ancient agrarian societies (like the Roman Empire) was the development of a universal faith that transcended social boundaries, and in particular the emergence of three new religions: Buddhism, Christianity (through Judaism) and Islam. In contrast with local gods tied to specific peoples these major religions eventually spread across vast stretches of land. These developments, it is claimed, resulted from advances in technology, transportation and trade relations, helped in no small part by empire-building, another major feature of ancient agrarian societies. These material developments all contributed toward a greater awareness of, and connections between, different societies. These various socio-economic changes led to broader overarching divine systems.[1]

What is particularly unusual about this argument is the idea that some form of universal monotheism was not, so it would seem, more widespread in the ancient world and apparently restricted to what were initially fairly obscure groups in the Roman world (Jews and Christians). But if the argument linking empires, communication and monotheism are correct then it would be particularly striking that monotheism had not emerged elsewhere for the obvious reason that major empires and systems of communication had been around for millennia by the time of Christian origins. Alternatively, then, it might follow from this sociological approach that something akin to monotheism or a more universal faith should have been more widespread. We might add to this the widespread idea in the ancient world that the heavenly world was believed to reflect the social structures of this world, heaven as it is on earth if you like. As one text put it:

> The satrap of a Persian or Roman monarch, or ruler or general or governor, yea, even those who fill lower offices of trust or service in the state, would be able to do great injury to those who despised them; and will the satraps and ministers of earth and air be insulted with impunity?
>
> (Origen, *Cels.* 8.35)

If we move away from such generalizations we can actually find some strong arguments put forward for a more widespread view of monotheism at the time of Christian origins. Contrary to popular belief and

---

[1] P. Nolan and G. Lenski, *Human Societies: An Introduction to Macrosociology* (9th edn; Boulder and London: Paradigm, 2004), 169–72. See further R. Stark, *One True God: Historical Consequences of Monotheism* (Princeton and Oxford: Princeton University Press, 2001).

certain Christian scholarly belief, there are examples from the Roman period suggesting that monotheistic ideas might have been more widespread in this era of notable developments in communication and empire-building. But first we need to establish more precisely what we mean by monotheism.

What do we mean by 'monotheism'?

The basic definition of monotheism[2] is the idea of one God. It is now widely recognized that Jewish monotheism around the time of Christian origins involved the idea of one God who ruled the universe and is distinct from all other beings in the cosmic hierarchy. Yet, as we have seen in previous chapters, there were figures that can be generally described as 'divine', 'supernatural', exalted human beings or someone or something holding a significant role in the cosmic hierarchy, often dwelling on the heavenly side of things. These figures include angels and archangels or named figures such as Melchizedek, Metatron, Moses, Michael, messiah and Enoch. Figures such as Wisdom and the Word of God have roles that sometimes appear distinct from God (e.g. Wisdom 18; Ecclus. 24.1–7; Philo, *Conf.* 49; *Det.* 116; *QG* 2.62; 4.97; *Dreams* 1.227–232).

Others too could be thought to have an extremely 'high' role in the divine cosmology or even take on some of God's characteristics, coming close perhaps to full divinity . . . but not quite. For example, among the Dead Sea Scrolls, scriptural texts referring to God as *elohim* (Ps. 82.1) and *el* (Ps. 7.8–9) can be re-interpreted to refer to the mysterious figure of Melchizedek (11Q13 2.10–11) and elsewhere similar language used of God can refer to angels (4Q405). Yet here it is the divine/linguistic *category* that is re-interpreted without entertaining the idea that God's overall role is compromised, as the Dead Sea Scrolls show abundantly. Monotheism functions as a restraining factor on these figures.

While there is much debate over how it got there, Christianity developed its own particular view of monotheism that had to work with the Jewish system and, thanks to the retaining of the Hebrew Bible/Old Testament, this would remain a concern even when Christians were identifying themselves over against Judaism. In this system, Jesus was incorporated

---

[2] The following definition of ancient 'monotheism' is based on my 'Moses and Pagan Monotheism', in *La construction de la figure de Moïse*, ed. T. Römer (Paris: Gabalda, 2008). See further L. W. Hurtado, *One Lord, One God: Early Christian Devotion and Ancient Jewish Monotheism* (Philadelphia: Fortress, 1988), 17–69; M. Casey, *From Jewish Prophet to Gentile God: The Origins and Development of New Testament Christology* (Louisville: Westminster John Knox; Cambridge: James Clarke, 1991), 78–96; J. J. Collins, *The Scepter and the Star: The Messiahs of the Dead Sea Scrolls and Other Ancient Literature* (New York: Doubleday, 1995), 136–94.

into the role of God, at least in the forms of Christianity that would go on to form Western Christian 'orthodoxy'. By incorporating a human being into this role, many non-Christians have been sceptical over the years as to whether Christianity is monotheistic but it is well known that 'orthodox' Christians identify themselves as monotheists. Indeed, whatever form Christianity would take in the ancient world, and for all its disagreements, it did not go toward polytheism (many gods) and remained constrained by monotheism. Like the Jewish system, Christians were able to retain the idea of supernatural or elevated figures that did not compromise their particular view of monotheism. In many ways, the generalized Jewish and Christian views of monotheism remain and should be generally familiar. For example, there are many people who believe in angels, saints and/or an elevated role of the Virgin Mary without compromising the idea that God is the ultimate ruler.

It is for such reasons that it is helpful to avoid providing an analytical definition of monotheism in its strongest sense: such a definition can be of more harm than good and can end up excluding too much of relevance, including, it might be added, much of early Jewish and Christian thought. Instead, when I speak of 'monotheism', I will be using it in the sense scholars of early Judaism and Christian origins use it: God is above all. There may be some kind of emanations of this God in some form; and there are beings that can be labelled divine but who do not compromise the overarching God. When the term 'monotheism' is used in this sense we can see that it is extremely well attested outside Judaism and Christianity.

Pagan monotheism

Recently some classicists have been challenging the view that Christianity via Judaism brought monotheism to the wider world which, until that point, was largely polytheistic. In fact it has been suggested that Christianity was partly successful because it shared so much in common with more widely held views on monotheism.[3] Various monotheistic movements across the Roman Empire have been noted by scholars, from Rome to Egypt, to the famous eastern Mediterranean 'cult' of what is generally labelled Theos Hypsistos, the highest and frequently abstract god. A common occurrence is the idea that the Jewish and/or Christian concept of God is not any different from pagan theologies, as opponents of Christianity pointed out. Celsus, for instance, claimed with reference to Jewish views of God, 'that it makes no difference whether you call the highest being Zeus, or

---

[3] P. Athanassiadi and M. Frede (eds), *Pagan Monotheism in Late Antiquity* (Oxford: Oxford University Press, 1999).

Zen, or Adonai, or Sabaoth, or Ammoun like the Egyptians, or Pappaeus like the Scythians' (Origen, *Cels.* 5.41). The second-century CE Christian Justin Martyr was aware his opponents would latch on to the idea that monotheism was found in the works of the Greek philosopher Plato (*c.* 427–347 BCE): 'For while we say that all things have been produced and arranged into a world by God, we shall seem to utter the doctrine of Plato' (Justin Martyr, *1 Apol.* 20). Indeed, monotheistic trends have long been noted in ancient interpretations of Plato, a central figure for philosophers in the Roman period, and Christian theology would famously proceed to incorporate Platonic ideas.

Another obvious example of possible pagan monotheism, or something so universal that it is comparable with monotheism, would be the Stoics who believed that an unchanging eternal divine power governed the entire universe (see e.g. Plutarch, *Comm. not.* 1051e–f, 1052a; 1077e). Yet another pagan idea that has traits in common with monotheistic understandings, and has been noted by New Testament scholars, is the cult of the emperor, notably developing around the time of Christian origins and stressing the emperor's world rule, with a divine mandate transcending alternative heaven and earthly powers. Whether this is technically monotheism is in some ways academic because its universalism means we are at least dealing with something comparable. It is for good reason that a great deal of recent scholarship has seen the rise of Christ-devotion as a movement paralleling the emperor cult. As Gerd Theissen put it:

> In both connections one found forms of solidarity which transcended the regions, a promise of a change of life, a cohesion which transcended classes, and a certain privilege which others who lived without such a relationship to the 'ruler of the world' did not have.[4]

Interestingly, some ancient pagans could describe their divine system in the same way as Jewish and Christian monotheism(s) have been described by ancients and moderns alike, in that there is the idea of one God over all and upon whom everything depends. Yet at the same time, lesser divinities or emanations are allowed their place in the supernatural system. This major similarity is conveniently summed up by the pagan philosopher referred to by Macarius Magnes (*c.* 400 CE):

> At any rate, if you say that angels stand before God who are not subject to feeling and death, and immortal in their nature, whom we ourselves speak of as gods, because they are close to the Godhead, why do we dispute about

---

[4] G. Theissen, *A Theory of Primitive Christian Religion* (London: SCM Press, 1999), 53–4.

a name? . . . The difference therefore is not great, whether a man calls them gods or angels, since their divine nature bears witness to them . . .

(*Monogenes* 4.21)

Monotheism and the empires

Looking at pre-Roman periods we can see how such beliefs had a long history and this is no surprise given the long history of empires in the Mediterranean and Ancient Near East. In terms of the development of Jewish monotheism it is worth recalling also the location of Palestine and its environs. Even as early as the second millennium BCE the area also functioned as a crossroads for trade routes between east and west, from the Aegean to the Punjab. It is further worth recalling the inhabitants of the area of Palestine and their historic encounters with empire. Palestine was constantly surrounded by the material longings of empire after empire after empire: the Egyptians, Assyrians, Babylonians, Persians and, later, the Greeks and Romans.

Tendencies in the direction of monotheism have been detected in the Ancient Near East as early as the second millennium BCE, especially in Egypt where links between monotheistic traits and the development of empire and international contact have long been noted.[5] In fact using Ancient Near Eastern empires is a particularly useful way of analysing the problem because, as noted, political and religious systems tended to mirror one another in the ancient world. Moreover, there is an obvious imperialistic element to certain ancient Near Eastern accounts of the divine world. It was a fairly standard procedure, it seems, to take away statues of a defeated god as spoils of war (cf. e.g. *ANET* 286, 287, 293, 299, 302, 304). With the Neo-Assyrian and Neo-Babylonian empires there is the idea of a god of all gods (e.g. Ashur, Marduk, Sin), conquered gods demoted, and thereby reflecting the conquered status of the respective territory. So here we have a kind of structural head role into which whatever deity was in the ascendancy could conveniently slot (cf. e.g. *ANET* 307, 310, 311, 312). It is no coincidence that the term 'king of the gods' was common in the ancient Near East, dating from at least the second millennium.

But perhaps the most widespread vigorous development towards a more universal monotheistic worldview arises with the emergence of the massive Persian Empire in the fifth century BCE. As might be expected from such a vast empire, the Persians advanced the monetary system, legal administration and postal networks. There were notable linguistic devel-

---

[5] Commentary on *ANET* 367. See also Donald B. Redford, *Egypt, Canaan, and Israel in Ancient Times* (Princeton: Princeton University Press, 1992), 209–10, 380.

opments as Aramaic was the widespread language of the Persian Empire, with major precursors under the Assyrians and the Neo-Babylonians. The Persians also provided what was to be a major development of the travel and communication system: the enormous Royal Road stretching from Susa in the east to the area around Sardis and Ephesus on the western edge of Asia Minor (e.g. Herodotus 5.52–53).

And in this general context we have a major movement toward a universalistic monotheism in the rise of Zoroastrianism, the religion emerging at the heart of the Persian system, with Ahura Mazda eventually becoming the major deity.[6] And, lest we forget, this was a religious movement that not only dates back centuries before the Persian Empire but also continued to flourish in the East through the time of Christian origins and, more generally, right up to the present day.

Persian religion at the time of the origins of Judaism developed ideas that are entirely compatible with the definition of monotheism I have given. The Persians have the idea of Ahura Mazda as the one eternal creator God (cf. e.g. Naqsh-e Rostam A 1–8; *ANET* 316). Other supernatural beings, at least on the side of good, were firmly subordinate to, or emanations of, Ahura Mazda, similar to the ideas we saw in early Jewish monotheistic thought. Similarly, Zoroastrianism is often said to be a dualistic (two opposing forces) system, but a belief that good would triumph is certainly present. Of course, it can be argued that dualism is not technically monotheism but, as has long been recognized, it seems that ideas of this variety were taken up in staunchly monotheistic Jewish thought (e.g. apocalyptic literature and the Dead Sea Scrolls: cf. 1QS; CD; 1QM). Yet the similarities may be even closer; the Greek writer Plutarch (46–127 CE), citing a much earlier source (*c.* 300 BCE), talks of less balance between the two forces (e.g. Plutarch, *Is. Os.* 46–47). There were two sides, but one *would* win.

The connections between developing monotheistic trends and empire are particularly clear in a fifth-century BCE inscription:

> Ahuramazda is the great god who gave us this earth, who gave that sky . . . who made Xerxes, the great king, the king of kings, the king of (all) countries (which speak) all kinds of languages, the king of this (entire) big and far(-reaching) earth . . . These are the countries – in addition to Persia – over which I am king under the 'shadow' of Ahuramazda, over which I hold sway . . . May Ahuramazda protect me, my family and these countries from all evil.
>
> (*ANET* 316–17)

---

[6] For an overview of ancient Persian religion, see P. Briant, *From Cyrus to Alexander: A History of the Persian Empire* (Winona Lake: Eisenbrauns, 2002), 240–54.

One notable development with the Persian Empire that remains firmly within the boundaries of monotheism as defined above was the equation of local or conquered deities with Ahura Mazda. This is not only one logical outworking of the universalism of the Persian variety but also a pragmatic measure with such a vast empire. The magnificently general 'the God of Heaven' in the Old Testament/Hebrew Bible (cf. Gen. 24.3; 2 Chron. 36.22–23; Ezra 1.2; Neh. 1.5; 2.4; Isa. 54.5; Jer. 10.11; Jonah 1.19) probably reflects Persian ideas. For example, there are the biblical instances of a decree from the Persian emperor Cyrus in 2 Chron. 36.22–23 and Ezra 1.1–4 (cf. Ezra 7.12–26) where the authority of Cyrus comes from 'the Lord, the God of heaven' who has given Cyrus 'all the kingdoms of the earth' and enabled the development of the Jerusalem cult. From the outside, the fifth-century BCE Greek historian Herodotus claims that it is not the custom of the Persians 'to make and set up statues and temples and altars, but those who do such things they think foolish, because, I suppose, they have never believed the gods to be like men, as the Greeks do; but they call the whole circuit of heaven Zeus, and to him they sacrifice on the highest peaks of the mountains' (Herodotus 1.131).

The influence of Persian religion on Judaism has long been noted – the parallels are simply too numerous to be simply coincidental – and it is particularly noteworthy that strongly universal monotheistic thought explicitly developed in Persian-period Judaism. It could be speculated that with the head(s) of Israelite divine hierarchy apparently defeated on the ground more than once, ideas of the divine allowing defeat (after defeat) as punishment (cf. e.g. Deut. 11) only needed specific changing circumstances to make the shift to a more universalistic monotheism where this god is in control of all. There is also the problem that, after the Babylonian exile, there is no king and so Judaism has God to take over this role. The emergence of a more universalistic system in an empire that could equate local or conquered cults with its own and show a significant degree of tolerance may also have been a major point in the emergence of Jewish monotheism, thereby supporting recent claims that the full-blown Jewish-style of monotheism emerged much later than conventionally thought, namely, in the Persian period (fifth and fourth centuries BCE). As I say, this is speculative but the key point is that Judaism was vigorously developing its own view of monotheism in the context of empire and it was firmly established several centuries before Christian origins.

The Greeks also had one eye on the Persians, and with their own political and cultural imperialism the Greeks also witnessed major developments in monotheistic-style thought. And, as we saw with Herodotus

(1.131), they were not ignorant of the similarities with Persian thought. Most famously, toward the end of the fourth century BCE, Alexander the Great not only conquered the Persian Empire but also effectively inaugurated a period of massively wide-ranging Hellenistic cultural expansion. This included the development of Greek cities, for example, alongside developments in international trade and what would become a widely used language, common Greek. The dissemination of ideas associated with Plato, which, as we saw, had strong monotheistic tendencies, went hand-in-hand with this expansionism.

Indeed, there had already been other significant shifts away from the hierarchical models of the gods, associated with Homer and Hesiod, to philosophical monotheism. It has often been remarked that the first 'unmoved mover' in the work of the fourth-century BCE Greek philosopher, Aristotle, equated with 'God', is at least compatible with monotheism, if not significantly monotheistic (e.g. *Metaphysics* L 7, 1072b 13–14, 25–30; 8, 1074a 36–37; 10, 1075a 11). Moreover, Xenophanes of Colophon (*c.* 570–480 BCE) had already made strides in the direction of monotheism (e.g. B 1, 15–16, 24–26). It seems that monotheistic tendencies were also understood in Aristotle's reception of Xenophanes: 'But Xenophanes, the first exponent of the Unity . . . gave no definite teaching, nor does he seem to have grasped either of these conceptions of unity; but regarding the whole material universe he stated that the Unity is God' (Aristotle, *Metaph.* 986b, 20).

Early monotheistic-like traits are found elsewhere in Greek traditions. In fact, as the strongest god of the typically polytheistic Greek pantheon, Zeus lends himself to a potentially monotheistic role. Aeschylus (525–456 BCE) not only makes a close association between Zeus and Fate (*Eum.* 1044) but can talk of Zeus in ways certainly not alien to Jewish and Christian concepts of God,

> Lord of lords, most blessed among the blessed, power most perfect among the perfect, O blessed Zeus, hear! And from your offspring ward off in utter abhorrence the lust of men, and into the purple sea cast their blackbenched madness.   (*Supplices* 524–30; cf. 599, 823; *Ag.* 160–66; 1487–88)

It is telling that the renowned expert in this area, Walter Burkert, can describe the rise of Greek philosophical religion in terms that once again echo the broader sociological developments of monotheism outlined above:

> [T]here is the still growing independence of the individual in a civilisation marked by economic growth: Greeks have conquered the Mediterranean, new colonies springing up, trade and industry are on the increase, and Greek forms are being imitated everywhere. Possibilities for development

are offered to the individual which are no longer confined to family, city, or tribe . . .[7]

Assimilating local gods to one great god is something found in the Graeco-Roman world. A good example of how this internationalist practice relates to developments in monotheism is the vigorous development of the Egyptian goddess Isis of whom all other goddesses across the Mediterranean and beyond could be seen as mere manifestations (Apuleius, *Metam.* 11.5). Similar developments in the direction of monotheism include the ways in which local deities were identified with the supreme god Zeus. In 2 Maccabees 6.1–2 we read of an imposed version of the practice, 'to pollute the temple in Jerusalem and to call it the temple of Olympian Zeus, and to call the one in Gerizim the temple of Zeus-the-Friend-of-Strangers, as did the people who lived in that place' (6.2). It may well be no coincidence in the light of the rise of monotheism with broader human interaction that Zeus is identified as the friend of the stranger, a great unifying figure.

It may be tempting for some to label many of these Greek and all the other non-Greek ideas discussed above, in terms of, for instance, a divine hierarchy rather than monotheism in the strongest possible sense of one God and no other. That would no doubt be a legitimate thing to do, but the fact remains that we are much closer and the ideas are structurally similar to the monotheism conventionally associated with early Judaism and Christianity, thereby highlighting the restrictive nature of the harder definitions. In fact, if we use the definition of monotheism given here, then these Greek views are as monotheistic as Jewish and Christian theologies. Indeed, in a Jewish context, monotheistic similarities with the broader Hellenized world were not missed. The Hellenized Jewish *Letter of Aristeas* has the gentile Aristeas claiming that Jews worship the God who is the creator and overseer of all while Gentiles such as himself refer to this divine figure as Zeus or Dis (*Ep. Arist.* 16; cf. 140).

It should be stressed that the comments made here are also *qualifying* the view that Christians and Jews virtually invented monotheism. This means that we should not lose sight of the polytheistic tendencies across the pagan world at the time of Christian origins. They were certainly still present. Yet in light of all the above evidence from the Ancient Near East and the Mediterranean – evidence covering centuries before, during and after the time of Christian origins – monotheism, or at least the idea of a universal faith, was deeply embedded and part of long-term trends in the ancient

---

[7] W. Burkert, *Greek Religion* (Oxford: Blackwell, 1985), 306.

world, particularly with the development of empires. These long-term trends, *in part*, allowed Christianity to develop as a religion in its own right. These were also long-term trends which Christianity had to negotiate, a task made more complicated by the fact that a human, Jesus, was at the heart of the Christian faith, alongside a god inherited from a long-standing monotheistic system in Judaism. So the question now becomes, in what ways did Christianity negotiate the long-term monotheistic trends in the ancient world?

The origins of Christian monotheism

As well as inheriting deeply embedded monotheistic tendencies from Judaism, Christianity also had the advantage of emerging from a religion that had communities and networks right across the ancient world. In this light, it could be countered: why did Judaism not spread to become the religion of empire in this context of wider developing monotheism? There was certainly an interest in Jewish monotheism in the pagan world, as we can see in the following example:

> Some who have had a father who reveres the Sabbath, worship nothing but the clouds, and the divinity of the heavens . . . and in time they take to circumcision. Having been wont to flout the laws of Rome, they learn and practise and revere the Jewish law, and all that Moses handed down in his secret tome . . .   (Juvenal, *Sat.* 14.96–103)

However, although some have detected missionary tendencies in early Judaism, there was little concern to spread the message far and wide. Additionally, as we saw in the chapter on Paul, one stumbling block to gentile conversion would have been circumcision for males (see page 75). Closely related was a major stress on ethnicity and kinship in early Judaism, being born a Jew and marrying others also born Jewish. The shift away from physical kinship in earliest Christianity, tied in with a willingness to associate with 'gentile sinners' and shifts in Law-observance, opened the way for Christians to exploit the existing wide-ranging Jewish networks and spread a monotheistic religion.

At this point it is worth retracing some of the steps taken in my sections of this book. We have seen that one of the important reasons for the development of Christianity away from a Law-observant Jewish movement to a movement where some were no longer observing major biblical commandments was caused by differing levels of practice, inevitable in the conversion of households and the loosening attachments of friends of friends of friends, all through pre-existing social networks. This link, first to Gentiles interested in Judaism, was made primarily through the structural similarity of Jesus' association with 'the sinners', itself a product of socio-economic changes in Galilee as Jesus was growing up (e.g. the destabilizing effects of the rebuilding/building of Sepphoris and Tiberias). Christianity, as many others have also pointed out, was able to exploit pre-existing social networks, including pre-existing Jewish *monotheistic* social networks.

If the above analysis is anywhere near correct, it potentially provides another context in which the deification of Jesus can be analysed. It is sometimes argued that exalted figures (e.g. angels, Enoch, Moses), such as we have noted here and in the chapters on Paul and the Gospels (see pages 116–32), were a major driving force behind the initial exaltation of Jesus. But these figures fall short of providing an explanation of the full deification of an individual. So how do we explain the key decisions toward the final step of fully deifying Jesus? Significantly, we have a Christian movement which has clear indications of differentiation from Judaism but which also had its beliefs (such as Christology) grounded in Jewish thought. As is sometimes asked, what happens when an increasing number of Gentiles, with a whole host of differing influences through pre-existing social networks (cf. e.g. 1 Cor. 8—10; Gal. 4.8; 1 John 5.21), including knowledge of human beings deemed divine in the pagan world (e.g. Roman emperors), start reading a passage such as Philippians 2.6–11? We might now add to this, what happens with those gentile Christians interested in Jewish monotheism, but identifying themselves not only over against Judaism but also in contrast to various pagan systems where long-term trends in monotheism had also been developing?

It has been argued (rightly in my opinion), that the big step toward deifying Jesus after he had been so heavily exalted and the shift towards a distinctive Christian monotheism only requires a changing social situation and the perception of socio-ethnic alienation from the Jewish community, just like the conflicts underlying John's Gospel.[8] Here we can recall the details in my section on the Gospels, where it was argued that the controversial deification of Jesus occurred in the context of a dispute with people identified as 'the Jews', a dispute that was potentially deadly (see pages 70–85, 97–102 and 116–32). We might add to this that with John's Gospel keen to identify itself over against 'the world' as well as 'the Jews', the broader monotheistic tendencies in the ancient world could again have contributed to a situation where new and distinctive ways of developing monotheism were being created.

---

[8] M. Casey, *From Jewish Prophet to Gentile God: The Origins and Development of New Testament Christology* (Louisville: Westminster John Knox; Cambridge: James Clarke, 1991), 114–15.

But John's Gospel was hardly the end of the story. The Gospel itself had some struggle to make it into the canon as its view of Jesus, so argued the early third-century Christian Gaius of Rome, seemed *too* heretical, written as it was, thought Gaius, by the 'heretic' Cerinthus (Epiphanius, *Pan.* 51.4.5), a point also raised in Bird's section on the Gospels (see pages 103–116). More immediately, some of the Christological claims made in John were too much and constructed too heavily over against Judaism for some among the Christian movement, as John's Gospel is only too aware (John 6.60–66). Christianity, and its take on the deification of Jesus, would have a variety of strands going in different directions, ranging from those who did not have such an exalted view of Jesus (e.g. the group called the 'Ebionites') to those who incorporated Jesus into their own intricately developed supernatural system (e.g. groups conventionally labelled 'Gnostic').

Yet such groups would not win the day in terms of what would go on to become orthodox belief. Groups like the Ebionites may well have been too easily identifiable as 'Jewish' to make Christianity distinctive whereas those usually identified as 'Gnostic' perhaps had too much emphasis on remaining internal-looking, secretive and being sectarian in nature to take on a more wide-ranging official status. I am, of course, speculating, but what we do know is that, in terms of longevity and power, it was those who are sometimes called proto-orthodox – those whose heirs would go on to develop orthodox Christian theology (at least in the West) – who would be the ones to go on and be among history's winners.

The construction of distinctive Christian theology with the fully deified Christ at its heart (at least among proto-orthodox Christians) would be a hugely important factor in identifying the Christian movement as distinctive. The dramatic spread of Christianity among friends of friends of friends through a variety of social networks, as Rodney Stark has shown,[9] and as this chapter and previous chapters have touched upon, put Christianity in a demographically strong position. And this victory was virtually sealed in the early fourth century CE when Constantine became the first Christian Roman emperor and the Council of Nicaea was held (325 CE). It was at this wide-ranging council that the details of Jesus' divinity were further hammered out for the Church across the Roman world. The Christian god, with whom Jesus was identified, had now to become a suitable god for the empire.

But that is not quite the end of the story either. There was a final pagan flourish at the highest level when Julian became Roman emperor (361–3

---

[9] Rodney Stark, *The Rise of Christianity: A Sociologist Reconsiders History* (Princeton, NJ: Princeton University Press, 1996).

CE), renounced his Christian past and attempted to turn the Christian tide. No surprise, then, that Christian tradition would leave him with the title Julian the Apostate. This is not only interesting for its own sake but it also shows that the links between empire and monotheism are not simply an academic guess by sociologists of ancient religion. Choosing the right god was in so many ways central to Roman imperialism.[10]

In late antiquity, arguably the major assessment of Jewish, Christian and pagan beliefs concerning the divine, and usually centred on a comparison of Moses with Plato, is that of Julian. It has been questioned whether we should define Julian as a monotheist, but if we use the conventional definition of monotheism usually applied to Judaism and Christianity then it should be quite clear that Julian is as monotheistic as Jews and Christians. Julian's theological and philosophical assumptions are a mixture of interpretations of Plato, sun-worship and popular cultic practices. Julian accepted the many gods of pagan thought but for him they were aspects or emanations of the great divine system as the following example suggests:

> The sun which is visible to our eyes is the likeness of the intelligible and invisible sun, and again the moon which is visible to our eyes and every one of the stars are likenesses of the intelligible. Accordingly Plato knows of those intelligible and invisible gods which are immanent in and coexist with the creator himself and were begotten and proceeded from him. Naturally, therefore, the creator in Plato's account says 'gods' when he is addressing the invisible beings and 'of gods' meaning by this, evidently, the visible gods. And the common creator of both these is he who fashioned the heavens and the earth and the sea and the stars, and begat in the intelligible world the archetypes of these.[11]

Julian continued to support local cults and so his monotheism can be seen as an intellectual justification of the traditional cults, a view not uncommon in pagan thought.

As with many monotheistic disputes, the big problems arise at the level of detail. Julian simply does not like the way his Christian opponents define 'monotheism'. And for Julian to out-think his Christian opponents over the issue of true monotheism, he has to fire at Moses because Moses was

---

[10] See further Crossley, 'Moses and Pagan Monotheism'. For a more general discussion of Julian's thought, see R. Smith, *Julian's Gods: Religion and Philosophy in the Thought and Action of Julian the Apostate* (London: Routledge, 1995).

[11] *Against the Galileans* 65b–c, *The Works of the Emperor Julian*, ed. and trans. W. C. Wright (London: Loeb, 1913–23).

the monotheist *par excellence* in the Judeo-Christian tradition, just as Plato was for many pagans. Julian therefore suggests a point-by-point comparison between Moses and Plato to show whose monotheism is the right monotheism for the empire.

Predictably enough Moses comes out a poor second on all the big issues. For example, Moses is said not to give a proper account of the god behind creation, and this is seen as a good sign of his general inconsistency. This is particularly important because with Julian there is always one eye on the most suitable divine system for the empire. Julian holds a common view that there are parallels between the divine world and the earthly world. He is very clear that each group of people in the world has its own particular god with local king-like authority but dependent on the one overarching God (e.g. *Against the Galileans* 143ab). In this context, Julian raises the problems of the supposed universal god of Moses being tied to a specific group of people. And, of course, this meant Moses' god would be an unsuitable god for the *empire*:

> [I]t is natural to think that the God of the Hebrews was not the begetter of the whole universe with lordship over the whole, but rather, as I said before, that he is confined within limits, and that since his empire has bounds we must conceive of him as only one of the crowd of other gods.
>
> (*Against the Galileans* 100c; cf. 143a–e)

But if Moses was bad then the Christians hardly constituted an improvement. In fact the Christians, Julian's real opponents behind all the analysis, do not even come up to Moses' standards of monotheism (*Against the Galileans* 290b–e; cf. 146a–b). Crucially, for Julian, the Christians contradict their monotheistic mentor by worshipping two or three gods. Note the reference to the key monotheistic texts of Deuteronomy:

> Moses, therefore, utters many sayings to the following effect and in many places: 'you shall fear the Lord your God and him only shall you serve (Deut. 6.13; 10.20).' How then has it been handed down in the Gospels that Jesus commanded: 'Go therefore and teach all the nations, baptising them in the name of the Father, and of the Son, and of the Holy Spirit (Mt. 28.19)', if they were not intended to serve him also?
>
> (*Against the Galileans* 290e–291a)

So, from the perspective of Julian, how can the Christians *possibly* be suitable monotheists and how could the god of the Christians *possibly* be fit to be the god of the empire?

But unfortunately for Julian and all his intellectual labours, the Christian god was to win out and be the god of the empire. Needless to say, this construction of the divine was a far cry from the ordinary human figure of the historical Jesus, active all those years ago in an obscure part of the empire, and a point that has not been lost on many Christians. But making Jesus more-or-less the god of Rome would arguably be the most important factor in Christianity becoming a world religion to this day.

Michael F. Bird

The King James Bible often uses the translation 'peculiar people' or 'peculiar possession' to designate Israel (Exod. 19.5; Deut. 14.2; 26.18; Ps. 135.4) and the Church (Titus 2.14; 1 Pet. 2.9). The word 'peculiar' is not meant in the sense of being odd or weird, but rather it is used in the sense of being distinct, unique and different. This highlights the chosen-ness of God's people. Israel and the renewed Israel that is the Church are the special possession of God with a unique mission in this world: to be a kingdom of priests, the light of the world and the salt of the earth. In the early centuries of the Church, Christians stood out for a variety of reasons: they worshipped only one God; they identified this God with Jesus; they refused to worship the emperor; they had members from different races and classes; and they didn't expose infants. Christians lay somewhere between a religious anomaly and a subversive threat to the social order in the eyes of both Jews and Pagans. In the Jewish context, Christians could be slandered as heretics and expelled from Jewish syn-agogues (John 9.22; 12.42) for exceeding the limits of common Judaism. Pagans in contrast could denounce Christians as riff-raff blowing in from the Orient and accuse them of fostering civil unrest, advocating a perni-cious superstition and promoting atheism. The first major apologist to respond to these accusations was Luke. According to Luke, Jesus and the Church are the fulfilment rather than the annulment of God's promises to Israel. Jesus is the one who will bring redemption (Luke 24.21) and times of refreshing for Israel (Acts 3.20). I find it remarkable that *almost* every Roman official in the book of Acts is portrayed as being either corrupt or incompetent. I think that Luke is deliberately snubbing his nose at one of the standard pagan criticisms of early Christianity, that Christians are somehow a threat to the justice of Rome. Luke's response is that, for some within the empire, Roman justice is not quite so just. Thus, if we are to understand the origins of Christianity then we must wrestle with how it forged a unique identity from its Jewish roots and how it developed in its Roman context.

Why did Christianity become predominantly gentile?

Historian Robin Lane Fox contends that histories of Christianity usually tell a story of unimpeded growth and frequently omit the complexities and setbacks of its emergence. Fox says: 'Nonetheless, Christians spread and increased: no other cult in the empire grew at anything like the same speed, and even as a minority, the Christians' success raises serious questions about the blind spots in pagan cult and society.'[12] Despite the fact that studies of the emergence of the Church are often romanticized and embellished with nostalgia, Christianity spread quite rapidly across the Mediterranean, traversing significant geographic, ethnic and social barriers in the process. Martin Hengel writes that: 'The irresistible expansion of Christian faith in the Mediterranean world during the first 150 years is the scarlet thread running through any history of primitive Christianity.'[13] How did this happen? The short answer is: Jesus and Paul. Jesus was a Jew, he ministered to other Jews, his closest followers were Jews, and Jesus never embarked on a worldwide preaching tour. In the Gospels we are given solid indications that he specifically limited his ministry to Israel (Matt. 10.5b–6; 15.24; Mark 7.27; cf. Rom. 15.8). And yet we find that a mission to Gentiles was launched in his name and a call to mission appears to have been part of the resurrection experiences of the disciples (Matt. 28.19–20; Luke 24.47–48; Acts 1.8). There are hints in the Gospels that Jesus anticipated his mission and ministry as having important ramifications for the Gentiles (e.g. Matt. 8.5–11; Mark 11.15–17; Luke 4.25–27). In my estimation Jesus' intention was to renew and restore Israel, in order that a restored Israel would bring God's salvation to the whole world. Since this restoration was already being realized in Jesus' ministry, it was becoming possible for Gentiles to share in the benefits of Israel's restoration already. What is more, Jesus understood himself and his disciples as the beginning of the new temple and the vanguard of the renewed Israel who would appropriate for themselves the mission of Israel and the temple in being a light to the nations. Thus, a gentile mission is implied in the aims and intentions of Jesus and was pursued in a transformed environment by members of the early Jesus movement.[14]

---

[12] Robin Lane Fox, *Pagans and Christians in the Mediterranean World from the Second Century A.D. to the Conversion of Constantine* (2nd edn; London: Penguin 2005), 271.

[13] Martin Hengel, *Between Jesus and Paul: Studies in the Earliest History of Christianity* (trans. John Bowden; London: SCM Press, 1983), 48.

[14] Michael F. Bird, *Jesus and the Origins of the Gentile Mission* (LNTS; LHJS; London: T&T Clark, 2006).

In the early Church the inclusion of the Gentiles was never a matter of dispute – it was the basis of their inclusion that prompted division: did Gentiles need to take on the Jewish Law in order to enter the Church (cf. Acts 15; Gal. 2)? It was largely Paul and like-minded Jewish Christians (and not Paul alone!) who secured the freedom of gentile converts from the Law and removed what was the single largest stumbling block that prevented Gentiles joining a Jewish sect.

In addition, the energy and drive of Paul to reach the Gentiles from 'Jerusalem and as far around as Illyricum' (Rom. 15.19) and ambitiously even on to Spain (Rom. 15.24, 28), underscores his determination to make Christ known where he had not previously been preached (Rom. 15.20–21). It is also likely that Paul expected his converts to replicate to some degree his evangelistic efforts in their own respective contexts (e.g. Phil. 1.14) and one of the offices that emerged in the early Church was that of the 'evangelist' (Acts 21.8; Eph. 4.11; 2 Tim. 4.5). Martin Goodman asserts: 'Christianity spread primarily because many Christians believed that it was positively desirable for non-Christians to join their faith and accrete to their congregations.'[15] There was undoubtedly an assortment of social, cultural and historical factors that accelerated and assisted the Christian expansion in the eastern Mediterranean, such as the widespread usage of the Greek language in urban centres, a network of roads and sea ports, as well as increased travel and trade.[16] But a distinctive characteristic of the Christian movement seems to be a desire to reach out to others, and this gained them a bad reputation. So much so that Paul and his companions in Acts are accused of turning the world upside down (Acts 17.6).

Why did Christianity split from Judaism?

Christianity originally started out as a messianic sect within Judaism and eventually became a religion separate from Judaism. Judaism itself was diverse and pluriform in the ancient world but there came a moment when followers of Jesus could no longer be accommodated (or would no longer accommodate themselves) within the matrix of Jewish belief and practice.

---

[15] Martin Goodman, 'Jewish Proselytizing in the First Century,' in *The Jews among Pagans and Christians in the Roman Empire*, eds J. Lieu, J. L. North and T. Rajak (London: Routledge, 1992), 53–78 (53).

[16] Adolf von Harnack, *The Expansion of Christianity in the First Three Centuries* (2 vols; trans. James Moffatt; London: Williams and Norgate, 1904–5); A. D. Nock, *Conversion: Old and the New in Religion from Alexander the Great to Augustine of Hippo* (Oxford: Oxford University Press, 1933), 187–211; Rodney Stark, *The Rise of Christianity: A Sociologist Reconsiders History* (Princeton, NJ: Princeton University Press, 1996).

This resulted in what has been called the 'parting of the ways' between Judaism and Christianity. On this subject a few caveats are in order. The gradual split between Judaism and Christianity is a complex one and the various details are mooted in scholarship.[17] Relations between Jews and Christians varied in time and location and it is safe to say that there never was a clean break between the two groups. This is evidenced by the fact that Ignatius of Antioch (*Magn.* 10.3; Phild. 6.1), Justin Martyr (*Dial.* 47) and John Chrysostom (*Adv. Jud.* 2.3; 3.5) all bear witness to Christians who remained in some relationship with Jews and Judaism in the first four centuries of the Christian era. The Neronian persecution of Christians in Rome in the mid-60s CE clearly distinguished Jews from Christians. In contrast, the pagan author Celsus could say that there was not a dime of difference between Jews and Christians (Origen, *Cels.* 3.1).

Over the course of time, however, there were several watershed events that led to the eventual split. First, an underrated factor that caused the parting was the ministry of the historical Jesus.[18] I am not suggesting that Jesus was trying to wipe aside Judaism and replace it with Christianity, nor was Jesus anything other than a devout Jew who proclaimed and enacted the message of the kingdom to other Jews. And yet Jesus eventually earned the indignation of the Judean leadership, resulting in a charge of blasphemy, and was handed over to the Romans as a messianic pretender. Jesus' heated disputes with his contemporaries (i.e. the Pharisees, Sadducees and Herodians) were not because he taught a religion of love and grace and they taught a religion of legalism. The bone of contention was who spoke for God, who's way of being Israel should be followed, and what must Israel do in order to be restored? If one adds to that Jesus' interiorizing of the purity laws, that is to say his prioritizing of moral purity over ceremonial purity (e.g. Mark 7.1–23), and his criticism of the Temple (Mark 11.15–17), then Jewish agitation at his actions and message is comprehensible. The Jewish scholar Joseph Klausner maintains that, 'Jesus was a Jew and a Jew he remained till his last breath' but he also adds that: '*Ex nihilo nihil fit* [from nothing nothing comes]: had not Jesus' teaching contained a kernel of opposition to Judaism, Paul could

---

[17] See Judith M. Lieu, ' "The Parting of the Ways": Theological Construct or Historical Reality?', *JSNT* 56 (1994), 101–9; Stanley E. Porter and Brook W. R. Pearson, 'Why the Split? Christians and Jews by the Fourth Century', *JGRChJ* 1 (2000), 107–9; Adam H. Becker and Annette Yoshiko Reed (eds), *The Ways That Never Parted: Jews and Christians in Late Antiquity and the Middle Ages* (TSAJ 95; Tübingen: Mohr/Siebeck, 2003).

[18] Michael F. Bird, 'The Historical Jesus and the "Parting of the Ways"', in *The Handbook of the Study of the Historical Jesus*, Stanley E. Porter and Tom Holmén (eds) (4 vols; Leiden: Brill, forthcoming).

never *in the name of Jesus* have set aside the ceremonial laws, and broken through the barriers of national Judaism.'[19]

Second, the early Jewish Christian community in Jerusalem suffered periods of intense persecution resulting in the martyrdom of James the son of Zebedee (Acts 12.1–3) and James the brother of the Lord (Josephus, *Ant.* 20.200). The reason for this persecution was probably: (1) James, like Jesus, was accused of being a 'law-breaker'; (2) the proclamation of a crucified messiah was an offence to Jewish eschatological hopes; and (3) there appears to be evidence that Jewish Christians were already incorporating Jesus into patterns of worship normally reserved for Yahweh, as is evident from the formulae 'in the name of Jesus' used in baptism, prayers, healings and exorcisms (e.g. Acts 2.38; 4.30; 10.48; 16.18; 19.5, 17, and note the prohibition in 4.18 and 5.28 about speaking in Jesus' name) and invocation made to Jesus in Aramaic-speaking worship as *marana tha* 'our Lord, come' (e.g. 1 Cor. 16.22; Rev. 22.20; *Did.* 10.6).

Third, the Hellenists (Greek-speaking Jewish Christians) probably contributed something to the Jewish–Christian split as well. Whereas the Aramaic-speaking Christians emphasized those elements of Jesus' teaching in continuity with Judaism (e.g. restoration of Israel, call for national repentance, true covenantal righteousness, healing ministry, etc.), the Greek-speaking Christians began to emphasize those aspects of Jesus' teaching that were at variance with the views of his contemporaries. That would include Jesus' criticisms of the Temple and actions by Jesus that provoked accusations that he did what was 'unlawful' (Mark 2.24; 3.4).[20] A group of Hellenists in Jerusalem centred on Stephen began to attract opposition based on their views of Torah and the Temple (Acts 6.13–14). When a persecution broke out against the Hellenists those scattered abroad from Jerusalem began preaching Jesus in other locations (Acts 8.1–5). Luke reports that men from 'Cyprus and Cyrene' began to speak to 'Greeks' (i.e. Gentiles) in Antioch proclaiming the Lord Jesus and so the gentile divide was finally crossed once and for all (Acts 11.20). It was in the mixed setting of Antioch that believers were first called 'Christians' (Acts 11.26). At this juncture (early to mid-30s CE) it is probable that some Hellenists ceased to require circumcision of Gentiles as a condition for fellowship

---

[19] Joseph Klausner, *Jesus of Nazareth: His Life, Times, and Teaching* (trans. Herbert Danby; London: Allen & Unwin, 1929), 368–9. Similarly, another Jewish scholar, Richard L. Rubenstein, wrote (*My Brother Paul* [New York: Harper & Row, 1972], 121): 'In reality it was not Paul but Jesus who instituted the irreparable breach with established Judaism.'

[20] Cf. Michael F. Bird, 'Jesus as Law-Breaker,' in *Who Do My Opponents Say That I Am? Investigating the Accusations Against Jesus*, eds Joseph B. Modica and Scot McKnight (London: T&T Clark/Continuum, 2008), 3–26.

and as a prerequisite to salvation.[21] This opened them up to the charge of lowering the currency of Israel's election by including Gentiles into the people of God without conversion to Judaism and this prompted persecution from zealous Jews such as Saul of Tarsus.

Fourth, Paul and his heirs established a Law-free mandate for Gentiles in the Church by including Gentiles under the designation 'the Israel of God' (Gal. 6.16) and making them part of the group known as the 'circumcision', which was a symbolic word for Israel (Phil. 3.3). That prompted no small measure of opposition as is evident from 1 Thessalonians:

> For you, brothers, became imitators of the churches of God in Christ Jesus that are in Judea, for you suffered the same things from your own compatriots as they did from the Jews, who killed both the Lord Jesus and the prophets, and drove us out; they displease God and oppose everyone by hindering us from speaking to the Gentiles so that they might be saved. Thus they have constantly been filling up the measure of their sins; but God's wrath has overtaken them at last! (1 Thess. 2.14–16)

Fifth, the destruction of the Temple in 70 CE changed Judaism and Jewish–Christian relations for ever. For Jews it represented the end of the world of Judaism as they knew it, and for Christians it was an act of judgment against the Jews for rejecting Christ. This was significant because: 'The *parting of the ways* arose because, for most other Jews, that Christian Jewish claim was incredible. The inclusion of pagans and the devastation by pagans were irreconcilable.'[22]

Sixth, closely related to the destruction of Jerusalem was the imposition of the *Fiscus Judaicus* or Jewish tax as a means of reparation after the Jewish war. Instead of paying an annual tax to the temple for its upkeep and maintenance, Jews of the empire were forced to pay a tax to the Temple of Jupiter in Rome. This led to the question as to who was eligible to pay the tax? Who was Jewish? Did Jewish Christians have to pay the tax? The obvious temptation was for Jewish Christians to deny their Jewishness and so renege on paying the tax at the price of jettisoning their Jewish identity in favour of an entirely Christian one.

Seventh, the period of 70–100 CE witnessed some vitriolic and vehement debates between the only Jewish sects that survived the destruction of the Temple: Christians and the Pharisees. The Pharisees began to exert pressure on Christians either to give up their distinctive beliefs or to be expelled from Jewish communities (which meant expulsion from a whole

---

[21] Cf. Hengel, *Between Jesus and Paul*, 13, 23–6, 56.

[22] Jonathan L. Reed and John Dominic Crossan, *Excavating Jesus: Beneath the Stones, Behind the Texts* (San Francisco: Harper, 2001), 324.

network of social, business and familial relations). The Jewish leadership eventually regrouped in the aftermath of the disaster and set up an academy at Yavneh. At some point in its history a council composed the 18 benedictions (*Shemoneh Esreh*) and the twelfth benediction includes a reference to the heretics or *minim*: 'And for apostates let there be no hope, and may the insolent kingdom be quickly uprooted, in our days. And may the heretics [*minim*] perish quickly; and may they be erased from the Book of Life; and may they not be inscribed with the righteous . . .' In the second century, Justin Martyr disparages the Jews for cursing Christ and Christians in their synagogues (*Dial.* 16; 47; 96). While the significance of the Yavneh decree has usually been overstated, it was a watershed in the history of Jewish–Christian interactions and upped the ante of the conflict. At the same time, Christians gave as good as they got and echoes of this intra-Jewish polemic can be found in the New Testament. The Johannine Jesus says to the Jews: 'You are from your father the devil' (John 8.44). In Matthew's Gospel, the Jerusalem crowd cries: 'His blood be on us and on our children' (Matt. 27.25). And in Revelation, John the Seer records: 'I will make those of the synagogue of Satan who say that they are Jews and are not, but are lying – I will make them come and bow down before your feet, and they will learn that I have loved you' (Rev. 3.9). It is crucial to put these remarks in the context of sectarian rivalries within Judaism; they are not anti-Semitic per se, but one does notice that the intensity of the accusations and counter-accusations was becoming more acute.

Eighth, the Jewish revolt led by Simeon Bar Kochba in 132–5 CE constitutes an additional turning point in the Jewish–Christian divide. Kochba persecuted Jewish Christians who refused to support the struggle against Rome. Justin wrote: 'Bar Kochba, the leader of the revolt of the Jews, gave orders that Christians alone should be led to cruel punishments unless they would deny Jesus Christ and utter blasphemy' (Justin, *1 Apol.* 31.6). A similar polemic edge is found in the second-century document the *Apocalypse of Peter*, which very probably identifies the coming of false Christs and martyrdom for believers with the persecution of Christians under Bar Kochba.

Ninth, we can note the gradual transformation of Christian attitudes from internal Jewish polemics to full-blown anti-Semitism. For instance, in the fourth century John Chrysostom could say this about the Jews to the churches of Antioch: 'They sacrificed their own sons and daughters to demons. They refused to recognize nature, they forgot the pangs of birth, they trod underfoot the rearing of their children, they overturned from their foundations the laws of kingship, they became more savage than any wild beast' (*Adv. Jud.* 1.6). By the time we get to Constantine the ways have well and truly parted and the anti-Semitism of Christianity had horrendous effects in the subsequent history of Jewish–Christian relations.

Why did Christianity win over the Roman empire?

As to why Christianity won over the Roman empire the obvious Christian answer is, 'because God made it so'. One could point to the unparalleled spread of Christianity, the survival of Christianity despite cruel persecutions and countless martyrdoms, the fortuitous conversion of Constantine through an apparent vision, and the success of the Christian proclamation among pagans. Christian apologists can say that the rise of Christianity is so miraculous and so amazing that the Christianizing of the Roman empire itself constitutes a miracle sufficient to evoke faith. While I agree that in the sovereign purposes of God the Church did eventually win over Rome, this does not negate the crucial historical, cultural and social factors that enabled Christians to survive and thrive. The rise of Christianity did not occur in a vacuum – there were factors and currents beneath the surface that facilitated that rise and it is worthwhile to chart and study them. That is no threat to a belief in the sovereignty of God since history is *His Story* or about the story of God and what God is doing and has done in the sphere of space-time history. God achieved his purposes, through Nero and Constantine, and he is supreme over any historical processes that he sought to use to that end. The factors that enabled the success of Christianity included the spread of Greek as the lingua franca of the Graeco-Roman world, the network of synagogues which Christian missionaries and immigrants could use to disseminate their beliefs, the relative freedom of movement across the Roman roads and international sea ports, and Western interest in religions from the Orient.[23]

Was Christianity influenced by pagan religions?

Christianity was certainly influenced by pagan religions. For instance, several of the second-century Christian heresies show clear signs of influence by pagan religions. The origins of Christian Gnosticism, though complex and disputed, probably occurred through some disenfranchised

---

[23] Earle E. Cairns, *Christianity through the Centuries* (3rd edn; Grand Rapids, MI: Zondervan, 1996), 39–46.

Jewish Christians rejecting their Jewish heritage and embracing a hyper-platonic dualism that separated the saviour God from the creator God. There was a group called the Montanists who had peculiar beliefs about the Holy Spirit and they were arguably to some extent indebted to the indigenous religions of Phrygia for their beliefs.[24]

Even the orthodox canonical writings indicate a willingness to express ideas in the language and thought-forms of the Graeco-Roman context.[25] In the prologue to the Fourth Gospel, John uses the designation *ho logos* ('the Word') to describe the pre-existence and revelatory function of Jesus as the eternal Word of God (John 1.1, 14). The concept is indebted to Jewish understandings of God's wisdom (*hokmah* in Hebrew, e.g. Prov. 8.22–31; cf. Ecclus. 1.1–10) or Speech (*memra* in Aramaic, e.g. *Tg. Onq.* on Gen. 15.1) found in the Jewish Scriptures. Yet the word also has a background in Greek thought where philosophers wrestled with the problem of how the noumenal realm of eternal forms and ideas connects with the phenomenal or physical world. Greek philosophers came up with the idea of the *logos* which mediates between these two realms. According to Plato and Heraclitus the *logos* is the ever present wisdom which steers and guides all things. In Stoic philosophy the *logos* was the common law of nature (e.g. Diogenes Laertius 7.87; Epictetus, *Diatr.* 1.20). The Jewish philosopher, Philo, thought of the *logos* as the eternal expression of God's wisdom. Philo even asserted that men can know God only through the *logos*. The *logos* is the architect of the universe (*Opif.* 20–25; *Her.* 205). For Justin Martyr the *logos* was the all-pervasive unifying principle of reason that governs the universe. It is this *logos* that is identified with Christ in his incarnation since he is the one who is pre-existent and mediates between the human and divine realms (Justin, *1 Apol.* 5, 46; 2.8, 10, 13). John uses *logos* because he wants his readers to know that God's Word that went forth in creation, God's Word that echoes out in revelation, redemption and renewal is none other than Jesus the Christ. John takes a term like *logos*, a word invented by pagan, polytheistic philosophers, and he empties it of certain connotations, fills it with others from Jewish wisdom theology, and then uses it to describe Jesus Christ the Son of God. Thus, while the vocabulary is indebted to Greek philosophy and religion, and while some of its concepts carry over into John's usage, he has essentially redefined *logos* with a distinctively Christian meaning.

---

[24] Vera-Elisabeth Hirschmann, *Horrenda Secta: Untersuchungen zum frühchristlichen Montanismus und seinen Verbindugen zur paganen Religion Phrygiens* (Historia-Einzelschriften 179; Stuttgart: Steiner, 2005).

[25] J. Daryl Charles, 'Pagan Sources in the New Testament,' in *Dictionary of New Testament Background*, eds Craig A. Evans and Stanley E. Porter (Downers Grove, IL: IVP, 2000), 756–64.

The images and language that Paul and John used may have reminded gentile Christians of things from the pagan religious sphere or echoed certain concepts, perhaps deliberately. That should come as no surprise to us as Christians were part of the pan-Hellenic context of their day and they used language and concepts that were in the air, which also partly explains why Paul and John were effective in their communication and why they were so persuasive in their proclamation. Neither of these two authors was using a secret language that only Christians understood. The qualifications that we need to add are:

1 analogy does not prove genealogy, and the question of who borrowed from whom is a complex one, especially when it comes to the mystery cults;
2 many of the words and categories taken over from paganism are clearly redefined with specifically Christian nuances;
3 the seedbed from which Christian theology grew and what it owes its conceptual architecture to was common Judaism (e.g. monotheism, election, Temple, Torah, Messiah, etc.) and the Jewish Scriptures; and
4 it is important to keep in mind the Christian critique of pagan ethics, politics and polytheism as Christians refused to go down the route of pluralism by saying that Jesus is Jupiter by another name.

As Paul says, while for others there are many 'gods' for Christians 'there is one God, the Father, from whom are all things and for whom we exist, and one Lord, Jesus Christ, through whom are all things and through whom we exist' (1 Cor. 8.6).

When did Jesus become God?

As to when Jesus became 'God', any Christian with a theological grounding will say, 'in eternity past'. But does the history match the theology? A popular line of thought in the twentieth century has been that of the history-of-religions school, which argued that the title *Kyrios* ('Lord') for Jesus emerged out of the Hellenization of the Christian faith in gentile Christian circles. The problem with this view is that the title *Kyrios* does not represent a terminological or theological innovation among gentile Christians, who appropriated the term from pagan cults:

1 The term was used by Greek-speaking Jews for the Hebrew tetragrammaton (Yahweh) and was part of the religious vocabulary of Greek-speaking Jews.
2 Claiming that Jesus was 'Lord' goes back to Jewish Christian circles, as evidenced by 1 Corinthians 16.22, where Paul cites the Aramaic invocation *marana tha*.

3 Several pre-Pauline passages refer to Jesus as Lord and involve reorientating biblical phrases and applying them to Christ, for example, 1 Corinthians 8.5–6; Philippians 2.9–11.[26]

This goes to show that the highest Christology in the New Testament is also among the earliest.[27] In the previous chapters I have already argued that Jesus understood himself as embodying the divine presence and possessing divine authority and that the early Jewish-Christian community had begun incorporating Jesus into patterns of religious devotion normally reserved for Yahweh (see pages 28–31). If we add to that the Christology of Paul and John there is no question of an evolution from Jewish prophet to gentile God, but a gradual development as Christian authors began to reflect and think over the significance of Christ's life, work and exaltation and how he related to the divine identity and divine activity.

This approach that I am setting forward can be contrasted with that of Crossley, who invests a great deal of time looking at the various sources and influences that shaped Jewish and Christian monotheism. He establishes what we already know: Jews were not the only monotheists in the ancient world; there are debates about how 'strict' Jewish monotheism was, not to mention endless debates about who was monotheistic first and who influenced who and when and where.

What I will contest, however, is his view that the development of Christian monotheism was owing to a change of social situation and the shifting perception of Christian gentile communities alienated from Jewish communities. This sounds to me like the early twentieth-century German history-of-religions school that contended that Palestinian Christianity saw Jesus as a prophet, an angel or as a mysterious figure exalted to heaven, and when Christianity moved into its Hellenistic and gentile environs it produced a syncretistic concoction of Jewish messianism and paganism that eventually became proto-orthodox Christianity. I think it worth pointing out that the Aramaic-speaking church in Jerusalem probably had a more divinized understanding of Jesus than Crossley allows for, as evidenced by 1 Corinthians 16.22 (cf. *Did.* 10.6), which puts Jesus in the position of 'Lord'. Indeed, early Jewish persecution of Christians pre-70 CE may well have been because of their incorporation of Jesus into patterns of worship that many Jews found blasphemous.[28]

---

[26] Larry Hurtado, *Lord Jesus Christ: Devotion to Jesus in Earliest Christianity* (Grand Rapids, MI: Eerdmans, 2003), 20–1.

[27] G. B. Caird, *New Testament Theology* (ed. L. D. Hurst; Oxford: Clarendon Press, 1994), 343.

[28] Cf. Hurtado, *Lord Jesus Christ*, 1–26.

My own view is that most Christians held something akin to *messianic monotheism* where the word 'God' is redefined and invested with new meaning in the light of faith in Jesus as the personification, presence and personal representation of God (see for instance 1 Cor. 8.6). The Fourth Evangelist goes so far as to imply that Jesus is the exegesis of God or the one in whom God is made known, seen and experienced (John 1.1–2, 14, 18; 14.9). Keep in mind that the Fourth Gospel, despite its polemics against 'the Jews', can hardly be categorized as un-Jewish in its worldview. Such a perspective of Christ as participating in the divine identity resulted in charges of blasphemy against Jewish Christians by leaders of the synagogues in the post-70 CE period and also accusations of atheism and treason against gentile Christians by Roman officials, for their failure to worship the emperor. In other words, you do not need a bunch of gentile Christians with a religious framework steeped in pagan monotheism to make Jesus one with 'God': on the contrary, it developed in the environs of Palestinian Christianity.

Conclusions

Some time around 112 CE the Roman governor of Bithynia, Pliny the Younger, wrote to the emperor Trajan asking what to do with persons who had been denounced as Christians. He wrote: 'For the matter seemed to me to warrant consulting you, especially because of the number involved. For many persons of every age, every rank, and also of both sexes are and will be endangered. For the contagion of this superstition has spread not only to the cities but also to the villages and farms' (Pliny the Younger, *Ep.* 10.96.9). It is interesting that the cross-section of persons involved include those of every age, rank and gender. Christianity succeeded in doing what the philosophers, pagan priests and military generals had never done, namely, unite together diverse tribes, classes and races under a single banner. Paul could write in Ephesians: 'There is one body and one Spirit, just as you were called to the one hope of your calling, one Lord, one faith, one baptism, one God and Father of all, who is above all and through all and in all' (Eph. 4.4–6). It was the cosmopolitan vision of Christianity which explains the ultimate separation from Judaism and its success in the Graeco-Roman world. Christians were able to accommodate within their ranks an ethnic, economic and social diversity that few movements could sustain, and include them under the designations of the renewed human race and the true Israel. In the words of the second-century Christian Apologist, Aristides, alongside Greeks and Jews was a 'Third Race', the Christians (*Apol.* 2).

Response from James G. Crossley

Once again, there is much with which I can easily agree in Bird's analysis of the 'early Church'. Much of his basic detail on the 'parting of the ways' is solid, well documented and helpful. However, there are points with which I would strongly disagree and much of this disagreement once again involves, I think, Bird's evangelical and Christian contexts dictating his narrative at the expense of basic evidence. I hope to show that Bird has provided a view of history that coheres far too neatly with Christian ortho-doxy without sufficient historical support. Moreover, I also think that Bird's narrative is part of a broader Western tradition whereby this orthodoxy uses and praises categories of 'Jews' and 'Judaism' while at the same time such categories only have a limited use in order to make sure Christianity transcends its Jewish context (often 'Judaism' and 'Jewish context' as con-structed by scholarship).

The function of 'Judaism'

Indeed, various scholars have now shown that much scholarly concern with 'Jewish context' has a duplicitous function. By stressing the Jewish context, it is argued, the category 'Judaism' preserves Christianity, keeping it 'pure' from pagan or 'idolatrous' influence, while maintaining the all-important link with the Old Testament/Hebrew Bible to a stunningly high degree. At the same time, however, the transcendence of the constructed 'Jewish context' helps preserve the myth of Christian superiority, and this is usually done by conspicuously *ignoring* key Jewish evidence – namely, Jewish evidence too closely paralleled with early Christian evidence and therefore not useful for the myth of Christian superiority – and by pushing Christian orthodoxy onto texts when it simply is not present. This scholarly love for 'Judaism' clearly has its limits.[29] Such trends are ('unconsciously') at work in Bird's reconstruction of Christian origins.

While Bird clearly tries to emphasize just how Jewish he thinks Jesus and his followers were ('Jesus was a Jew, he ministered to other Jews, his

---

[29] I am amalgamating arguments from the following: J. Z. Smith, *Drudgery Divine: On the Comparison of Early Christianities and the Religions of Late Antiquity* (Chicago: University of Chicago Press, 1990), e.g. 83; W. Arnal, *The Symbolic Jesus: Historical Scholarship, Judaism and the Construction of Contemporary Identity* (London and Oakville: Equinox, 2005); T. Penner, 'Die Judenfrage and the Construction of Ancient Judaism: Toward a Foregrounding of the Backgrounds Approach to Early Christianity', in P. Gray and G. O'Day (eds), *Scripture and Traditions: Essays on Early Judaism and Christianity* (Leiden: Brill, forthcoming); J. G. Crossley, *Jesus in an Age of Terror: Scholarly Projects for a New American Century* (London and Oakville: Equinox, forthcoming), chapter 6.

closest followers were Jews'), we see a subtle shift in his argument in relation to Judaism. Here I would object to Klausner's use of 'opposition to
Judaism', which is cited positively by Bird alongside the claim that the split
from Judaism had to originate with Jesus (see page 155). While there is
no doubting Bird's claim that Jesus came into conflict with others, he was,
as I have pointed out in previous chapters (see pages 1–17, 33–7 and 116–32),
hardly the first Jewish figure to come into conflict with his fellow Jews and
this phenomenon can hardly be classed as 'opposition to Judaism'! Bird's
evidence does not support his case either. As for Jesus 'prioritizing' key
aspects of the Law such as purity, this was hardly new in early Judaism
and in fact it was completely uncontroversial (e.g. *Ep. Arist.* 234; cf.
170–171; and e.g. Isa. 1.10–17; Jer. 6.20; 7.21–28; Amos 5.21–27!). Furthermore, criticizing the Temple was hardly unheard of in the first century
(see my section on Jesus, pages 1–17), neither was levelling allegations of
blasphemy (see my section on the Gospels, pages 116–32) at other Jews,
and neither was being killed by the Romans.

Historical explanation

If all these views concerning clashes were found in early Judaism, then
how can Bird's explanation of Christian origins work? Why is it that the
Jesus movement and not some other Jewish movement became the new
religion? Without addressing such questions, Bird's analysis does not
have strong explanatory power.

Similarly, Bird's account of the origins of Gentile inclusion in earliest
Christianity has to be traced back to Jesus. Leaving aside the question of
historical accuracy, some of his evidence does not suggest a strong concern for Gentiles. Mark 11.15–17 is a protest about the state of the Temple
and talks of a house of prayer for all nations, which is standard Temple
theology (e.g. Isa. 56.6–7!). The idea of Jesus and his followers being some
kind of new Temple, as mentioned by Bird, owes more to Christian imagination than any evidence from the Synoptic Gospels (see my chapter on
Jesus, pages 1–17 and 33–7). Yet I would agree with Bird that Jesus probably believed in a future inclusion of Gentiles. However, Bird's view of Jesus
again suggests nothing new in early Judaism. As he knows, there is plenty
of Jewish evidence for an inclusion of Gentiles at end times, so this leaves
Bird's argument once again lacking in explanatory force because he does
not explain why the movement associated with Jesus was the one that
attracted the Gentiles. Why not another Jewish movement that looked
forward to the incoming of the Gentiles?

Looking further at Bird's arguments can help explain why they lack explanatory power. For a start, the arguments based on the strong grounding

of later Christianity in the teaching of Jesus do not necessarily work. It could easily be argued – rightly or wrongly – that Paul could have set aside parts of the Law because, for instance, he had a vision after Jesus' death or that there were plenty of Gentiles associated with the Christian movement who were no longer interested in parts of the Law, so Paul attempts to deal with the problem by justifying non-observance. Clearly, this does not necessarily require Jesus to have said something so dramatic as to effectively create a new religion. There is simply no logical reason why the split from Judaism must *necessarily* have come from Jesus' teaching (see also my response to Bird's section on Jesus, pages 33–7). Here the words of Dale Allison are also worth keeping in mind:

> One should freely confess that there need be no necessary continuity between what Jesus taught about the law and what some of his followers taught about it. We cannot ascribe everything in early Christianity to its founder. We can no more praise him for all that went right than we can blame him for all that went wrong. His followers sometimes reaped where he did not sow.[30]

Klausner may argue that nothing comes from nothing but this should imply that a range of factors must be investigated and not hung at the end of an argument, as Bird does, about Jesus' clashes with his opponents. Intriguingly, Bird briefly acknowledges that a range of social, economic and geographical factors contributed to the rise of Christianity, which would suggest that things can happen and change without heavy reliance on individual influence. Yet Bird still relies primarily on ideas and individual influence when talking about Jesus and the rise of Christianity. In terms of conventional historical explanation among historians (though not in terms of most historians of Christian origins), this near-complete reliance on ideas and individual influence is odd and outdated. Bird's avoidance of, or token acknowledgment of, broader issues in the emergence of Christianity has an important ideological function: it allows Jesus to be responsible for the key aspects of the religion in his name.

Hellenists

Again, the overly polarizing rhetoric of Christianity versus Judaism is present in Bird's retelling of the first years of Christian origins after Jesus' death. Of a group of 'Hellenists in Jerusalem centred on Stephen', Bird claims that they 'began to attract opposition based on their views of Torah and

---

[30] D. C. Allison, *Resurrecting Jesus: The Earliest Christian Tradition and Its Interpreters* (London: T&T Clark, 2005), 150.

the Temple (Acts 6.13–14)' (see page 156). For a start, Bird makes no argument in favour of the events of Acts 6 reflecting the historical Stephen.
Maybe everything told in Acts 6 really did happen and really was said, but
with the lack of any sort of useful complementary evidence it is extremely
difficult to make any clear judgment on the matter. But even if we assume
that everything Acts 6 tells us is accurate, Bird's argument is still shaky.
In my sections on Paul (see pages 70–85 and 97–102), I pointed out that
the dispute in Acts 6 provides no example of any specific biblical law
having been broken and could easily be taken as a dispute over the interpretation of biblical Law. Indeed, the passage even says that Stephen was
accused of critiquing 'the customs that Moses handed on to us' (Acts 6.14),
which is the sort of language used to describe expansions and interpretations of biblical Law (see again my sections on Paul). Therefore the
conflict could, for all we know, be one of perspective. In other words,
Stephen's opponents may think he is opposing the Law from their perspective but from Stephen's perspective he may have thought he was
behaving within the boundaries of Law-observance.

Bird also argues that in the 30s CE the Hellenists were engaged in disputes over Torah and Temple and started to engage openly with Gentiles.
Fine; there is, as Bird shows, some evidence (no matter, for the moment,
how reliable or unreliable it is) for this. But then Bird claims, with reference to the hugely influential Martin Hengel, that it is 'probable that some
Hellenists ceased to require circumcision of Gentiles as a condition for
fellowship and as a prerequisite to salvation' (see page 156–7). Yet when
we look closely at Acts we find that it is not that specific on the details of
the disputes. As it happens, there is *not one* mention of dropping circumcision for Gentiles wanting to become part of the Christian movement.
Yet, with reference to a hugely influential scholar who relies heavily on the
still powerful but historically dubious and very old-fashioned Law versus
Gospel tradition of some Protestant thinking, Bird tells us that it is 'probable' that some Hellenists dropped circumcision for Gentiles. For all we
know, some Hellenists may have done as Bird and Hengel say they did but
there is no evidence for it. For all we know, they might not have done. It
is precisely this kind of argument by Bird that leads me to suspect that
the quest for the ancient origins of orthodox Christianity over against
Judaism is guiding Bird's narrative rather than basic evidence.

Pagans and monotheism

And then there are the pagans. Bird does claim that 'Christianity was certainly influenced by pagan religions' (see page 159). That would seem to
contradict some of the general claims I have made about Bird's arguments.

However, he makes the significant qualification that 'several of the second-century Christian *heresies* [my italics] show clear signs of influence by pagan religions', before mentioning the Gnostics and Montanists. The term 'heresy' already implies a history from the perspective of orthodox Christianity. Bird does claim that '*Even* [my italics] the orthodox canonical writings indicate a willingness to express ideas in the language and thought-forms of the Graeco-Roman context' and mentions the term *logos* in the prologue to John's Gospel. Yet, for Bird, there is nothing like the kinds of pagan influence attributed to the so-called 'heresies', and his language is decidedly different when it comes to 'orthodox Christianity' ('a willingness to express ideas in the language and thought-forms of the Graeco-Roman context'). Given that Christians (however we define them) found themselves all around the Roman world, is it not suspicious that only that which was deemed to be outside orthodox canonical Christianity is the Christianity really *influenced* by 'pagan religions'? Is it not far too convenient that history has apparently worked out in such a theologically convenient way, effectively preserving orthodoxy and tainting non-orthodoxy? Would Bird go so far as to say that pagan religions did not influence the New Testament and orthodox Christianity? I suspect that the world is a lot messier place than Bird credits.

Bird criticizes my apparent view that, in his words, 'the development of Christian monotheism was owing to a change of social situation and the shifting perception of Christian Gentile communities alienated from Jewish communities' (see page 162). Against this, however, I did not say that specifically *gentile* Christian communities became isolated from Jewish communities. On the contrary, given my explanation for the strongest deification of Jesus as being based on John's Gospel and that John's Gospel contains heavy influence from Jewish tradition, I see no problem in arguing that the group behind John's Gospel who made major steps in the construction of a Christian identity contained a lot of people from an ethnically Jewish background. Bird then proceeds, without evidence, to tie my explanation in with the German history-of-religions school and their claims of a stark difference between Palestinian versus Hellenistic Christianity. I have never made nor endorsed such claims and, for the record, like Bird I do not think such a sharp distinction between Palestinian Christianity and Hellenistic Christianity is particularly helpful in this context. Indeed, I tried to focus on the bigger picture of the Christian movement *in general* and how Christian identity was constructed in the broader Roman world.

It seems, therefore, that Bird is (wrongly) tying my arguments on pagan monotheism with 'gentile Christianity' and the old debates about

'Hellenistic' versus 'Palestinian' Christianity. For example, he claims that 'you do not need a bunch of gentile Christians with a religious framework steeped in pagan monotheism to make Jesus one with "God": on the contrary, it developed in the environs of Palestinian Christianity' (see page 163). I certainly do not recognize my argument here. My argument was not about what was 'needed' to make Jesus God but rather it was about providing, with conventional historical hindsight, the sorts of reasons that might explain why Jesus was made God in the strongest sense. I emphasized that the idea of monotheism was widespread in different traditions in the context of empire. I then gave specific social circumstances – those reflected in John's Gospel – as the most significant aspect of the development of a specifically Christian view of monotheism in a world of monotheistic ideas. This is quite different from Bird's representation of my argument.

Dating divinity

Bird's arguments for the emergence of Jesus-as-God in a 'Palestinian' context is lacking in serious evidence. Bird believes that it is 'worth pointing out that the Aramaic-speaking church in Jerusalem probably had a more divinized understanding of Jesus than Crossley allows for, as evidenced by 1 Corinthians 16.22 (cf. *Did.* 10.6), which puts Jesus in the position of "Lord" (see page 162).' As it happens, I did not allow or disallow anything concerning the 'Aramaic-speaking church' so it is difficult to know precisely what I was supposed to have said about the Christology of the 'Aramaic-speaking church'. A big problem here is, however, that Bird has not provided a definition of 'divinized understanding'. Does Bird imply that I do not see this use of 'Lord' in the strongest possible sense, just as I did not see Paul's description of Jesus in Philippians 2 as necessarily having Jesus-as-God in something like the orthodox Christian sense? This seems to be the case and, if so, it ought then to be recalled (see further my sections on Paul and the Gospels) that such use of language usually reserved for God could be applied to other figures in early Judaism without implying equality with God in the strongest possible sense. Furthermore, the term 'Lord', for what it is worth, does not automatically imply 'God' and could also be used of figures from humans to angels (cf. Zech. 4.4–5; Matt. 7.21–22; Mark 7.28; Luke 6.46).

However, what is particularly significant about Bird's rhetoric is that it seems to push the link to the key Christian doctrine of the full divinity of Christ right back to the earliest days. As he says, 'the highest Christology in the New Testament is also among the earliest' (see page 162). Yet for all the emphasis on Jews and Judaism, Bird does not interact with the known Jewish parallels with the application of divine language to certain figures (see my sections on Paul). 'Judaism' ceases to be useful for this kind of argument. Furthermore, Bird even claims that the 'early Jewish persecution of Christians pre-70 CE may well have been because of their incorporation of Jesus into patterns of worship that many Jews found blasphemous' (see page 162). But again there is simply no explicit evidence to back this claim up. The point has been made before and will need making again: as I pointed out in my sections on the Gospels, Paul and Early Christianity, prior to John's Gospel there is no evidence of any disputes over the high deification of Jesus as co-equal with God in contrast with the massive problems Paul had with the Law. If there were persecutions or controversies over such claims of the highest deification of Jesus, why are they never mentioned explicitly?

Further reading

Athanassiadi, P. and M. Frede (eds), *Pagan Monotheism in Late Antiquity* (Oxford: Oxford University Press, 1999).

Barnett, Paul, *Jesus and the Rise of Early Christianity* (Downers Grove, IL: IVP, 1999).

Cameron, R. and M. P. Miller (eds), *Redescribing Christian Origins* (Atlanta: SBL, 2004).

Dunn, James D. G., *The Partings of the Ways: Between Christianity and Judaism and Their Significance for the Character of Christianity* (2nd edn; London: SCM Press, 2006).

Harland, P. A., *Associations, Synagogues, and Congregations: Claiming a Place in Ancient Mediterranean Society* (Minneapolis: Fortress, 2003).

Hurtado, Larry, *How on Earth Did Jesus Become a God? Historical Questions about Earliest Devotion to Jesus* (Grand Rapids, MI: Eerdmans, 2005).

Nash, Ronald H., *Christianity and the Hellenistic World* (Grand Rapids, MI: Zondervan, 1984).

Smith, R., *Julian's Gods: Religion and Philosophy in the Thought and Action of Julian the Apostate* (London: Routledge, 1995).

Stuckenbruck, L. T. and W. E. S. North (eds), *Early Jewish and Christian Monotheism* (London: T&T Clark, 2004).

Stark, R., *The Rise of Christianity: A Sociologist Reconsiders History* (Princeton: Princeton University Press, 1996).

Wright, N. T., *The New Testament and the People of God* (COQG 1; London: SPCK, 1992).

6

Responses from other Jesus experts

Response to James G. Crossley by Scot McKnight

It is easier to find fault with another scholar's statements (and I find plenty to fault both in substance and in logic in James G. Crossley's sketches in this book) than it is to write a compelling alternative. Crossley's work is at its best when he is in critique mode but suffers, fatally I think, from a failure to provide perspective and scope in his overall sketch of both Jesus and the birth (and rise) of earliest Christianity. If I offer some critique of Crossley in what follows, which again is the easier task of the two, I have chosen more importantly to offer an alternative narrative to that provided by Crossley.

But let me begin with the sword. I was annoyed that Crossley claimed Bird's evangelicalism was a bias while he simultaneously claimed his view was more objective, empirical, socially shaped, and less theologically oriented. (Yes, I know Crossley 'states' that his method is no more object-ive, but I would like to have seen him tip his hat at times to the outworkings of his own biases). There was a day when Geza Vermes could pretend to sit down with Gospels, open them up, and claim he could write a sketch of Jesus 'with a mind empty of prejudice' and study the Gospels 'as though for the first time'.[1] Those days are gone. Not only did Bultmann warn us all of *Vorverständnis* ('pre-understanding'), which should have been warn-ing enough, but sitting within the walls of Nottingham University, the home of Crossley's doctoral work, is the world's expert on hermeneutics, Tony Thiselton, and his voluminous writings should forever prevent the idea that we do not each bring our own agendas and 'bias' to the text. Crossley's method, in other words, suffers from bias too. His attitude suggested to me he didn't see his bias.

What struck me as singularly odd about Crossley's sketches above was the juxtaposition of two seemingly contradictory claims: first, that his own method is sociological and his work is socially shaped (he connects his

---

[1] Geza Vermes, *Jesus the Jew: A Historian's Reading of the Gospels* (London: Fontana/Collins, 1973), 19.

views to a Marxist historiography) instead of theologically driven; and, second, that the sketches he gives us are nearly entirely theologically shaped and lack a thorough socially shaped method. By calling attention to some social and economic factors, Crossley begins on what I thought would be a social reconstruction of the Jesus movement that would explain things in a Marxist vein, but instead those insights fell through his hands and he began instead to deconstruct theology without proposing a plausible, compelling account of the birth of earliest Christianity in socially shaped categories. In other words, Crossley's account is just as theological as is Bird's.[2]

Another methodological point: Crossley's claims to be a 'historian' lack an articulation of historiographical method. Perhaps he has fully laid out his mind on this issue in another context, but it is more than a little presumptuous for him to make the routine claim to know how historians operate, that Bird evidently does not, and not provide for us at least a fair-minded and comprehensive sketch of what his historiography looks like. So, let me say a few things. We historians work with three things: data, facts and theories. *Data*, things like a text of the Gospel of Mark or a shard from Galilee or a coin from Jerusalem or a report from a Roman emperor, can be chronicled in a fairly objective manner. One needs simply to lay such things on the table. *Facts*, in contrast, are thin interpretations of the data. Thus, 'this shard is from approximately 30 CE' could be a fact if the evidence seems compelling enough.[3] *Theory and history*, however, are *the historian's attempt to render the data and fact into a credible, compelling account, narrative or story that makes sense of those data and facts.* Here we come to a fundamental conclusion: *all history is literary, is imaginative and is a reconstruction.* It more or less corresponds to what happened, to be sure, but it remains the construct of a historian's mind now put onto paper. Because such constructions emerge from the mind of a historian as he or she interacts with the data and facts, no theory is without bias, without prejudice or final. Good histories string together data and facts in the most compelling of ways because they make best sense of those data and facts; that is, they both correspond to and make sense of the data and facts. Bad histories involve a string that either does not string together the data and

---

[2] I am aware of Crossley's book, *Why Christianity Happened: A Sociohistorical Account of Christian Origins (26–50 CE)* (Louisville, KY: Westminster John Knox, 2006), but I haven't been asked to assess that book; instead, I have been asked to assess the sketches in this book.

[3] Though beset with philosophical and methodological problems, both Bird and Crossley more or less seem to operate with a correspondence theory of truth when it comes to rendering historical judgment. I have no desire to dispute such a theory in this context for my own historiographical reflections move along similar lines.

facts in a way that corresponds to those data and facts or they do not offer a compelling string. Crossley's sketches above, in my judgment, fail to offer a compelling string because, and now I shall drop my sword, they ignore too much of the data and facts. So, now to another sketch of that evidence, and I hope it is more comprehensive and credible than that offered by Crossley.[4]

Jesus

Embedded in a context of yearning for God's kingdom, whether we call this the 'end of exile' or not,[5] John (later called 'the Baptist') and Jesus emerged to announce that the day had arrived. Many today question the historicity of the Lucan infancy narratives, but few doubt the historical credibility of an *Anawim* theology (i.e. the lost and forgotten ones) at work behind the scenes of John's and Jesus' ministries. So, even if one quibbles with lines here and there, what we find in both the *Magnificat* (Luke 1.46–55) and *Benedictus* (1.67–79) reflect the culture, the faith and the hope of the wombs from which both John and Jesus grew (also cf. 2.25, 38). Several themes emerge from this *Anawim* context: first, the yearning for *God* to act to establish *justice* for the *poor*; second, the *downfall* of the oppressive rulers, most notably Herod the Great and, perhaps second, Caesar Augustus; third, the *establishment* of God's good and holy and pious people into positions of leadership; fourth, provision of food for the *hungry*; fifth, *peace* in the Land; sixth, re-establishment of holiness and worship in God's *Temple*; seventh, the focusing of these hopes on a *messianic person* who apparently will reign in (or through) Jerusalem over Rome and all of Israel's enemies.

The subtle tension of some of these themes with what actually happened as well as the congruence of others with the central features of John's and

---

[4] Crossley's obsessions are obvious: dating Mark's Gospel in 40 CE, besides being methodologically impossible to verify at anything more than a speculative level makes his judgments and inferences on the basis of that dating tenuous: the observance and non-observance of Torah as a distinguishing characteristic; and the rise of monotheism. Torah observance is important enough and the rise of monotheism overdrawn, but the absence of the central themes of the New Testament cut into his sketches like a jagged knife. I shall attempt to rectify those absences in the sketch I provide below.

[5] I have fewer quibbles with N. T. Wright's famous 'end of exile' emphasis than most, not because I think the word 'exile' was breathed out of everyone's mouth daily but because as a heuristic tool that expression anchors us into a credible, Jewish expectation of that time. See N. T. Wright, *Jesus and the Victory of God* (COQG 2; Minneapolis: Fortress, 1996). Notably, Wright has seemingly dropped the exile theme as he has moved into his newer paradigm, the 'fresh' (anti-Rome ideology) perspective. See now *Paul: Fresh Perspectives* (London: SPCK; Minneapolis: Fortress, 2005).

Jesus' ministries render these themes credible – and in fact conform to some of Crossley's socio-economic emphases. Notice that John's own message, found now at Luke 3.7–14, which found application in the very household of Herod Antipas (3.18–20), shaped a vision of a more just and holy society. John's own answers to questions about what to do are entirely shaped by a socio-economic vision for the Land and for Israel. John's vision conforms to Zechariah's, as does Jesus' with his mother Mary's.

Jesus' kingdom vision

The famous inaugural sermon of Jesus anchors the entire vision of Jesus in a socio-economic paradigm that creates an Israel noted most emphatically by justice. Thus, Luke 4.18–19:

> The Spirit of the Lord is upon me, because he has anointed me to bring good news to the poor. He has sent me to proclaim release to the captives and recovery of sight to the blind, to let the oppressed go free, to proclaim the year of the Lord's favour.

If this text is paradigmatic for Jesus, it also emerges neatly out of the *Anawim* themes sketched above: Jesus' vision is for a just society in which there will be the elimination of oppression, both socio-economically (Jubilee-like) and physically, and an overwhelming sense of God's good favour upon God's people in the Land.

The Beatitudes, often mistakenly interpreted as a list of virtues, declare the favour – perhaps also Jubilee-like – of God upon the very groups both Mary and Zechariah knew were about to see the blessing of God. Furthermore, Luke's account entails – as do both *Magnificat* and *Benedictus* – woe upon the oppressors. Luke 6.20–26 contain those words and, if they are not the words of Jesus, they echo his vision. The Beatitudes, again, are not a list of virtues but a list of those *Anawim*-like characters who find the kingdom of God bringing justice into their condition. Accordingly, they also bring rectification into the world of those who distribute injustice into the world. Here again, we have a socio-economic vision on the part of Jesus that shapes everything he does.

I stick with the Lucan text, though each of these has forms in other Gospel traditions, and move now to Jesus' words to the imprisoned Baptist. Staring at his feet in prison, John wonders if the socio-economic vision of the *Anawim* will come to pass or not – at least within his lifetime. Further, with his view of Jesus as the one who is stronger than he, John petitions Jesus to see if he might 'do something about it'. Luke 7.19 has John asking, via intermediaries, 'Are you the one who is to come, or are we to wait for another?' Many have assumed, without much reflection I suggest, that 'the one who is to come' is a variant on 'Messiah', but closer inspection of Malachi 3—4 suggests that John is asking if Jesus is the Elijianic figure. (There is an entire set of issues here, which we can't indulge in this context, about John and Jesus debating 'who is who' in the script of Tanakh, but their resolution is not important here.) Jesus' answer, evidently then, is 'No, I'm not that figure. You are. My role can be found in the script of Isaiah 29.18; 35.5–6; 42.18.'

> Go and tell John what you have seen and heard: the blind receive their sight, the lame walk, the lepers are cleansed, the deaf hear, the dead are raised, the poor have good news brought to them. And blessed is anyone who takes no offence at me. (Luke 7.22–23)

And again, we are back to *Anawim* theology, to the kinds of things found in *Magnificat*, *Benedictus*, the repentance message of the Baptist, Jesus' inaugural sermon and the Beatitudes. From the very beginning, Jesus' vision is one of including the oppressed, healing the broken and rectifying the world now gone bad by injustices at the hands of evil oppressors.

Christology

What perhaps strikes any reader of such words is the emphasis they find at the end – and these words are but the tip of the iceberg in the Gospels: 'And blessed is anyone who takes no offence at *me*.' Here we find the radical 'Christological' factor at work in the Gospels. It may be accurate for a historian to conclude that John's Gospel outdoes what we find in the Synoptics, but they too are zipped up tightly with a Christological focus so clear that even what John does with his 'I am' sayings and his opening volley in John 1.1 is not a quantum leap.

A place to begin is Mark 3.31–35, where we find Jesus' mother and siblings annoyed (cf. 3.20–21) with Jesus' ministry and associations. Rapping on the door, they are invited to sit where everyone else sits when Jesus is present: *at his feet, encircled around him, listening to him as one listens to a rabbi.* No one disputes the symbol this tradition conveys: Jesus is teacher, his disciples sit at his feet, and Jesus is the middle of everything. In fact, one can say he is the middle; he is the Agent of God. (At the least, he believes this about himself and his followers do too.) Even the accusations lodged against Jesus, what might be called a 'Christology from the side', witness to the same centrality of Jesus.[6]

---

[6] On this, see now S. McKnight and J. Modica (eds), *Who Do My Opponents Say That I Am? An Investigation of the Accusations against Jesus* (LNTS; Edinburgh: T&T Clark, 2008).

Long ago Elizabeth Anscombe, in her stunning little book *Intention*, made the claim that the best way into a person's head, mind and intention is to observe what that person does.[7] Several actions of Jesus, while not cumulatively adding up to 'Well, then, he thought he was God!', surely mount the case that became the next step for early Christians, and Murray Harris's exegetically precise and theologically profound monograph expounded each and every text of substance on the deity of Christ in the New Testament.[8] We'll not go that far here, but the following *actions* of Jesus are the raw materials out of which the centrality of Christ became his deity:

1 His calling of twelve apostles (Mark 3.13–19).[9]
2 His performance of stupendous deeds (Matt. 11.2–5; 12.28).[10]
3 His sitting at table with sinners, and other provocative, prophetic actions (Mark 2.13–17; Matt. 11.19).[11]
4 His disruptive action in the Temple courts (Mark 11.12–19).
5 His last supper actions (Mark 14.12–26).[12]

As *actions*, these five pieces of evidence need to be strung together, and at least one way of putting them together leads to this conclusion: *Jesus thought of himself as the eschatological leader who was both greater than the Temple and one whose death was atoning.* At a purely sociological level, I suppose, one would have to conclude that Jesus had an amazing *chutzpah* ('audacity'). But there is more.

If we add to these actions of Jesus some of his words, words that punctuate various sources and contexts in the Gospels, that *tell the story of his centrality*, then we are drawn into a vision of Jesus where he not only predicts and begins to enact a society of justice but also where his

---

[7] G. E. M. Anscombe, *Intention* (Library of Philosophy and Logic; London: Basil Blackwell, 1978). This was developed brilliantly in B. F. Meyer, *The Aims of Jesus* (London: SCM Press, 1979), and then also, in a different way, by E. P. Sanders, *Jesus and Judaism* (London: SCM Press, 1985).

[8] Murray Harris, *Jesus as God* (Grand Rapids: Baker, 1992).

[9] See S. McKnight, 'Jesus and the Twelve', *BBR* 11 (2001), 203–31.

[10] Crossley's aversion to miracles could be refined by a careful reading of J. P. Meier, *A Marginal Jew*, Vol. 2, *Mentor, Message, and Miracles* (ABRL; New York: Doubleday, 1994), 509–645.

[11] On prophetic actions and Jesus, see my study, 'Jesus and Prophetic Actions', *BBR* 10 (2000), 197–232. Crossley's contention that 'sinners' refers to economic oppressors (see page 5) deserves consideration, but I remain convinced that J. D. G. Dunn's study is more compelling; see J. D. G. Dunn, 'Pharisees, Sinners, and Jesus', in his collection *Jesus, Paul and the Law: Studies in Mark and Galatians* (Louisville, KY: Westminster John Knox, 1990), 61–88.

[12] On which, see S. McKnight, *Jesus and His Death: Historiography, the Historical Jesus, and Atonement Theory* (Waco, TX: Baylor University Press, 2005).

own role in that society is without parallel. Scholars dispute historicity on nearly everything in the Gospels, but the following agglomeration of texts might together compel some to see Jesus as playing an unparalleled centrality in his Jewish vision:

1 The 'I have come' sayings: Matt. 5.17; Mark 2.17; 10.45; Luke 12.49–51.
2 The demand to follow him: Matt. 8.18–22; 10.34–36; Mark 1.16–20; Luke 9.61–62.
3 The claim that final judgment is rooted in relationship to Jesus: Matt. 10.31–32.
4 The 'I am the way' saying that, however much developed by John, is little more than a crystallization of what we find in the Synoptics: John 14.6.
5 The claim to be Son of God: Matt. 11.27–29; Mark 12.1–9; 14.32–42; John's Gospel!

Chutzpah isn't enough. I don't pretend to outsider status looking in on this evidence; nor do I claim a neutral impartiality. What I do claim is that this evidence, and in one way or another much of it can pass muster with typical criteria of authenticity, witnesses to a centrality of Jesus that becomes the raw material for the fashioning of a Christology that leads straight to Nicea and Chalcedon.[13]

Jesus and his death

If two themes that find their way to the surface in any study of Jesus are his kingdom vision and the centrality of himself in that kingdom work of God, then a third one is his *attitude toward his death*. But, because I have both developed that theme in *Jesus and His Death* and because the next section will explain this more, I will leave my comments at this.

Earliest Christianity

The tension I had with Crossley's sketches above was their narrowed focus. I kept saying to myself as I read his work 'How would I sketch the birth and rise of earliest Christianity? And how would it flow out of the central concerns of Jesus – namely, his kingdom vision, his attention on himself, the atoning significance of his death?' I offer the following points.

---

[13] I appeal here to the magisterial work of Larry Hurtado, *Lord Jesus Christ* (Grand Rapids: Eerdmans, 2004), for fuller explanation and amplification. See also his *How on Earth Did Jesus Become God?* (Grand Rapids: Eerdmans, 2005).

Formation of an ecclesial community

The Story of the Bible is a story about God's dealings with Israel, and the New Testament portion of that Story is the Story of God's dealings with the *Church*. Crossley's sketches were about ideas; the socio-economic community Jesus envisioned became the 'church' of Paul and Peter and the community of James and the fellowship of Hebrews and the life-sharing fellowship of John. Of course there are differences, some of them major, but that is how stories develop and unfold.

I begin with Acts 2.42–47 and 4.2–35 which, at least at the level of narrative and probably also at the level of historical fact, bring to a kind of fruition the kingdom vision of Jesus. If Jesus' vision was about a socio-economic community of justice, peace, economic fellowship, and holiness, then one finds it on display in Acts 2 and 4. That community will find brotherly and sisterly communities in the Roman Empire, communities that will be both like and unlike what we find in Acts 2 and 4, and those communities are the focus of the New Testament. So, if one is interested in a sociological understanding of the birth and rise of Christianity, then one must give due attention to what the New Testament says about those communities.

A second stop on this journey finds its location at Corinth where Paul explains to the churches how they are to live as the community of Christ. The major idea he conveys is that the community is a community shaped by and enlivened by and empowered by *spiritual gifts*. Even if Paul's favourite term, *ekklesia* ('church'), can be connected to the Greek *polis* and even if his other favourite term, *soma* ('body'), can also be connected to the Greek concept of a community, Paul fills those terms with a Spirit-shaped and Spirit-prompted life. These words of Paul's, found in 1 Corinthians 12.4–13, say all that needs to be said:

> Now there are varieties of gifts, but the same Spirit; and there are varieties of services, but the same Lord; and there are varieties of activities, but it is the same God who activates all of them in everyone. To each is given the manifestation of the Spirit for the common good. To one is given through the Spirit the utterance of wisdom, and to another the utterance of knowledge according to the same Spirit, to another faith by the same Spirit, to another gifts of healing by the one Spirit, to another the working of miracles, to another prophecy, to another the discernment of spirits, to another various kinds of tongues, to another the interpretation of tongues. All these are activated by one and the same Spirit, who allots to each one individually just as the Spirit chooses.
>
> For just as the body is one and has many members, and all the members of the body, though many, are one body, so it is with Christ. For in

the one Spirit we were all baptized into one body – Jews or Greeks, slaves or free – and we were all made to drink of one Spirit.

A third example of this ecclesial consciousness, this time drawing the entire Old Testament to a head as now being expressed by the earliest Christians in Asia Minor – and I believe Peter wrote his letter to a socially disen-franchised group – can be found in 1 Peter 2.9–10.[14]

> But you are a chosen race, a royal priesthood, a holy nation, God's own people, in order that you may proclaim the mighty acts of him who called you out of darkness into his marvellous light.
> Once you were not a people,
>   but now you are God's people;
> Once you had not received mercy,
>   but now you have received mercy.

Evidently predominantly Gentile, this collection of churches in Asia Minor sees itself – or Peter casts them a vision in which they are to see themselves – as a 'chosen race, a royal priesthood, a holy nation' and 'God's own people', terms drawing deeply upon Israel's self-conscious covenant relationship with the God of Israel.

If Acts 2 and 4 reveal a socio-economic community of justice and Paul a community of Spirit-prompted gifts and fellowship and Peter a community fulfilling the role of Israel in Asia Minor, John's vision of the community is one that, now beset by persecution from without and defection within, is to be characterized by 'loving one another'. The expression is found almost monotonously in John's letters. Again, of course, there are debates. We can leave them to the side since we are not talking about precision dating. Instead, we are sketching the rise of earliest Christianity and, if anything characterizes it, it is a sense of community, a sense of fellowship, a sense of looking out for one another and a sense of dependence upon one another. Here we find the locus of the social realities of the first Christians, and a singular study of this that has carried the weight is that of Wayne Meeks, *The First Urban Christians*.[15]

Death, resurrection and Spirit

Any reading of the Gospels leads one inevitably to Jesus' cross. But if the Gospels are the *bioi* of Jesus, and if those *bioi* find their way to focus

---

[14] I follow in the main the studies of J. H. Elliott, *A Home for the Homeless* (Minneapolis: Fortress, 1990); *1 Peter* (AB 37B; New York: Doubleday, 2000).

[15] Wayne A. Meeks, *The First Urban Christians: The Social World of the Apostle Paul* (2nd edn; New Haven and London: Yale University Press, 2003).

on the death of Jesus, nothing in them anticipated the centrality the cross itself would take up in early Christian thinking. So, once again, a responsible sketch of earliest Christianity will reveal the obsession most of the earliest Christians had with the death of Jesus. Furthermore, if the emphasis is on the death of Jesus in those writings, they also give more than a little attention to his resurrection and the gift of the Spirit. (We will not focus on a theology of resurrection or Spirit in what follows, but only because space does not permit it.) To focus on Law has its merits, but there is so much more to Paul's theology and it is only this more that gives us a reliable sketch of Paul and the earliest churches.

I begin where Crossley remains: with the apostle Paul. Five themes summarize Paul's theology of the cross.[16] First, Jesus' death is an eschatological rescue operation, an act of God's paradoxically mighty power, from death (1 Thess. 5.10), sins and this evil age (Gal. 1.4), the curse of the law (3.13–14), bondage and slavery (5.1), the Passover-night wrath of God (1 Thess. 1.10), the powers of this age (Rom. 8.31–39) and unjust conditions (3.24). Second, Jesus' death brings an eschatological bounty of such things as sonship (Gal. 4.5), forgiveness (1 Cor. 15.3), justification (Rom. 3.21–26; 2 Cor. 5.21) and reconciliation (Rom. 5.10). Third, the death of Jesus is an actual recreation and empowerment – and not just a legal act in the heavenly courtroom. Something happens. Thus, 2 Corinthians 5.14–15: 'For the love of Christ urges us on, because we are convinced that one has died for all; therefore all have died. And he died for all, so that those who live might live no longer for themselves, but for him who died and was raised for them.' Fourth, for Paul the death of Jesus – clearly an act of Christ that is both 'instead of' and 'for the benefit of' others – is also an act on the part of believers who both die with and are raised with Christ. Paul's language is that of co-crucifixion, co-resurrection (Rom. 6.3–11; Gal. 2.20). There is a sense in which Jesus' death is both *substitutionary* and *representative*; that is, it is a cosmic act in which Christ dies and one in which believers die with and in Christ. Finally, Jesus' death is *exemplary*. This, of course, is how Jesus himself described his death – as one he died and one he called his followers to embrace (Mark 8.34). But Paul too sees the death of Jesus as a paradigm for the Christian life (2 Cor. 2.14–16; 4.1–18; Gal. 3.1; 4.14; Col. 1.24—2.5). It would be easy to trace the same theme in Hebrews, in Peter and in the Johannine writings, but space prohibits.

An account of the rise of the Church anchors concrete church life, the socio-economic and spiritual strivings and struggles of those early

---

[16] See my *Jesus and His Death*, 344–53.

Christian fellowships, in the life, death and resurrection of Jesus, at times in his ascension, and in the gift of the Spirit to empower the communities to live out the gospel.

Linguistic turn

Jesus preached the kingdom. Paul preached an ecclesial faith anchored in the soteriology of the Christ event that gave rise to a Spirit-empowered fellowship. Peter preached an ecclesial faith for the socio-economic disenfranchised as they lived out the life and death of Jesus as they awaited future salvation. The writer of Hebrews preached a cult-shaped theory of church life that gave rise to stern warnings and a holiness of life. James preached a wisdom-shaped life of obedience that gave rise to a community that had to learn how to navigate difficult socio-economic oppression. John urged his community to live in the light, to walk in love, to avoid the darkness and to abide in Christ in fellowship with one another.

If the rise of earliest Christianity teaches us anything it is the value of a dictionary and a lexicon in several languages! Our point is this: the explosive faith of the earliest Christians was mirrored by an explosive range of articulations of that faith. One way of putting it is this: no one language or rhetoric sufficed. What was conservative about the earliest Christians was the gospel, but that gospel was expressed in any number of ways and through any number of lenses. The linguistic turn in philosophy sheds light on how the early churches arose and became what they became: linguistic-shaped communities seeking to articulate the gospel in new ways for new days.

Behaviours

Any account of Jesus and the rise of the earliest Christians must give due attention to behaviours, behaviours that were articulated in different ways by different early Christian leaders. Since I have given little attention to this in the Jesus section above, I begin with Jesus.

Jesus' call is the call to *discipleship*. Paradigmatically, the Gospel of Mark begins with the baptism of Jesus, the temptation, and then the summons Jesus gives to Israel in light of the dawn of the kingdom of God (Mark 1.15). His words are foundational to the shape of New Testament ethics: repent, believe and follow me. How might these behaviours be manifest? The first answer for the New Testament is *to love God and to love others*.

A singular feature of Jesus' teachings, one that has reverberations throughout the New Testament, is Jesus' subtle but significant amendment to the *Shema* (Deut. 6.4–5).[17] The *Shema* commanded Israel to recite throughout each day the call to love God:

> Hear, O Israel: The LORD is our God, the LORD alone. You shall love the LORD your God with all your heart, and with all your soul, and with all your might.

When a scribe asked Jesus what was the Greatest Commandment, Jesus 'amended' the *Shema* by adding to it a daily recitation of Leviticus 19.18:

> The first is, 'Hear, O Israel: the Lord our God, the Lord is one; you shall love the Lord your God with all your heart, and with all your soul, and with all your mind, and with all your strength.' The second is this, 'You shall love your neighbour as yourself.' There is no other commandment greater than these. (Mark 12.29–31)

This amendment by Jesus, which does not mean that Jesus first taught folks to love others, merely attached the command to love others to the daily recitation of loving God. And it is this second half of (what I call) the Jesus Creed that found its way into the fabric of early Christian behaviours and ethics. First, the apostle Paul brings it forward in two letters: Galatians 5.13–14 and Romans 13.8–10. Second, James does the same in 2.8. And it is not amiss to see the same behind John's epistolary concern to love one another (1 John 3.11; cf. 3.14, 23; 4.21; 5.2).

The apostle Paul used yet another expression to get to the core of Christian behaviours. I close with this observation: for Paul the essence of Christian behaviour was *to live in the Spirit* (Gal. 5.16–22). Again, examples could be multiplied.

Conclusion

Observance of law and monotheism played a crucial part in the Jesus movement and the rise of earliest Christianity, but if one wants to sketch a social vision of what was going on, one must begin with kingdom, with the centrality of Jesus, and with the incredible verbal display and concentration those early ecclesial communities had on the life, death and resurrection of Jesus, along with the gift of the Spirit. That concentration shaped those communities in ways that empowered them to live out – when they did things as they were designed to be done – the kingdom vision of Jesus in the shape of a Church filled with Jews and Gentiles who loved God, loved others and lived a life empowered by God's Spirit. Observance, or

---

[17] By the time of Jesus it is probable, though hardly certain, that recitation of the *Shema* involved reciting the Ten Commandments as well. We cannot be sure how much of the later orthodox Jewish *Shema* was already in force in the first century.

non-observance, of Torah and even monotheism emerged from the rich and fertile womb the *Anawim* gave to John and Jesus and which they passed on to the apostles and any who chose to listen, learn and follow. The earliest Christian movement was a missional, ecclesial movement where theology emerged from the concrete realities of a missional, ecclesial life.

Response to Michael F. Bird by Maurice Casey

I read with interest the contributions of Michael Bird to this volume. He has made many points with which I agree. The purpose of my response is, however, to take issue with those of his points which arise out of his evangelical Christian convictions.

The earliest witnesses

Bird begins with his 'Christian view on the birth of Christianity' (see pages xv–xvi). He claims that what sets him apart from Crossley is that 'I accept the interpretation of the events by the earliest witnesses, I share their faith . . .' Bird's definition of 'the earliest witnesses' is biased, for he means only the Gospels, though he knows there were other early witnesses, who have not left written documents. For example, Bird draws attention to the evidence that Jesus could not do much healing in Nazareth owing to lack of faith on the part of its inhabitants (Mark 6.5–6), and 'the admission that Jesus' signs did not convince the inhabitants of Capernaum, Bethsaida and Chorazin (Luke 10.13–15/Matt. 11.20–24)' (see page 23). The evidence that some Jews were not convinced by Jesus is just as important as the evidence of the Gospel writers. Some of them were eyewitnesses, just as much as the first followers of Jesus, and their evidence should be taken just as seriously. Bird does not 'share their faith', for they had the faith of first-century Jews who did not accept Jesus.

Bird's claim to 'accept the interpretation of the events by the earliest witnesses' (see page xv) is misleading for a more complex reason. His interpretation of 'the earliest witnesses' is conditioned by later witnesses. Furthermore, his concept of 'the earliest sources' does not stretch to Aramaic sources of the Synoptic Gospels.

Four canonical Gospels

Bird believes in the witness of the four canonical Gospels. I accept his exclusion of other gospels.[18] One problem is Bird's defence of the historicity of

---

[18] Craig A. Evans, *Fabricating Jesus: How Modern Scholars Distort the Gospels* (Downers Grove: IVP, 2006), esp. 52–99, 240–5.

the Fourth Gospel. Critical scholars have long been aware that this is a theological document which, from a historical perspective, is not literally true.[19] I set out the main arguments against the historicity of this Gospel, and the evidence that it is seriously anti-Jewish, in *Is John's Gospel True?*[20] While he refers to this (see footnote 12 on page 111), Bird cannot be said to have answered its arguments.

Bird underplays the differences between John and the Synoptics, especially over their Christology. In so doing, he compares John with the completed Synoptic Gospels, rather than with the historical Jesus. For example, he suggests that 'the "I am" sayings cohere with the "I have come" sayings of Mark 1.38; 2.17; Matthew 5.17; 9.13; 10.34–35; Luke 12.49 that imply pre-existence' (see page 111). But it is not probable that Jesus said all these sayings. For example, Matthew 5.17 has an excellent *Sitz im Leben* in Matthew's Sermon on the Mount: 'Do not think that I have come to abolish the law or the prophets; I have come not to abolish but to fulfil.' Matthew was concerned that gentile Christians should observe the Torah. In the ministry of Jesus, however, this was hardly a live issue, so it is not probable that this was a saying of Jesus. Second, Bird over-interprets some sayings. For example, Jesus responded to hostile criticism by saying, 'I have come to call not the righteous (people) but sinners' (Mark 2.17). This does not mean that Jesus believed he was pre-existent: it told his opponents the purpose of his ministry. Bird has interpreted this saying in the light of later tradition.

In the Fourth Gospel, Jesus' pre-existence is openly stated and treated as a significant aspect of Jesus' deity. Jesus states it clearly: 'So now, Father, glorify me in your own presence with the glory that I had in your presence before the world existed' (John 17.5). The presentation of Jesus' pre-existence is more dramatic in chapter 8, where it concludes an acrimonious debate with 'the Jews'. At 8.23, Jesus declares that he is 'from above', not 'of this world'. As the discourse proceeds, he claims divine origin as well as divine inspiration. At the climax of the discourse, he declares, 'Very truly, I tell you, before Abraham was, I am' (8.58): the Jews therefore 'picked up stones to throw at him' (8.59). Stoning was the penalty for blasphemy. The Fourth Gospel's Jews, in public debate, have accepted the Johannine interpretation of Jesus' pre-existence as an aspect of his deity, thereby indicating the setting of this debate in the conflict between the Johannine community and the Jewish community, towards the end of the first century CE.

---

[19] Cf. e.g. C. K. Barrett, *The Gospel according to St John: An Introduction with Commentary and Notes on the Greek Text* (London: SPCK, 1955), 117 (2nd edn, 1978, 141–2).

[20] P. M. Casey, *Is John's Gospel True?* (London: Routledge, 1996).

The abundant evidence of Jesus' pre-existence in this Gospel entails that we interpret similarly its language about the sending, giving and coming of Jesus. In some passages, these terms are associated with a declaration of pre-existence. For example, the description of Jesus as 'the one who descended from heaven' at John 3.13 is followed by the description of him as 'the only begotten Son' (3.16, 18), and by the statements that God 'gave' and 'sent' him (3.16–17), and that 'the light has come into the world' (3.19). This is culturally different from 'the earliest witnesses', and should not be read into passages such as Mark 2.17.

Bird glosses over the major difference that the Fourth Gospel has almost removed Jesus' teaching about the kingdom of God, commenting, 'John retains "kingdom" in his repertoire (e.g. John 3.3–8) even if it is not his primary motif' (see page 111). This underlines Bird's inability to come properly to terms with Jesus' teaching that the kingdom of God was at hand. Responding to Crossley's conventional view of this, Bird comments, for example, 'Mark 9.1 is sandwiched in a context where Jesus connects his messianic identity and the kingdom to his appointed destiny to die in Jerusalem amid the messianic woes' (see page 26), apparently supposing that this is all that Jesus was referring to.

This involves not taking seriously what Jesus said: 'Truly I tell you, there are some standing here who will not taste death until they see the kingdom of God has come in power' (Mark 9.1). In the light of straight-forward Jewish evidence, the expression 'the kingdom of God has come in power' can only mean the final establishment of God's kingdom. When it was said, we do not know. Although it follows a collection of sayings, Mark introduces it with 'And he said to them', presumably because he found it in a separate source. He also caused trouble for subsequent interpreters by following it with the Transfiguration. Luke made this the reference of the saying, so that his gentile Christian audiences could see Jesus' predic-tion fulfilled in the experience of the Transfiguration by Peter, James and John. He removed 'in power', and altered the introduction to the Trans-figuration to read 'Now about eight days after these sayings' (Luke 9.28).

Matthew, however, was still part of first-century Jewish culture. When he wrote, Jesus had been dead for some time, and his return was found in the Scriptures, including Daniel 7.13, from which the term 'Son of man' was taken (Mark 8.38; 13.26; 14.62). Matthew therefore altered Mark 9.1 to include Jesus, adding in the term 'the Son of man' which Mark used in the previous verse (Mark 8.38, vigorously edited at Matt. 16.27): 'Truly I tell you, there are some standing here who will not taste death before they see the Son of Man coming in his kingdom' (Matt. 16.28). The editorial work of both Matthew and Luke falls within the parameters of the reactions of faithful Jews, and subsequently Christians, to predictions which were not fulfilled. While Matthew clarified Jesus' prediction, believing that God would fulfil it soon, Luke saw it fulfilled in an event which took place at the time. Both maintained the unshakeable faith in God which inspired Jesus' original prediction. Neither of them was disappointed, or considered Jesus to be mistaken. Accurate history, however, demands that we take a different view from them. Jesus was mistaken, and the kingdom did not come as he predicted.

In this case, Bird does not share the faith of Jesus, and has not taken seriously Jesus' first-century culture. Moreover, the expectation of the coming of the kingdom has been removed from the Fourth Gospel, surely because the Johannine community's opponents, 'the Jews', knew that Jesus' expectations were not fulfilled.[21] Hence the only two occurrences of the term in John's account of the ministry are deliberately interpretative:

> Very truly, I tell you, no one can see the kingdom of God without being born from above . . . no one can enter the kingdom of God without being born of water and spirit. (John 3.3, 5)

The first of these sayings ensures that 'see the kingdom of God' cannot be interpreted eschatologically as part of an unfulfilled prediction, as at Mark 9.1. The second ensures that 'enter the kingdom of God' cannot be so interpreted either, as it might for example at Mark 10.15. Both sayings refer to Christian baptism instead, a repeated event of central importance to the Johannine community.

Miracles

Bird believes in miracles, and declares this a major divide between 'Evangelicals and Secularists' (see page 21). He defines a miracle as 'an extraordinary event that is brought about by a god and possesses religious significance' (see page 21).[22] No one coming in from a secular perspective would accept this definition. For historical purposes, I propose to work with the following definition as well:

> A miracle is a remarkable deed performed by an unusual person believed by his followers to be in close touch with a deity.

In this sense, I believe that Jesus performed a significant number of miracles, more precisely, exorcisms and other healings. My definition takes

---

[21] Casey, *Is John's Gospel True?*, esp. 81–3, 127–30, 162–3, 184–5.

[22] Likewise, e.g. R. Swinburne, *The Concept of Miracle* (London: Macmillan, 1970), 1.

account of the fact that Jesus' followers did believe in his miracles, and other Jews did not accept their validity. Bird's definition makes it easy to leave out one of the main points: Bird believes in the miracle stories in the four Gospels, and apparently not in any others. This requires more justification than he offers. Many Christian scholars do not believe in the literal truth of miracle stories in the Fourth Gospel, because they do not believe in the literal truth of that Gospel as a whole. Moreover, some people love making up stories, and some of these include events which are not normally possible. We need to know which stories are of this kind. This is related to the fact that Bird classifies all kinds of miracle stories together. He takes together as Jesus' miracles 'exorcisms, healings, resuscitations and nature-miracles' (see page 21), and defends the historicity of Jesus' virgin birth and bodily resurrection. He appears to suppose that people believe in all the Gospel miracles or none of them.

Bird notes strength of attestation and embarrassing elements as positive reasons for believing in miracle stories about Jesus. What follows from this, however, is the historicity of Jesus' ministry of exorcism and healing, not the historicity of all the miracle stories in all four Gospels. For example, Bird refers to 'the accusation that Jesus performs miracles by the power of Beelzebub (Mark 3.22–23; Luke 11.19/Matt. 12.27)' (see page 23).[23] It shows that some of Jesus' most serious opponents could not deny the effectiveness of his ministry of exorcism, and this is unshakeable evidence that this ministry was effective. The accusation is attested in both Mark and in 'Q' material, and other Gospel evidence includes exorcism narratives (e.g. Mark 1.23–27), summaries (e.g. Mark 3.11–12) and indirect evidence, including a parable which indicates that an exorcized person who was not looked after might relapse (Matt. 12.43–45/Luke 11.24–26). The cumulative weight of this evidence is overwhelming: Jesus was an exceptionally effective exorcist.

This evidence does not, however, support the historicity of all the other Gospel miracles. It does not even show that all the exorcism stories are true. The most conspicuous example of storytelling is often known as the 'Gadarene swine' (Mark 5.1–20/Matt. 8.28–34/Luke 8.26–39).[24] The demoniac is an extreme case, inspired by stories of Samson. The first aspect of the story that is untypical of Jesus, but widespread in stories of exor-

---

[23] For detailed discussion, including reconstructions of the Aramaic sources of Mark and 'Q', see P. M. Casey, *An Aramaic Approach to Q: Sources for the Gospels of Matthew and Luke* (Cambridge: Cambridge University Press, 2002), 146–84.

[24] For detailed discussion, including demonstration of this central point, R. D. Aus, *My Name is 'Legion': Palestinian Judaic Traditions in Mark 5:1–20 and Other Gospel Texts* (Dallas: University Press of America, 2003).

cism, is that, even after ordering the unclean spirit out of the man, Jesus has to ask it its name (Mark 5.8–9). This is narratively convenient, so the storyteller can give its name as 'Legion; for we are many', the first indication of disenchantment with Roman legions. Things that do not happen in the real world include the existence of a herd of 2000 pigs. Pigs were notoriously unclean animals, so especially suitable for unclean spirits to enter. The result of the exorcism was that 'the herd . . . rushed down the steep bank into the lake and were drowned in the lake' (Mark 5.13). This sends the demons back into the underworld, and dumps Legion where many Jews would have loved to see Roman legions go. But Mark was not concerned about the geography of the Decapolis. Whether this was in the country of the Gerasenes (according to the manuscripts ℵ * B D, etc.) or the Gadarenes (according to the manuscripts A C, etc. which assimilate the text to agree with Matthew's version) makes the difference between whether the pigs had to run 33 miles, or 6 miles, to get to the lake of Galilee! This tale is a warning to be wary of the wiles of storytellers.

Bird classifies exorcisms as miracles in the sense in which he has defined that term. Exorcisms are well known all the world over. However, they occur only in societies where most people believe in demons, and in subgroups of our society who maintain such traditional beliefs, much to the dismay of their fellow Christians.[25] Exorcism was well known in Israel. For example, Josephus recounts one effect of Solomon's wisdom: 'Now God granted him understanding of the skill used against demons for the help and healing of men. He also composed incantations by which diseases are alleviated and he left methods of exorcisms by which those who are entangled drive out demons so that they never return' (*Ant.* 8.45). This is followed by an account of successful exorcism by Eleazar, witnessed by Josephus.

Moreover, Jesus approved of the ministry of other Jewish exorcists. When accused of casting out demons by the prince of demons, he responded:

> If I cast out demons by Beelzebul, by whom do your sons cast them out?
> Therefore they will be your judges.[26]   (Matt. 12.27/Luke 11.19)

Jesus was so convinced that exorcism was part of a cosmic battle between God and Satan that he was confident that exorcists associated with his opponents would vindicate him.

---

[25] For discussion, including much useful material, G. H. Twelftree, *Christ Triumphant: Exorcism Then and Now* (London: Hodder and Stoughton, 1985) and *Jesus the Exorcist* (Tübingen: Mohr Siebeck, 1993).

[26] For detailed discussion, including reconstruction of the Aramaic source of this saying, see Casey, *Aramaic Approach to Q*, 148–9, 164–7.

All this is consistent with these exorcisms being miracles as I have defined them. Bird has not given sufficient reason to suppose that any or all of them were owing to the direct action of God rather than a feature of societies whose members believe in demons.

Other healings are also a feature of many different societies. Significant light on what is normally possible has come from two different fields, the anthropology of medicine dealing with many societies, and psychosomatics, a branch of Western biomedicine. In general, cross-cultural work on healers shows a massive variety of phenomena.[27] Many cultures have healers to whom people go when they are ill, and who perform, or instruct them or their relatives to perform, many different rituals, including prayers and taking potions. The intellectual structures surrounding these events are quite varied, and include the placation or intervention of a wide variety of deities and spirits. The perception that someone is ill may depend on the person themselves and/or on the social group to which they belong. The perception that they are better always includes a change in the social classification of the person, and may or may not include a change in symptoms.

As examples of Jesus' healing ministry, I have discussed elsewhere two cases of paralysis, which he healed (Mark 2.1–12; 3.1–6).[28] Some kinds of paralysis have psychological causes, and may be subject to spontaneous remission and/or therapy. They are accordingly within the range of what traditional healers can heal. So are some kinds of blindness, which Jesus also healed. An example is the healing of a blind man at Bethsaida (Mark 8.22–26). Here people urged Jesus to touch the man (8.22). Jesus took him by the hand, and led him out of the town. There, Jesus spat in his eyes, and laid his hands on him, specifically on his eyes, as we must infer from the next part of the story. Jesus then asked if he could see anything. 'And the man looked up and said, "I can see people, but they look like trees, walking"' (Mark 8.24). Keir Howard has shown that this means first that this man's blindness was acquired, not congenital.[29] Acquired blindness was common in the Middle East, and sufferers often developed cataracts.

---

[27] There is a very large bibliography, much of it written by specimens rather than analysts. Recent discussions directly relating to NT studies include J. Wilkinson, *The Bible and Healing: A Medical and Theological Commentary* (Edinburgh: Handsel, 1998); J. J. Pilch, *Healing in the New Testament: Insights from Medical and Mediterranean Anthropology* (Minneapolis: Fortress, 2000); J. Keir Howard, *Disease and Healing in the New Testament: An Analysis and Interpretation* (Lanham: University Press of America, 2001).

[28] For detailed discussion, including additional references to work on healing paralysis, and reconstructions of Mark's Aramaic sources, see P. M. Casey, *Aramaic Sources of Mark's Gospel* (Cambridge: Cambridge University Press, 1998), 138–9, 173–92; and *The Solution to the 'Son of Man' Problem* (London: T&T Clark, 2007), 144–67.

[29] Keir Howard, *Disease and Healing*, 106–12.

Jesus' use of saliva will have encouraged the man, who will have been aware of the healing properties ascribed to saliva. The saliva will also have removed dirt and dried secretions from the eyelids. The pressure of Jesus' fingers on the eyes caused the lens to fall back into the vitreous chamber. This is why the man saw men as large as trees, and suffered from blurred vision. He remembered what men and trees looked like, because they were familiar sights before he became blind.

The next stage of the healing followed: 'Then Jesus laid his hands on his eyes again; and he looked intently and his sight was restored, and he saw everything clearly' (Mark 8.25). Keir Howard explains that the man will have been someone whose

> eyes are excessive in length and excessively distendible. The vitreous body is extremely fluid and the cataracts are eminently couchable. Further, traditional healers are often able to recognise those sufferers who will benefit most from their ministrations. After the cataract has been removed, such people tend to see much more sharply and clearly than the normal cataract patient.[30]

It follows that, like the two cases of paralysis which I have discussed elsewhere, this healing was a miracle in the sense in which I have defined miracles, but not necessarily in Bird's sense. The same cannot be said of the healing of a blind man in John 9. This has the man blind from birth, so this story has been deliberately written to make the healing a normally impossible event. It has also been written up in a culturally Johannine context. Here, Jesus breaks the Sabbath by making a paste from mud (John 9.6, 14–16), as the synoptic Jesus did not do.[31] He repeats his declaration 'I am the light of the world' (9.5), which set off the Johannine discourse of chapter 8. The miracle is followed by a lengthy dispute which includes complex theological use of the symbolism of light and blindness, and an anachronistic threat that if anyone confessed Jesus as Christ they would be kept out of Jewish meetings (John 9.22).

I therefore conclude that the exorcisms and healings in the bottom layer of the tradition were genuine and remarkable events. They do not require us to believe that they were owing to direct divine intervention, which helps to explain why many Jews were not as impressed as Jesus' followers were. Already in the Gospels, however, they are accompanied by storytelling and by deliberate theological writing, both of which entail Bird's view of

---

[30] Keir Howard, *Disease and Healing*, 111.

[31] For detailed discussion of the Sabbath disputes at Mark 2.23–28, see Casey, *Aramaic Sources of Mark's Gospel*, 138–92.

miracles. Accordingly, he has not followed the 'earliest witnesses'. He has followed selected early witnesses, interpreted in the light of later tradition.

Virgin birth and resurrection

Bird defends the historicity of the 'virgin conception' (see pages 18–21). He again fails to take account of ancient storytelling. For example, the birth of Melchizedek in *2 Enoch* 71 takes place without a human father. Sothonim was an old and sterile woman, and when Nir her husband found out she was pregnant he was so angry that she fell down dead. They had not had sex together for years. Melchizedek was born from Sothonim's womb nonetheless, fully developed like a three-year-old, speaking and blessing the Lord. This is the same culture as produced the stories of Jesus' miraculous birth.

Bird also omits the work of Aus, who has given decisive support to the widespread view that the Matthean birth narratives were inspired by stories of the birth of Moses.[32] For example, according to Josephus, one of the sacred scribes, referred to in other Jewish sources as 'astrologers', announced to 'the king' that 'there would be born to the Israelites at that time one who would humble the power of the Egyptians but exalt the Israelites'. It was because 'the king' was 'afraid' at this, that he ordered that every male child born to the Israelites should be killed (*Ant.* 2.205–6). According to Pseudo-Philo, Moses' sister Miriam saw a dream in which an angel declared 'I will do signs through him, and save my people' (*L.A.B.* 9.10). When Moses was born, he survived Pharaoh's orders to kill all male Hebrew children (Exod. 1.15—2.10). Many such elements show that these stories inspired Matthew.

Bird's positive arguments are also defective. For example, he notes that 'Jesus is called the "son of Mary" and not the son of Joseph in Mark 6.3' (see page 20). The virgin birth is not mentioned in Mark, and the inhabitants of Nazareth did not believe in it when they rejected Jesus. It follows that this cannot have been what they meant. However, Jesus' mother Mary was active during his ministry (Mark 3.21, 31–5; cf. Acts 1.14), whereas Joseph is never mentioned. We should follow the common view that Joseph was long since dead. Hence the description of Jesus as 'son of Mary'.

There is biblical precedent in Joab son of Zeruiah (e.g. 2 Sam. 2.13) and his brothers, for Zeruiah was the sister of David: we should assume

---

[32] R. D. Aus, *Matthew 1—2 and the Virginal Conception in Light of Palestinian and Hellenistic Judaic Traditions on the Birth of Israel's First Redeemer, Moses* (Lanham: University Press of America, 2004).

that their unmentioned father was unimportant, and probably dead too. Later examples include Josephus' references to Antipater as 'son of Salome' (e.g. *Ant.* 17.230). This is usually thought to be because Salome was important at Herod's court. Josephus also refers to a high priest as Simon son of Kamith (*Ant.* 18.34). A later source, naming him 'Shim'on son of Qimhith', discusses the virtues of his mother Qimhith (*y. Yoma* 1,1/33 [38d]). He was not born of a virgin and, had there been doubts about his parentage, he could not have been high priest. It follows that there had to be a reason for a man to be described as the son of his mother rather than his father. There could be a variety of reasons for this, and no examples are known to have been caused by virgin birth or illegitimacy.

Bird's defence of the *bodily* resurrection of Jesus (see pages 38–50 and 64–9) is equally unconvincing, for reasons including the following.[33] First, Bird underestimates the importance of Jewish belief in survival after death without the resurrection of the body. For example, Josephus describes the Pharisees' belief in 'souls' which survive death, and he does not mention resurrection of the body (*Ant.* 18.14). Paul appealed to their belief, declaring, 'I am a Pharisee, a son of Pharisees. I am on trial concerning the hope of the resurrection of the dead' (Acts 23.6). Jesus portrayed Lazarus going to join Abraham straight after his death: neither of them left their tomb empty (Luke 16.19–31).

Second, Bird underestimates the visionary traditions of Judaism. In caricaturing the view that the resurrection appearances were visions, he refers to 'a few grief-stricken and frightened Jewish women', 'subjective visions' and 'group hallucinations' (see page 49). But faithful Jews believed in the reality of visions. The most striking is St Paul. Paul had a vision of the risen Christ on the Damascus road, and after relating a very early tradition of appearances to Cephas, the Twelve and others, he equates his vision with these appearances, declaring 'last of all . . . he appeared also to me' (1 Cor. 15.3–8). This equates a vision with a resurrection appearance. The Gospel writers wrote up the true fact that the first appearances were to women partly because they could follow them with appearances to men, including the Eleven in Matthew (Matt. 28.16–20), and Simon in Luke (Luke 24.34). Paul's summary tradition dropped the women.

Third, Bird underestimates the importance of the fact that Jesus predicted that his resurrection would take place a short time after his death

---

[33] See further P. M. Casey, *From Jewish Prophet to Gentile God. The Origins and Development of New Testament Christology* (Cambridge: James Clarke; Louisville: Westminster John Knox, 1991), 65–7, 98–105.

(e.g. Mark 8.31).[34] This is essential to understanding why his most faithful disciples believed that he rose from the dead.

Fourth, Bird does not follow the earliest traditions about Jesus' burial. The early tradition quoted by Paul (1 Cor. 15.3–7) does not mention the empty tomb, nor do the early speeches in Acts. The Pauline tradition refers to his burial, a true fact which showed that he was dead, and the early speeches refer to his resurrection and interpret Scripture to mean that he was at the right hand of God (e.g. Acts 2.24, 32–4, using Ps. 110.1). This is not compatible with the literal truth of the stories of the empty tomb. Nor is its absence from the early chapters of Acts, since it would have been an important site if the stories were true. Bird has read the early traditions in the light of later ones. He does the same with many details. For example, he describes Joseph of Arimathea as 'a sympathetic member of the Sanhedrin . . . who placed Jesus' body in his own personal tomb' (see page 39). Mark does not say he was sympathetic or that the tomb was his own, but Matthew does (Mark 15.43; Matt. 27.57, 60; cf. Luke 23.51; John 19.38).

Fifth, Bird again ignores the nature of ancient storytelling. The resurrection stories are legitimating tales.[35] For example, one of the latest stories legitimates the deity of Jesus (John 20.28). The earliest stories legitimate the resurrection itself. Some Jews believed, like Bird, that resurrection involved the resuscitation of the earthly body. Those who converted to Christianity would naturally assume that if Jesus rose from the dead and appeared to his disciples, there must have been an empty tomb. The resulting stories are too much like a marvellous proof to be unwelcome in the churches. For example, Mark's story has the unimpeachable witness of an angel, who 'shows that Jesus' remains had gone from the correct tomb. He points out the part of the tomb where he was laid (16.6), so the women could not have failed to recognize a rotting body and imagined that he had gone from an empty space left for the next one. He also gives the information that Jesus had risen, and legitimates a purely Galilean tradition of appearances (16.7).'[36]

Sixth, Bird ignores the witness of most Jews who were in Jerusalem at the time. They celebrated the miraculous delivery of Israel from Egypt, and many of them hoped, like Joseph of Arimathea, that he would miraculously deliver Israel again soon, and that he would raise the dead. They did not, however, believe that God had raised Jesus from the dead.

---

[34] For detailed discussion, see now Casey, *Solution to the 'Son of Man' Problem*, 200–11.
[35] Casey, *From Jewish Prophet to Gentile God*, 99–100, 103–4.
[36] Casey, *From Jewish Prophet to Gentile God*, 104.

I conclude that the evidence for early appearances, from the women to St Paul, is unimpeachable, but we should not believe in the literal truth of the resurrection stories.

The Jesus of history and the Christ of faith

Two of the above points are especially important in leading Bird effectively to abandon the Jesus of history and put forward a picture of Jesus characteristic of the Christ of Faith. One is his defence of the historicity of the Fourth Gospel, in which Jesus is fully divine. The second is his habit of reading the earliest witnesses in the light of the later ones, and ignoring the witness of Jews who did not join the Jesus movement. This leads him to adopt too high a Christology in the Synoptic Gospels, which he then attributes to Jesus and the earliest witnesses. I have noted some examples above. Another notable example is his use of Johannine texts and Luke 10.22/Matt. 11.27 to allege multiple attestation for Jesus referring to himself as the 'Son'. The Fourth Gospel is too inaccurate to be brought into multiple attestation. The notion that 'no one knows the Father except the Son and anyone to whom the Son chooses to reveal him' (Matt. 11.27) entails that diaspora Jews who were too poor to travel to Israel and/or did not join the Jesus movement did not know God. That is not part of the teaching of Jesus – it reflects the sectarian nature of early Christianity, and it is a step not only towards the Christology of the Johannine community but also towards their rejection of 'the Jews'.

Bird's brief comments on the use of the term 'Son of man' also belong to evangelical tradition. Like most New Testament scholars, he cannot read the language Jesus spoke, and consequently he cannot even begin to explain how the underlying Aramaic idiom could have been used in 'a deliberately veiled and cryptic messianic claim' (see page 27).[37] For the same reason, he cannot consider whether sayings which he attributes to Jesus could have been spoken in Aramaic.

Conclusions

I conclude that Bird is seriously mistaken. His evangelical convictions lead him to believe in the historicity of much secondary material in the canonical Gospels, to read early traditions in the light of later ones, and to view the Christ of evangelical faith as if he were the Jesus of history.

---

[37] For a complete discussion of this problem, see now Casey, *Solution to the 'Son of Man' Problem.*

7

Final reflections

It is probably quite obvious by now that we (that is Michael Bird and James Crossley) disagree about a great deal. We differ quite violently about the possibility of miracles, the resurrection of Jesus, the historical reliability of John's Gospel, when Jesus was first hailed as 'God', the nature of Jewish Law-observance in the earliest churches, and how to situate Christianity in its wider religious and social contexts. It is worth pointing out that both Bird and Crossley would also differ from Scot McKnight and Maurice Casey over several matters as well. This has prompted various salvos of criticism from both sides, including claims, counter-claims, allegations of misunderstanding what was written, accusations of mishandling the evidence, a few mocking jibes, and even some rhetorically loaded remarks about each other's positions. But it has all been done in a spirit of candour and collegiality and we remain good friends at the end of it all. In our own respective viewpoints relatively little has changed. Michael Bird has not renounced his faith and holy orders in order to join the British Humanist Society and neither has James Crossley repented of his (manifold) sins and sought entrance into a monastery where he might cultivate the virtues of humility, temperance and chastity. So what have we achieved in this book, then?

First, we hope we have clearly set out two differing ways of interpreting the New Testament texts and the history of early Christianity, written from the perspectives of belief and unbelief accordingly. By analogy what has been presented here is much like two people describing what a cathedral looks like. One person is standing outside the cathedral in the cemetery, brushing past streams of tourists, and gazing at the Gothic architecture whereas the other one is standing inside the cathedral walls amid the stained-glass windows and listening to the choir rehearsing. Both see and hear something completely different, but as to which report contains the most verisimilitude and is best able to explain the interior and exterior features of the cathedral itself will be a matter for others to decide.

Second, we have established that the fields of New Testament studies and Christian origins are very complex and disputed and we both bring some fresh and interesting proposals to the discussion. Neither of us is naïve enough to presume that we are completely objective or one hundred per cent correct in all that we say. There is something to be said for a non-Christian perspective on Christianity that is relatively insulated from the debates and divisions of the past two thousand years of Christendom. Then again, one can commend a sympathetic reading of these Christian texts by readers who value them as sacred objects and therefore seek to venerate them in a most profound way by trying to understand them on their own terms. That said there is little doubt where the main faultlines are in this book and it is therefore all the more amazing when bipartisan consensuses develop on certain topics. For instance, we both agree on the necessity of applying the very best of literary, social and historical tools to the study of early Christianity, even if we differ in how to apply them and what the results are. Perhaps most surprisingly in a period of intense Christian and secular disputes, there is a notable agreement of the historical reliability of the Synoptic Gospels at least, even if there are notable differences over interpretation.

Third, in the words of Robert Burns, it would be great if we could 'see ourselves as "others" see us'. This book is partly an exercise in criticism of our respective secular and Christian view points. As long as history tarries, both perspectives will co-exist beside one another in the street, in families, in politics, and even in the academy. It is, therefore, helpful for us to learn what one thinks of the other and through that experience to make sure that any future disagreements between us and our peers are anchored in evidence and not prejudice. We also want to ensure that our exchanges are done in a spirit of learning and not of animosity and fear.

Fourth, while we differ in our relative understanding of what creates and sustains reality and moral values, we can still share a real consent in some of these areas. We both affirm the intrinsic goodness of humanity, express a desire for the collective suffering of human beings to end, seek the genuine enhancement of the human condition, hope for the religious Church and the secular State neither to control nor to tyrannize each other, believe in the freedom of religion and in the exercise of free conscience in religious matters. Perhaps it can even be argued that Christianity remains good for the secular world, but that is more likely to be the subject of another book.[1]

---

[1] For one constructive attempt at a union between believers and non-believers, including a mutual appreciation of biblical heritages, against politically dangerous uses of the Bible, see now R. Boer, *Rescuing the Bible* (Oxford: Blackwell, 2007).

Index of biblical and ancient texts

Index of modern authors